THE SECRET TWENTIES

Also by Timothy Phillips

Beslan: The Tragedy of School No. 1

TIMOTHY PHILLIPS

THE SECRET TWENTIES

BRITISH INTELLIGENCE, THE RUSSIANS AND THE JAZZ AGE

GRANTA

Granta Publications, 12 Addison Avenue, London W11 4QR
First published in Great Britain by Granta Books, 2017

Copyright © Timothy Phillips, 2017

The list of illustrations on page xi and the illustration credits on page 366 constitute extensions of this copyright page.

Lines from 'The Case for the Miners', copyright Siegfried Sassoon, are reprinted by kind permission of the Estate of George Sassoon.

Timothy Phillips has asserted his moral right under the Copyright, Designs and Patents Act, 1988, to be identified as the author of this work.

A CIP catalogue record for this book is available from the British Library.

1 3 5 7 9 10 8 6 4 2

ISBN 978 1 84708 251 0
eISBN 978 1 84708 884 0

Typeset by Avon DataSet Ltd, Bidford on Avon, B50 4JH
Printed and bound by CPI Group (UK) Ltd, Croydon, CR0 4YY

MIX
Paper from
responsible sources
FSC
www.fsc.org   FSC® C020471

For Nini Rodgers

'They're the last Marxists,' said Johnny unexpectedly. 'The last people who believe that class is a total explanation. Long after that doctrine has been abandoned in Moscow and Peking it will continue to flourish under the marquees of England. Although most of them have the courage of a half-eaten worm,' he continued, warming to his theme, 'and the intellectual vigour of dead sheep, they are the true heirs to Marx and Lenin.'

'You'd better go and tell them,' said Patrick. 'I think most of them were expecting to inherit a bit of Gloucestershire instead.'

Edward St Aubyn, *Some Hope*, 1994

'It had nothing to do with any real person. Why do you bother yourself with us? Go back to Whitehall and look for more spies on your drawing boards [. . .] It's an old illness you suffer from, Mr Smiley,' she continued, taking a cigarette from the box, 'and I have seen many victims of it. The mind becomes separated from the body; it thinks without reality, rules a paper kingdom and devises without emotion the ruin of its paper victims. But sometimes the division between your world and ours is incomplete; the files grow heads and arms and legs, and that's a terrible moment, isn't it? The names have families as well as records, and human motives to explain the sad little dossiers and their make-believe sins. When that happens I am sorry for you.'

John le Carré, *Call for the Dead*, 1961

CONTENTS

ILLUSTRATIONS

PROLOGUE

MISS LUNN'S MISFORTUNE

Hidden away in the National Archives in Kew, west London, are a series of documents that recount a sad story from the 1920s.

The story relates to a Miss Ida Lunn (usually known as Edith), who in 1925 took her summer holiday in Devon in the company of her friends, the Mitroff family. The party went to Salcombe, a newly fashionable seaside resort about fifty miles from Exeter, where Miss Lunn lodged with a Mrs Dymond, and the Mitroffs stayed in an adjacent house with a Mrs Stone. The whole party met to take meals together. After some days enjoying the South Devon coast and Salcombe's steep, narrow cobbled streets, Miss Lunn was suddenly taken ill and a doctor had to be called. On being examined by the doctor, whose name was Twining, she heard that she had had a miscarriage and was ordered to a hospital some miles away, in Kingsbridge, where she was prescribed several weeks of bed rest under close medical supervision. For the first few days of her stay, her health was said to be so poor that there was even some brief concern for her life.

Miss Lunn was thirty-eight years old, an age at which, in those days, it was considered risky for women to have their first child. Throughout her life, she had marked herself out as a thoroughly modern individual. Eager to earn her own living, politically engaged and well-educated (she spoke three languages fluently), she had just begun to share a flat with another woman in north London, and, of course, she had got pregnant while still unmarried. She had not seemed in the least upset about this. She was, as one friend put it, 'rather an exceptional person altogether'.[1]

Edith miscarried in the fourth month of pregnancy. The unborn child's father, Andrew Rothstein, was not with her at the time, but this does not mean that she had been abandoned. As soon as possible after the event, Edith wrote a postcard to him telling him of the bad news. Thereafter, Mrs Zika Mitroff took responsibility for keeping him updated, sending regular letters until he was able to come to Devon. 'The important thing now is that Ida is <u>out of danger</u>,' Mrs Mitroff told Andrew on 17 August. 'She, of course, wants very much to see you as soon as possible,' she added.[2] A few days later, Andrew was finally able to get away from London and arrived in Kingsbridge, checking into the Albion Hotel and going straight to Edith's bedside, where he comforted her and commiserated.

Edith was discharged on 3 September, travelling back up to London in the company of the devoted Mrs Mitroff and her son (both Mr Mitroff and Andrew had returned to the capital some time earlier). Edith then spent a further period in a residential nursing home in Hampstead before finally receiving doctor's advice that she could resume her normal life. It was, nevertheless, to be a difficult autumn. Edith seems to have avoided her family after what happened. They lived just south of the Thames in Battersea, but her mother wrote in somewhat hurt tones in November, 'We were expecting you every Sunday. Why have you not been?'[3] Edith also received many letters from friends who asked about her poor health and continued to wish her a speedy and full recovery, all of which suggests that, while she was on the mend, her convalescence took longer than expected.

Only in December did a little brightness return, ironically against the backdrop of some bleak winter weather. Edith, daring as ever, took the decision to move in with Andrew, giving up her flat in Parliament Hill Mansions and transferring to his house in Woodchurch Road a couple of miles away. Such a thing would have been almost unthinkable just a few years before, but times and, in some quarters, morals had changed. Andrew, again absent on business at the moment when the move occurred, sent Edith a love letter from Berlin on 8 December. 'Only just arrived [. . .] and already I am writing to you,' it began. 'I'm sure that in London there is fog, rain and all the rest of it. Perhaps you have already moved? That would be such a lovely surprise [. . .] I embrace you warmly and kiss you a hundred times.'[4] A hard year was ending on a happier note.

Edith's and Andrew's personal lives may seem familiar enough, yet the intimate nature of this story is far commoner in fiction than non-fiction for the simple reason that it is rare to find primary source material of this kind. People guard their private lives carefully; in the past, they did so even more carefully than now, and documents relating to miscarriages, romantic affairs and other personal matters – particularly about people who were not celebrities – tend not to survive. Such things were frequently not spoken of either, meaning that oral history is unable to fill in the gaps. To read such intimate details about individuals like Edith and Andrew, expressed in their own words, is surprising. And the surprise only grows when we consider that these documents are contained not in some family attic but in the declassified archives of MI5: the vast, sweeping, intriguing and sometimes shocking repository of material that Britain's principal domestic intelligence organisation gathered over the decades and is now making available in progressively greater quantities for all to see.

Left to their own devices, Edith and Andrew might well have chosen to tell almost no one about their misfortune in the summer of 1925; it seems probable that Edith did not tell her own mother and father. She may also never have shown anyone else the letter that Andrew sent her from Berlin; often people destroyed such letters in later life in order to keep them truly private. Consequently, although this glimpse of an unconventional couple's life in the 1920s is fascinating, it brings with it a sense of intrusion – not just because we are reading about the couple now, but also because this personal correspondence was intercepted and analysed in the first place.

Miss Lunn and Mr Rothstein were leading British Communists and, therefore, kept under surveillance by the British state throughout their adult lives. Almost all their actions were minutely scrutinised by MI5 and Special Branch, and sometimes by the Secret Intelligence Service as well; and vast swathes of their private communications were collected and preserved. Whenever they went on holiday; whenever they moved house; whenever they cashed a cheque at the bank, or wrote to friends and family, or even sometimes when they got a new hairstyle, government officials were there to observe and catalogue the developments, trying all the while to understand the motivations of the individuals involved. Even the ownership of a large Airedale terrier seemed briefly to be relevant to the authorities as they attempted to work out the identity of Edith Lunn's flatmate.

Sometimes the notes in the files went beyond the mere piecing together of a case, and instead offered a kind of moral commentary. One officer looking into Edith Lunn accused her of 'masquerading about the country' as Andrew Rothstein's wife, in what was a clear expression of distaste for her Bohemian choices.[5] Another described her move away from the family home in Battersea as a transfer to 'the Bolshevik Colony at Hampstead', while speculating, apparently on the basis of no evidence, that her father must have thrown her out.[6] But permeating all this, and implicit in both the selection of people who were followed and the interpretation of evidence gathered, was the clear impression that such individuals represented a threat to national security, and therefore deserved such intrusion as they got.

The 1920s was a decade of peace, yet for those charged with monitoring Edith's and Andrew's lives in microscopic detail, it felt like a time of war, and, absurd though it may sound, the tracking of holidays in Devon and the premature ending of a pregnancy were understood to be legitimate and even necessary elements in the fight.

Edith Lunn and Andrew Rothstein were only two among thousands of people who drew the attention of Britain's intelligence agencies during the 1920s because of their political sympathies and allegiances. There is little doubt that some of these people warranted official attention, but in the course of checking on their political activities, British spies sucked up and sifted through every other aspect of their existences as well, and at times seem not to have known what they were looking for or when it was appropriate to stop. The archives are fascinating for what they reveal about the innocent, and sometimes not so innocent, lives of those under surveillance. But they also provide a sobering introduction to the mindset, the morality and the political concerns of those who did the watching. What emerges from these secret documents is a mosaic of compelling and unexpected individual stories and a completely fresh perspective on one of the most alluring and important decades of the last century. MI5 chronicled these years in ways that no other organisation could and, consequently, it came to possess many secrets that no one else knew. *The Secret Twenties* is the story of those secrets.

Original in P.F.R. 3915. ROSTA. Vol.2. (54a).

TRANSLATION.

Monday 17.8.25.

c/o Mrs Stone
Shelter,
Coronation Road.
Salcombe. S. Devon.

Dear Andriousha,

You will know already from Ida's post cards of the sad event.   The important thing now is that Ida is out of danger, but she needs mental rest - and after the hospital a good rest - a full restoration of her strength.   She, of course, wants very much to see you as soon as possible.   Mrs ? Winnie ? Whinney has rung her up.   It is a pity that the hospital is at Kingsbridge and communication is bad, so far I have seen her every day.

...   .
    .   .   .   .

The hospital is not far from the station at Kingsbridge. We should like to see you after you have seen Ida, you can take a bus and come to Salcombe.   Perhaps I will ring you up to-morrow, in the morning.

I kiss you & Jania.

Yours

Zika or Zioha.

In this letter Edith Lunn's friend, Zika Mitroff, gave Andrew Rothstein an update on his lover's condition following her miscarriage. This is MI5's translation of the original, which Zika had written in Russian.

INTRODUCTION

SOMEONE TO WATCH OVER ME

I have been fascinated by espionage and intelligence since I was a boy. I used to imagine I was a spy when playing on my parents' farm in Ireland. For a while, I even liked to pretend that, by using 'secret technology' enclosed in my Casio digital watch, I was able to monitor goings-on in London and communicate with my cousin Rachel, who lived there.

A few years ago, re-engaging with this childhood passion, I decided to devote some time to looking at the newly declassified archives of MI5. Sometimes a person undertakes such an exercise with a specific writing project in mind, but in this case I went along to the National Archives in Kew out of sheer fascination during what I thought was a break between writing assignments. I can still recall the excitement I felt as I opened my first intelligence file and saw the words 'Secret' and 'Top Secret' stamped across its pages, and how indiscriminately I ranged over the material, initially paying little heed to subject or year and only keeping a running tally in my head of the bewildering array of suspects and conspiracies I was encountering. Already by the end of my first morning, I was certain that I had stumbled upon what was, for me, the perfect treasure trove.

The 1920s is the decade of British history for which the most complete intelligence record has so far been made available. As I write now, I have made a detailed study of more than two hundred files from those years, containing well over ten thousand pages of British Intelligence intercepts, transcripts, minutes and reports. At some point early on in my investigations, I became convinced that I needed to write a book about this material. There was so much here that was unknown, despite being of obvious interest and importance. A small number of historians had used the files but, so great was the volume of evidence, their work had only scratched the surface of the riches the documents contained.[1] Some researchers had gone to work instrumentally, with very specific questions in mind, often wanting to prove or disprove long-standing hypotheses. Others were primarily interested in the era as a prologue to what came next, the age of the great dictators and the Second World War. Meanwhile, large parts of the files' remarkable contents had been left untapped, and I also felt that some of their animating spirit – the spirit of that famous decade – had been neglected.

I decided that I would try to use the intelligence archives in a new way: to show both the breadth of human life that they cover and the way in which British Intelligence recorded and participated in one of our most studied periods. I found myself taking on the twin roles of detective and secret policeman, spying on the recipients of surveillance all over again, and trying to reassemble both the facts of their own lives and the connections with the era's wider tensions and trends. Undeniably, the 1920s look bright and shiny, even familiar, from afar. But up close these years can seem cold and alien, a time when political fears about the future consumed many people, and when thoughts and emotions frequently ran along different lines than today.

This decade began in a maelstrom of turmoil and hope.[2] For British people, conditions were undoubtedly safer than during the Great War, but not necessarily more prosperous, and there was an understanding that society was changing more rapidly than before – something that was by no means universally welcomed. People wanted a new order, but while for some this meant wholesale change and an upending of a social and political *status quo* that had caused the unnecessary deaths of tens of millions of people, for others it involved a recommitment to older values and certainties after four years of unprecedented conflict. The resulting tension, between cautious gradualism or stagnation on the one hand and dizzying experimentation on the other, was to be a key source of the decade's energy, and this naturally is reflected in the MI5 archives, which show how Britain's spies and their masters tried to hold on to the reins of change even as others attempted to wrench them from their grasp.

In the political sphere, it was the first era when the fight between socialism and conservatism became predominant, as the milder liberal movement, which had held power in Britain for much of the late nineteenth century and in the Edwardian period, struggled to remain relevant. In the world of culture, two countervailing forces also competed: one, a desire for iconoclastic artistic expression, which was embraced with particular enthusiasm by the intellectual elite; and the other, a proliferation of new kinds of popular entertainment, which brought fresh opportunities for leisure to the masses, broadening many people's horizons but also, in the eyes of others, lowering the tone.

Above all else, Britain in the 1920s was a nation deeply connected to the rest of the world. The country's enormous empire still extended from the frozen wastes of Canada in the north to New Zealand in the south, and across most of the continent of Africa and all but a tiny fraction of the Indian subcontinent. Four hundred million people lived under British rule and Britain remained a Great Power, whose opinion on all international issues mattered. The country and the empire were hugely affected by contact with others. Culturally, this was most obvious in the relationship with the United States, whose shared language now began to weaken Britain's control over the stories, films and plays that British people consumed. In politics, by contrast, the main external influence was Russia, a country that had long been a rival and that had demonstrated, through its brutal revolutions in 1917 and the ensuing civil war, what could happen if regimes did not adapt to changing realities. Russian Communism, or Bolshevism as it was usually known at the time, would be a constant preoccupation for British rulers in the 1920s.

As we shall see, the Bolshevik influence was also the principal concern of MI5 and Britain's other intelligence organisations. Though they would often be proved wrong about the specifics, these agencies correctly identified the momentousness of what was occurring in Russia: Lenin and his followers really had changed the course of history through their actions during and after the storming of Petrograd's Winter Palace, and they really did have global ambitions. Although we now date the start of the Cold War to 1945, in many ways it had already begun by the end of 1918. During the 1920s, it, or something very like it, whirred constantly, and disruptively, in the engine room of world affairs.

This book is my attempt to tell the story of a decade from the perspective of its spies. The story's obvious heroes and anti-heroes are the officers, agents, informants and secretaries of British Intelligence on the one hand, and the spies, revolutionaries, moles and followers of Soviet Russia and Britain's extreme left on the other. But to do full justice to the material in the archives, the boundaries of plot and narrative need to be stretched much wider to encompass, among other things, the history of cinema, jewel thieves, philanderers, drunken evenings in nightclubs and, of course, Miss Lunn's miscarriage – and to recognise that it is by no means always clear who the heroes were and who the villains.

Modern digital technology, cyber hacking and the Edward Snowden scandal have made all of us much more aware of how our own lives are being captured for posterity. The exhaustive approach modern intelligence agencies take to the accumulation of information is awe-inspiring. Yet it is not as novel a development as we might think. Even in the 1920s British Intelligence was able to collect data indiscriminately, in massive quantities, and to hold on to it indefinitely. It now transpires that thousands of British people unwittingly had their lives intruded into by the state during the interwar period. But was MI5 well served by this capacity to know so much about so many people? Too often the quality of its analysis could not keep pace with the quantity of information it obtained. As we shall see, the gap between this meaningless data and the meaningful intelligence that might have been produced was one of the factors that allowed 1920s paranoia and prejudice to grow, fed by preconceived notions of right and wrong, and leading to a vicious cycle of suspicion and still more suspicion.

The journey we are about to take unfolds against a strikingly dramatic landscape. Pause for a moment to summon in your mind the vivid picture of the 1920s that you already know. Assertive young women and idealistic young men, perhaps. The golden age of cinema and the writers of Bloomsbury. Britain at the apex of its imperial pomp. And all the hopes and regrets of 'the war to end all wars' just passed. This was a place where, more than ever before, people could live controversial lives openly without worrying about the consequences; and yet it was also a place of many dark secrets and hidden judgements. The MI5 archives embody these contradictions and open our eyes anew to this lost world, a world of seemingly infinite possibilities but equally limitless fears.

PART I

A NEED FOR INTELLIGENCE

Almost every country in the world now has an intelligence agency. Even tiny peaceful places like Luxembourg and Monaco have secret services with which to protect their citizens and vital interests, while the five permanent members of the United Nations Security Council spend tens of billions of pounds annually between them on espionage and counter-espionage activities. According to recent data, Britain itself spends over £2 billion a year through its Single Intelligence Account, which pays for most, but not all, of the country's secret-service work, while France reportedly spends about €1 billion. Of the three biggest intelligence nations, the United States through its Central Intelligence Agency (the CIA) spends around $50 billion a year, with US military intelligence costing a further $15 billion or so. Meanwhile, estimates for Russia and China currently reside in the realm of speculation, but undoubtedly the amounts must be very large.

State-sponsored spying is as old as the idea of the state itself. The cliché that spying is the second oldest profession, after prostitution, is certainly apt: both occupations have been shameful but indispensable parts of powerful men's lives for a very long time. As early as 450 BCE, Herodotus relates the story of Deioces, whom he describes as the first king of the Medes.[1] Deioces, Herodotus tells us, was selected from among his people for his openness and ability to arbitrate fairly in disputes, yet no sooner had he achieved formal power than he sent 'people spying and listening for him throughout his kingdom' (ostensibly – as always – for his subjects' own good).[2]

Deioces's network of informers sounds like a very organised operation, as do many other ancient spying outfits. Yet it has really only been in quite recent times that official espionage has taken on the permanent, highly orchestrated and quasi-industrial characteristics that we now associate with it. Growth spurts in the development of espionage have coincided with the religious unrest of the Reformation, the American War of Independence, the French Revolution, and the varied responses of European governments to radical grassroots politics from the mid-nineteenth century onwards – as well as with techno-logical advances like the introduction of mass postal services, the railways, the telegraph and the telephone.[3] In Britain, the emergence of espionage as a pervasive feature of everyday life was more halting than in many major states. Most of today's intelligence agencies can only trace their history back to the beginning of the 1900s, which means that, at the point when our story begins, it was by no means certain that they would go on to enjoy the long lives they have had; at that time, they were still comparatively unestablished parts of the establishment.

Britain held out longer than any other major European power before acquiring the formal apparatus of secret state surveillance for the simple reason that it doubted the need for it. 'Never put anything in writing if you can avoid it' has been something of a mantra for the British state throughout its history, and so it was with espionage. British monarchs and their courtiers certainly spied on friends and foes alike, both domestic subjects and foreigners, but they did so in ways that tended towards informality and that waxed and waned (sometimes almost to nothing) depending on the character of the age. Only at the end of the eighteenth century, as the American War of Independence concluded, did the British parliament institute an annual Secret Vote in order to give government the funds to pay for routine undercover operations.[4] This was the first permanent feature of Britain's intelligence landscape and funded things like the creation and decoding of ciphers, and subventions to overseas and domestic informants. It did not, however, amount to an espionage infrastructure *per se*. That only began to emerge in the 1880s, with the creation of the Metropolitan Police Special Branch.

Every European state faced grave internal threats during the nineteenth century; the pace of economic development, the iniquities and inequities of imperialism, and the spread of education made this inevitable. In Britain, the greatest perceived danger came from Ireland, whose people lived, increasingly unhappily, under direct rule from London. When a small group of Irish nationalists began bombing the British mainland after 1881, politicians and officials were initially at a loss to know how to stop them. In 1883, after successful bomb attacks in Salford, Chester, Liverpool, Glasgow and London, they finally responded by creating the Special Irish Branch of the Metropolitan Police, a department whose role was to track and, where possible, frustrate terrorists.[5] The Fenian bombing campaign came to an end only a couple of years later, with some claiming the credit for the new police body. This assessment was contested, but what is important from the point of view of our story is that, in a very short space of time, the Special Irish Branch had made itself seem indispensable to those who mattered in the corridors of power. Thus, after dropping the word 'Irish' from its title, it was allowed to endure and become the first major component of Britain's twentieth-century national security network.

The next element in that network also had roots in colonialism. The Indian Department of Criminal Intelligence (the DCI) was established in 1904 under the then Viceroy of India, George Nathaniel Curzon, a man who will play a prominent role in this tale. Though the DCI's purpose was initially less clear than Special Branch's, it too went on to have a long life, becoming the main means by which the Raj secretly tracked Indian nationalists, both at home and abroad right up until Indian independence in 1947.[6]

Only in 1909 did the United Kingdom acquire what are surely its two most famous clandestine organisations, both initially part of a single Secret Service Bureau but soon developing their own distinct identities. These were the domestic secret service that came to be known as MI5, and its foreign counterpart, the Secret Intelligence Service (SIS), later known as MI6. Once again, the bodies owed their creation to an immediate and specific threat, in this instance the perceived danger of an expansionist Germany. And it was that same German threat – now fully realised and transported from the realm of fantasy to the realm of fact[7] – that led a few years later to the establishment of the Government Code and Cypher School (GC&CS, later renamed GCHQ), the youngest of Britain's principal intelligence-gathering capabilities.

As is well known, four of these five institutions continue to watch over Britain, and to some extent the rest of the world, today. Yet their survival even as far as the 1920s was by no means a foregone conclusion. The perceived need for state intelligence had grown greatly during the 1900s and 1910s, when other aspects of the state's role had also been expanding. The Liberal governments of Sir Henry Campbell-Bannerman and Herbert Asquith had introduced free school meals, old-age pensions, labour exchanges, national insurance and unemployment benefit, just as they created MI5 and SIS; and after war broke out the country's leaders had taken railways, coal mines and other industries into state control, while also establishing systematic monitoring of signals and telegraphic communication, and legislating for curfews and other draconian restrictions on everyday life. Yet the 1920s was to be a decade of harsh retrenchment throughout the public sector, which shrank steadily, with every element of taxpayer-funded activity constantly having to justify and re-justify itself.

In this context, the surprising durability of British Intelligence after 1918 had little to do with the putative successes of the four previous years of fighting. Rather, it was a succession of new and pressing threats that rescued the intelligence system from abolition. Had they been asked, many ordinary Britons might well have expressed a wish to live in a country that played a quieter, less conspiratorial role in the global future; and many government ministers, we know for a fact, dreamt the same dream. Yet a combination of social unrest at home and new dangers abroad made the permanent regularisation of the surveillance *status quo* seem like the only sensible way to proceed.

Of immediate concern was a brief spate of mutinies and threatened mutinies that happened in the armed forces during 1918 and 1919, a result of the delayed demobilisation which angered many weary conscripts. In addition, there were strikes that hit several key civilian industries when trades unions – for the most part docile and patriotic during wartime – recommenced their struggles on behalf of members. Finally, in Ireland, a full-scale war of independence now raged, making the bomb plots of a generation earlier look tame.

Yet it was undoubtedly Russia that offered the most frightening prospect of all; Russia, which came to be viewed in many parts of officialdom as the era's Great Satan. The unique problem was that Bolshevism, as well as being thoroughly undesirable in its own right, also appeared to be implicated in every other difficulty Britain faced. Somehow, it was believed that Lenin and his followers were able to connect all these disparate dangers together and make them more dangerous than they would have been singly. Bolshevism was suspected in the mutinies and the strikes, and in Ireland, as well as in a host of lesser national and colonial problems. Bolshevik ideology was thought of as a poison gas, spreading invisibly throughout the world, invading unsuspecting societies noiselessly and scentlessly, choking off normal social relations, and with the potential to reach lethal levels of concentration. Russian money and revolutionaries were believed to range widely across the globe, supplying practical and moral support to Britain's enemies.

More than anything else, this fear of Russia explains why, when other parts of the newly created public sector disappeared after 1919, it seemed impossible to imagine a Britain without British Intelligence. Yes, MI5, SIS and GC&CS would all have to deal with cuts during the first decade of the interwar period – sometimes savage cuts – but they nevertheless survived without radical reconfiguration. Over the same period Special Branch broadly maintained its strength, reflecting the fact that, increasingly, Britain's new battles were waged in the civilian sphere. To many in Whitehall, the threat from Russia loomed so large that the need for a robust intelligence community had never been greater. To keep the nation safe in peacetime was arguably going to be a more formidable task even than winning the war.

I

FOR THE GOOD OF THE NATION

The Secret Service Committee was created just ten weeks after the Armistice in one of the first decisions taken by the new cabinet in 1919. The committee met amid an atmosphere of national celebration. Millions of women and working-class men had just cast their first ever votes in a general election on 14 December 1918. An entire empire had welcomed in its first peaceful new year for half a decade. And so, decidedly there seemed to be reasons to be cheerful. Only a few hundred yards up the road from where the committee would gather, at the Coliseum theatre, a British orchestra was experimenting with jazz music for the first time. *The Times*'s assessment was curmudgeonly, describing the orchestra's sole object as being 'to produce as much noise as possible; the method of doing so [appearing] immaterial'.[1] But the music would achieve instant popularity and become the soundtrack for much of the next quarter century.

The committee itself shared some of the general buoyancy. Many of Britain's victories in the Great War had been attributed to her excellent intelligence work, and the committee members took this opportunity to congratulate themselves. 'Heavy as [the] outlay [had] been', they found it easy to conclude that this expenditure was 'thoroughly justified by the results' – results that they felt were 'equal, if not superior' to those 'obtained by any other country engaged in the War'.[2] Yet the men had come together to talk not about the past but the future, and on that subject they felt much less hopeful. It was a strange state of affairs, given the apparent unlikelihood of any threat even remotely similar to Germany or Austro-Hungary emerging in the immediate years to come, but their overwhelming response to the world was pessimism, felt not just professionally but also deep in their bones.

The committee's membership included key personalities from the war effort. Many of them would also be major players in the decade ahead. Their chairman was Lord Curzon of Kedleston, the Viceroy of India who had presided over the creation of the Indian secret service back in 1904; he was Britain's Acting Foreign Secretary while Lord Balfour was away at the Paris Peace Conference. Also on the committee was a host of other senior Whitehall personages – Walter Long (the First Lord of the Admiralty), Edward Shortt (the Home Secretary), Lord Peel (the Under-Secretary of State for War), and Ian Macpherson (the Chief Secretary for Ireland), all of whom were full committee members – and British Intelligence's various chiefs: Sir Vernon Kell at MI5, Sir Mansfield Cumming at SIS, and Basil Thomson, the head of Special Branch, all there to provide evidence and expertise and fight their own particular corner.

During the meetings, which took place in January and February 1919, these men collectively stared the post-war world in the face and tried to devise a fitting response. They set out their own priorities for clandestine activity, which resulted in recommendations to the government as a whole. Inevitably, they worked in the realm of predictions and guesses but they had decades of collective experience in domestic and global affairs behind them. Repeatedly in the secret report they produced for the cabinet, the problem of Bolshevism came to the fore. The group had assembled with the 'utmost promptitude', the document stated, so as to establish how intelligence work could 'best be coordinated' in peacetime; and they had all quickly agreed that the biggest threat to British and world security came from 'revolutionary or anarchical movements'. This, therefore, had been the issue to which they had 'devoted their attention especially'.[3]

It was hardly surprising given the state of international affairs.[4] Despite the giddy revelry in many quarters, Europe had been shattered by the war and, in the manner of shattered things, was at risk of falling apart. Russia had been the earliest and most spectacular example of disintegration to date and its implosion was continuing at the time of the committee's work. Back in the spring of 1917, the Russian Tsar, Nicholas II, had been deposed and the entire system of government he and his forebears had maintained over so many centuries had been supplanted, first by an unstable provisional administration and then by the Bolshevik faction of the Social Democratic Party (quickly renamed the Communist Party), which was one of the world's most radical groups.

While the final year of the Great War had crawled towards its conclusion, British politicians had watched with growing incredulity as the situation in Russia went from bad to worse. The extremist government of Lenin, Trotsky, Stalin, Bukharin, Zinoviev and others – all of whom had been little more than nonentities just a short time before their sensational seizure of power – had swiftly dismantled the pre-existing bureaucracy and all other sources of authority. The new laws they summarily passed banned regular property ownership and nationalised people's private savings, among a host of other unprecedented developments. And these were twinned with brutal reprisals against representatives of the old regime, including many individuals who were apparently low-ranking or harmless. There had been an inevitable refugee crisis, and this had been compounded from the middle of 1918 onwards by a bloody civil war. Foreign bystanders had initially hoped

– and many had assumed – that the Bolsheviks would last no more than a few weeks, and that Russian liberals, army generals, aristocrats or some other group would swiftly reassert control. But each month that passed brought a growing realisation that Bolshevism, far from being a short-lived phenomenon restricted only to Russia, was capable of thriving and spreading, just as its leaders had predicted.[5]

In the same month that the Secret Service Committee was formed, the Spartacist Uprising occurred in Berlin, underlining the strength of the far-left threat. Although quickly put down by the paramilitary Freikorps, which also assassinated the uprising's ringleaders, Karl Liebknecht and Rosa Luxemburg, this was the first concerted attempt to establish a revolutionary socialist regime, similar in many respects to Lenin's, in another European capital city. Simultaneously, a Bavarian Soviet Republic based in Munich tried to copy Bolshevism, and the Bolsheviks' own Red Army was having success retaking former Tsarist territory in both Ukraine and Estonia.

When they spoke about 'revolutionary' and 'anarchical movements', and what Britain needed to do to keep them in check, the members of the Secret Service Committee had all these issues in mind. SIS was active in Berlin and Munich and in the theatres of war where Russia's White (anti-Bolshevik) forces were fighting the Reds, yet inevitably British politicians were even more concerned with incidents closer to their own doorstep. The December general election in Britain had returned to power a version of the successful wartime coalition, thanks to landslide victories in English, Scottish and Welsh constituencies. But in Ireland the same election had heralded the obliteration of the traditional moderate nationalists, who were replaced by Sinn Fein, a radical independence party, which won 73 out of 105 seats. In the poll's aftermath, Sinn Fein refused to send its MPs to sit in the Westminster parliament and instead, on 21 January 1919, declared Irish independence in its own newly created Dublin assembly, the *Dail*. This declaration was in itself a revolutionary act and on the very same day the Anglo-Irish War of Independence began. What is often forgotten is the Marxist dimension to Sinn Fein's radicalism of this era. One of the first statements made in the *Dail* was the announcement of a Democratic Programme, a rallying cry in the language of socialism that set out the equality of all Irish people and the republicans' socioeconomic agenda for the future.[6]

Thousands of miles to the east, meanwhile, but nonetheless close to many committee members' hearts, especially Curzon's, the situation in India during the first weeks of 1919 gave almost as much cause for concern. Political terrorism and pressure for Indian self-government had been disturbing if peripheral aspects of the Great War, with a number of Indian separatist groups looking to Germany for assistance. Now the war was over, the ruling British feared that these same Indian groups would look to the Bolsheviks for succour, and they were deeply unsettled by growing signs of popular unrest on India's streets. While the Secret Service Committee met in London, a Sedition Committee was concluding its work in India and would recommend a new Anarchical and Revolutionary Crimes Act (commonly known as the Rowlatt Act) which authorised additional repression in order to try to keep a lid on things.[7]

Finally, on mainland Britain, there were events that could also be seen as revolutionary, especially by anyone who felt spooked at the general leftward turn in contemporary affairs. The so-called Battle of George Square in Glasgow was probably the most unsettling occurrence. It had begun as a protest by the Scottish Trades Union Congress – a call for nothing more extreme than a shorter working week – but had turned into something akin to a citywide general strike and then, on 31 January 1919, a riot between workers and police. The government, watching with anxiety from London, became gravely concerned at the rhetoric of some organisers and the police's failure to deal decisively with the disturbances. The Secretary of State for Scotland, Robert Munro, stated that the strikers' actions were a 'Bolshevist uprising' and ordered the deployment to Glasgow of ten thousand soldiers, armed with machine guns and backed by tanks.[8]

For an intelligence establishment contemplating the formal advent of peace, these developments made it entirely logical to continue speaking and thinking in the language of war; logical, too, to continue advocating some of the tactics of war. The committee examined the current capabilities of each arm of the secret services and, although there was general recognition that the state's resources would be under great pressure in future and that efficiency would have to increase, members found not a single area of intelligence work that they deemed surplus to requirements or wanted to stop altogether. If anything, there was a desire to broaden British Intelligence's purview.

Since its creation, SIS, 'under the general control of the Foreign Office', had had responsibility for 'obtaining secret information from abroad on military, naval and other matters', including by means of 'all kinds of secret operations'; and this, the Secret Service Committee agreed, should continue.[9] The independent naval and army intelligence offices which had been developed during wartime, and which also sometimes worked abroad, would continue too. And an additional intelligence office was even proposed for the new air force. Similarly, the need for an extra Ireland-only body to help the military and civil powers there to combat the independence movement was accepted, while the Indian Department of Criminal Intelligence – though not formally within the committee's scope – was also expected to go on with its work protecting the Raj.

MI5, 'under the general control of the War Office', was to continue being 'concerned with counter-espionage', namely 'measures for detecting foreign agents working in [Britain,] and for frustrating their efforts'.[10] This had been its role since its inception. But it would also retain a number of the wider roles it had acquired during wartime in 'questions relating to aliens and suspects in this country, particularly in regard to the entry and departures of persons to and from British ports'.[11] 'Aliens' and 'suspects', it will be noted, were not necessarily the same as 'foreign agents', a fact that was repeatedly to bring Sir Vernon Kell's officers up against the remit of Special Branch. For Special Branch itself was to go on having the principal responsibility 'for obtaining information in regard to anarchists and other dangerous political criminals' in the United Kingdom.[12]

As it concentrated on seamlessly switching the focus of British intelligence work from Germany to Bolshevism, the Secret Service Committee of 1919 undoubtedly passed up a unique opportunity to address some of the problems with the existing system. Since 1909, duties and rights had accrued to various branches of the intelligence community in a higgledy-piggledy way, leading to confusion and a succession of often rancorous rivalries. The Secret Service Committee was well aware of these overlaps and conceded in its analysis that cooperation between the agencies had 'not always' been a strong suit.[13] But its report ultimately allowed this state of affairs to persist, and in some ways even exacerbated it. It made a half-hearted attempt to unify intelligence analysis in the hands of the chief of Special Branch, who found himself appointed to a new role as head of an overarching Secret Service Department. However, this idea was stillborn, as Basil Thomson was hobbled both by his own ego and by other senior officers' determination to ignore and frustrate him.

The Secret Service Committee might also have been expected to provide high-level strategic guidance on how the intelligence system should best apply its vast wartime powers in the very different context of peace, and potentially to recommend a reduction in those powers, yet it did not. Of course, this is less surprising when we consider the committee's prevailing analysis that the peace itself would be far less different from the war than people might have hoped. British Intelligence actually had its formal powers strengthened through a new Official Secrets Act in 1920 – thus implying that even more secret laws were needed than in the tumultuous 1910s! The authorities' ability to seize telegrams was expanded; the presumption of guilt for people found to be in contact with foreign agents was increased; and it was made easier to charge people with incitement, aiding and abetting, and other ancillary kinds of subversive crime. Similarly, the wartime Defence of the Realm Act, which restricted people's freedom of movement and increased state censorship powers, would remain on the statute book until 1927.

The Secret Service Committee made one very bold suggestion of its own about expanding the remit of British Intelligence. In the last two pages of its nine-page report it addressed head-on the issue of the British state's role in active propaganda. This had largely been an innovation of the Great War, when the British government had felt obliged to devote increasing resources to print, poster and film initiatives aimed at maintaining national morale and ensuring that ordinary people held the correct opinions about the conflict. Here was an area of expenditure that most officials had assumed would cease altogether once the fighting was over. But committee members warned that there was now a 'pressing need for some form of propaganda against Bolshevism in this country' in order to strengthen 'public opinion against the sinister influences which have been and still are at work'.[14] Once again, the Kaiser was instantly replaced by Communism as the rationale for government action.

The committee members conceded that propaganda activities would have to be undertaken with greater discretion than in wartime, when there was wider agreement about the state's right to interfere. Nonetheless, they thought there should be 'an agency [. . .] trusted to communicate [with] the press [. . .] in such a way as to secure [. . .] publication' of 'anti-Bolshevist propaganda', and they also recommended investment in 'cinematograph films'. Anti-Bolshevik commentators, whatever their medium of influence, needed to be 'kept supplied with all information which may bear on this subject' and 'seditious speeches' should not be 'left unanswered' as it was vital that 'people's eyes' were 'open[ed]' to the truth.[15]

Although no such government anti-Bolshevik propaganda agency was ever formed, many politicians and officials would continue to believe passionately that the state needed to wage an intangible war for British hearts and minds just as much as it needed to run tangible operations against specific individuals. This belief stemmed from a conviction that significant numbers of seemingly innocuous people were actually or could easily turn into radical left-wing threats. Workers, colonial subjects, intellectuals, and rank and file members of the armed forces were all believed to be susceptible to the Communist message in its various guises – all (that is to say, hundreds of millions of people in total) assumed to be vulnerable to what we would now call 'radicalisation'. It may seem surprising to see the 1920s presented in this way, given the decade's frothy, flighty reputation, but this is how it looked to the secret service community. In one passage of the committee's report, the members refer to the dangers posed by 'discontent among some body of men', without specifying the sort of discontent or body of men they had in mind.[16] Often intelligence agencies' worst fears during the ensuing decade were no more concrete than that.

Many of the committee's recommendations went on to be endorsed by the cabinet and put into effect immediately. While some would stand the test of time, others did not. Overall, the committee succeeded in setting a tone and establishing the rules of engagement for MI5 and other intelligence bodies on the threshold of a new decade. The beginning of 1919 was an especially troubled time in world history and many of the worst predictions about what might happen did not come to pass. Nonetheless, the immediate post-war analysis of British Intelligence's purposes proved remarkably durable in the years to come, as did the many fears that had been stirred up in those first post-war months. Cuts to intelligence institutions throughout the 1920s were greater than Curzon and his colleagues had anticipated (a result of altered economic realities rather than any principled change of opinion about intelligence-gathering); but the scale of British Intelligence's worries and ambitions never shrank.

With hindsight, it sometimes feels as if Britain's spies were simply scaring themselves with spectres of their own making. But, imaginary fears aside, perhaps the key reason why their concerns in 1919 were sustained into the next decade was the arrival in the United Kingdom midway through 1920 of a large contingent of high-ranking citizens from the very country they feared the most, Soviet Russia. Such a development would have been unthinkable just a year before, but – in the face of many protests – the British Prime Minister himself decided to invite the Bolsheviks in for trade negotiations. At a stroke, some of the people whom experts had identified as Britain's greatest current enemy suddenly materialised at the centre of British power. British Intelligence's challenge, which would always have been formidable, suddenly came to seem immeasurably more difficult.

Colonel Jones

ECRET.

12

REPORT OF SECRET SERVICE COMMITTEE.   CAB 24/76

PAGES 346A - 346F

T. 6965.

REPORT

OF

SECRET SERVICE COMMITTEE.

HOME OFFICE.
FEBRUARY, 1919.

The front page of the Secret Service Committee's 1919 report. This report determined the interwar structure of British Intelligence, deciding that it should change very little after the Great War and identifying the Bolsheviks as Britain's principal peacetime threat.

2

WE NEED TIMBER, FUR AND PIG BRISTLES

'One might as well legalise sodomy as recognise the Bolsheviks.'

Attributed to Winston Churchill in a conversation with
David Lloyd George, January 1919

Since the mid-nineteenth century, Britain had been viewed as something of a safe haven for political radicals, who were keen to take advantage of the country's relatively forgiving attitude towards dissent and its commitment to freedom of speech. Karl Marx himself had made London his base for more than thirty years, with many of his prototype Communist organisations headquartered there, and several of his seminal texts written in the city's libraries, most famously the British Museum Reading Room. Lenin had then followed in his hero's footsteps during the early 1900s, visiting the capital no fewer than six times between 1902 and 1911, accompanied by a host of other left-wing Russian exiles, and holding many early Bolshevik meetings there.[1]

It had always been a source of frustration to security officials that such a situation had been allowed to persist, but in the early years of the twentieth century crackdowns had tended to be piecemeal. Only with the Bolshevik seizure of power at the end of 1917 did the British state finally begin to take concerted action against resident Russian radicals. Many, of course, had already departed in order to support the revolution at home. But those who remained ran a heightened risk of being declared undesirable and expelled. The most prominent person to suffer this fate was Maxim Litvinov, whom Lenin named as his first envoy to Britain, but who found himself detained at His Majesty's pleasure in Brixton prison and put on a boat back to his homeland.[2]

As the Secret Service Committee met in early 1919, this policy of ostracising the Bolsheviks remained firmly in place. Indeed, the British government was still offering significant assistance to the forces inside Russia that were attempting to rid the country of Bolshevism. British troop detachments and naval and air force personnel had all been involved on the White side of the civil war from the beginning. After the November 1918 Armistice in the Great War, there had been some debate about whether British forces should continue to be stationed in Russia, but Winston Churchill, the new Secretary of State for War, had insisted on it, and also made sure that these troops periodically got involved in actual fighting. However, for all that they were said to have operated with 'courage and dash' – to borrow the words of a War Office press release from mid-February 1919 – these men came from a military machine that had been exhausted and depleted by four years of global conflict, and so their impact was limited.[3] As 1919 wore on, it became increasingly clear that neither Britain nor any other Allied power could commit enough troops and materiel to the Russian Civil War to make a decisive difference; meanwhile on the other side the Red Army had more and more success.

With the Bolshevik government likely to survive, Britain looked set to adhere to her policy of ostracism indefinitely: starving Russia of finance, maintaining a *de facto* blockade on Bolshevik ports, and refusing to compromise or have any contact with the regime's bloodthirsty leaders. Such an approach was presented by proponents not just as the best line of defence given the White armies' collapse, but also as a means to choke off, over time, the lifelines on which Bolshevism depended.

In the words of the government's Under-Secretary of State for Foreign Affairs, Cecil Harmsworth (who was also one of the owners of the *Daily Mail*), such measures would 'continue until a democratic Government which can be recognised by the Allies has been established in the part of Russia in question'.[4]

This was certainly a policy that Churchill supported – once he had come to terms with the fact that a military victory over Bolshevism was impossible – and it was also the policy favoured by Curzon. Moreover, we can infer from their reactions to later developments that the leaders of British Intelligence themselves backed the approach. Crucially, however, it was not what the British Prime Minister wanted. David Lloyd George had spoken out against Bolshevism often since the 1917 revolution and had been at the helm of the government throughout its participation in the Allied military intervention in Russia. But for most of that time he had been absent and distracted in Versailles and it was only on his return that he directed his thoughts fully towards Bolshevism; he quickly began to doubt that either military attack or cold-shouldering was really the best way forward.

Lloyd George could see that the world was a place where pre-existing economic certainties had been obliterated by the war and that the prospects for swiftly recovering former levels of wealth and productivity were highly fragile. The complete removal of Russian goods and raw materials from the international market would, he felt certain, drive commodity prices to perilously high levels, where they would then remain indefinitely. Without Russian raw materials – flax, timber, fur and pig bristles were particular items of concern – he also feared that some British businesses might not have the necessary components to make the items they had sold before 1914. To him, it was problems such as these, and not the direct threat of Bolshevik agitation or propaganda, that seemed most likely to lead the unemployed and impoverished of Britain to seek ever-more radical ways of improving their lot.

In a daring and deeply controversial move — a move that ran directly counter to the stance urged by the Secret Service Committee — Lloyd George invited representatives of the Bolshevik government to come to London in the spring of 1920 for talks about trade and peace. Up to then, the global boycott of Moscow had been almost total, so that shock was expressed not only by members of Lloyd George's own government but by many other world leaders. One newspaper noted that the Prime Minister had 'dragged his colleagues' into the negotiations against their will and also that he had done so 'to the amazed disgust and indignation of our French Allies'.[5] It was no exaggeration. And yet Lloyd George determinedly ploughed ahead (much as he would do on a number of other sensitive issues during the remainder of his premiership) initiating ten months of start-stop diplomacy and forcing many of his own ministers to hold their noses and treat as equals the very men whom they thought represented the worst of humanity.

Parliament, the right-wing press and London's establishment seethed about the Prime Minister's naive or, as some of them saw it, treacherous and immoral behaviour. At one point, Churchill and Curzon even threatened to resign. But the levels of incredulity were undoubtedly greatest among the intelligence and security community. As far as they could see, the Russian threat facing the country and its empire remained exactly the same as in 1919, when the Secret Service Committee had conducted its initial post-war analysis. Lloyd George's talks simply brought the threat closer to home, giving the Bolsheviks fresh opportunities to spread their poisonous ideology.

Early in the negotiations, members of British Intelligence felt fairly confident that the talks would fall apart before long. Never mind that the security community had lost the argument about avoiding Anglo-Soviet cooperation on principle, intelligence officers believed that there was so much evidence of wrongdoing and bad faith on the part of Bolshevik negotiators, just in the short time they had spent in London, that the talks would of necessity collapse. The very first party of Soviet citizens to arrive, on the steamship *Iris*, at Newcastle-upon-Tyne on 16 May 1920, included a number of dangerous troublemakers who had been chosen in spite of Moscow's promises not to send undesirable individuals or engage in agitational scheming.

The MI5 archives preserve a copy of the original Immigration Office document that a Mr J. W. Oldfield completed on the Sunday morning these first Bolsheviks arrived – the document may be thought of as an opening act of live surveillance on Soviet citizens on British soil during the 1920s.[6] Among the eight names listed were two who gave particular cause for concern: Viktor Nogin and Nikolai Klyshko. Both they and the others (apart from Michael Rosofsky, a fourteen-year-old boy travelling in the company of his father) were then painstakingly tracked by a combination of regular police, Special Branch and MI5, while SIS simultaneously attempted to gather information on them from officers and informants overseas.

Viktor Pavlovich Nogin was a seasoned Bolshevik who had been involved in revolutionary politics since at least 1898, the year in which he turned twenty. One of the organisers of the pioneering Soviet of Workers' Deputies in Moscow in 1917, Nogin had also participated in that city's armed uprising and had operated under numerous aliases over many years (including M. Novoselov, P. Yablochov, and the one-word moniker Makar). He was said to have escaped from prison and exile no fewer than six times. And according to SIS intelligence forwarded from Copenhagen, he was under instructions upon arrival in the United Kingdom to make underground contact with, and presumably offer support to, members of Sinn Fein and the Irish Republican Army.

Meanwhile, the defeat of the ostracism policy was embodied by no one better than Nikolai Klementievich

Klyshko. Involved with the Bolsheviks from 1904 onwards, he had spent a prolonged period in exile in Britain working as an engineer while also continuing to associate with and support Russian revolutionaries. His activities after the 1917 revolution had led to him being declared *persona non grata* by the British government and he had been one of the Russian citizens deported in 1919. Just a few months later, he was now returning triumphantly as an official negotiator. It was understandable that the secret services should feel this to be an acute humiliation and also entirely unsurprising that Klyshko quickly reactivated many of his old relationships with members of Britain's radical left.

Nogin and Klyshko were monitored exceptionally closely. Surveillance officers watched them day and night as they came and went from their rooms at the First Avenue Hotel, a respectable but far from luxurious establishment in Holborn in London. Intercept warrants were placed on their post, and towards the end of May 1920 Klyshko found himself hauled before Sir Basil Thomson for an interview which was intended as both an interrogation and a warning. Similar treatment was meted out to the two top negotiators who arrived in the days following the group on the *Iris*: Leonid Krasin and Lev Kamenev, the latter being the highest-ranking Bolshevik to visit Britain during the interwar period. They, too, were men with troubling backgrounds. During their initial months in Britain, they met British socialists and were suspected of passing money and secret instructions to them, while also making potentially incendiary remarks in the British left-wing press and at mass speaker meetings. During August 1920, news broke of a new Communist Party of Great Britain, founded with significant assistance from Moscow. At the same time, intelligence emerged that a member or members of the Bolshevik negotiating party had smuggled stolen diamonds and suitcases full of precious metals into Britain and were in the process of selling them off to fund the failing British socialist newspaper, the *Daily Herald*.[7]

British Intelligence presented this and other wide-ranging evidence of Soviet wrongdoing to the cabinet. While certain ministers declared themselves outraged, Lloyd George himself reacted calmly and even with seeming complacency. One of his favourite assertions at this time was that any resurgence of Russian trade would quickly knock the hard edges off Bolshevism, as its leaders found themselves tempted by the benefits of capitalism. 'We have failed to restore Russia to sanity by force,' he had said in February 1920, '[but] I believe we can save her by trade [because] the simple sums in addition and subtraction which it inculcates soon dispose of wild theories.'[8] It was in September 1920 that the Prime Minister faced the greatest clamour to end the Anglo-Russian talks, but he responded only with a tactical retreat, demanding that the most prominent Bolshevik, Kamenev, leave the country, while continuing his negotiations with Krasin, Klyshko and the others.

From the end of 1917 until 1920, British Intelligence had focussed its efforts against Russia on getting rid of the Bolsheviks altogether. After the end of 1920, this was no longer possible. Indeed, it was no longer even possible to imagine a Bolshevik-free Britain, much less a Bolshevik-free world. Intelligence officers now contemplated a future in which the Russian menace would be both permanent and proximate. As early as March 1921, the British government and the Bolsheviks declared themselves ready to conclude an official treaty to formalise their unexpected new relationship. The draft text declared it to be 'desirable in the interests both of Russia and of the United Kingdom that peaceful trade and commerce should be resumed forthwith'.[9] The treaty also contained what for intelligence officers were a long list of worst-nightmares-come-true. It allowed the Russians to send 'such number of [their] nationals as may be agreed' to live in Britain and also granted some among them the 'same privileges [. . .] as are accorded to the official representatives of other foreign Governments' including 'immunity from arrest and search'. It further permitted the importation of '3 kilograms per week' of parcels in 'sealed bags [which were] exempt from examination' and also allowed the use of 'wireless telegraphy in cypher'.[10]

In January 1920 there had been no Soviet citizens in Britain; but by March 1921 there were around thirty. Then, over the next seven years, literally hundreds of Soviet officials and their families travelled to Britain, and to other parts of the empire, availing themselves of the terms of the Anglo-Soviet treaty ostensibly to run the new institutions that it brought into being. Their community spread quickly, from the modest First Avenue Hotel – a place where it had at least been easy for the authorities to keep watch on suspects – to hundreds of separate flats and houses across London's new northern suburbs, in particular Hampstead and Golders Green. Throughout their time in the West, many, if not most, of these men and women would carry out secret work of some form or another, relying on the quasi-diplomatic protections that they enjoyed and also on the day-to-day cover of working for the Russian Trade Delegation or the All-Russian Co-operative Society, ARCOS, a British limited company that was to all intents and purposes a wholly owned commercial arm of the Soviet government.

Despite initial hopes that Lenin's regime might soften and moderate thanks to Lloyd George's intervention – the New Economic Policy, introduced in Russia at the same time as the treaty was signed, seemed especially propitious – the venom would never really leave Bolshevik rhetoric or actions. In fact, official bans on hostile activity, which had been written into the Anglo-Soviet treaty to make it acceptable to the likes of Curzon, were immediately flouted. It seemed as if the many-headed hydra of Soviet Communism had come to take up residence in the British Empire's heart, with its constituent parts choosing to live in a host of unassuming mansion blocks and two-up, two-down terraced houses just five or so miles from Trafalgar Square. Lloyd George had sought peace and prosperity, but in hindsight it would look to many as though he had laid the groundwork for a kind of first Cold War.

COPY.

IMMIGRATION OFFICE,

KING STREET,

NEWCASTLE-ON-TYNE.

May 16th 1920.

(Mr. Mugleston),
    H.M. Chief Inspector,
      Home Office, S.W.

        The undermentioned Russian subjects arrived from Bergen today, the 16th instant.

        They are the members of the Russian (Soviet) Trade Delegation and were met on arrival by Capt. A.P. Thompson of the Russian Trade Committee, and to whom all facilities were given.

    (1) TCHKOLINSKY, Victor *Ivanovitch*] R 3328 *Tcherdingen*
    (2) GOBDIN, Nicholas *Segonan*.
    [(3) KLISHKO, Nicholas .] *Set. in R.421.*
    (4) MILLER, Peter .
    [(5) METCHNIKOFF, Alexandra (F)] R Lists (o) .
    (6) NOGIN, Victor *Parlovich*.
    (7) ROSOVSKY, Solomon, and his son
                 Michael, 14 years.

The party are staying at the First Avenue Hotel, London and left Newcastle 10.10 a.m. today.

             (Signed) J.W. OLDFIELD.

                  H.M. Inspector.

J. W. Oldfield at the Immigration Office in Newcastle-upon-Tyne was the first line of defence in Britain's efforts to protect itself from Soviet negotiators in 1920, faithfully recording the arrival of Nikolai Klyshko and seven others, and immediately sending the information to London, where it was distributed to MI5 and other agencies.

3

THE BIGGEST JEWEL THIEVES IN HISTORY

'Kissing your hand may make you feel very good but a diamond bracelet lasts forever.'

Anita Loos, *Gentlemen Prefer Blondes: The Illuminating Diary of a Professional Lady*, 1925

In Anita Loos's celebrated Jazz Age novel, *Gentlemen Prefer Blondes*, the heroine, Lorelei Lee, an American flapper, is greatly fascinated by diamonds, precious stones and jewellery of all kinds, as she chronicles her journeys through Europe and in the shopping emporia of New York and other major cities. As the quotation above suggests, she is especially keen on diamonds. At the end of her story, the scatterbrained and highly demanding Lee tries to extricate herself from an unwanted romantic relationship by implying to her suitor that she is the sort of woman who might even expect to receive the Russian crown jewels as a gift. When told that these jewels, in addition to being very expensive, might also prove extremely 'unlucky' – given their owners' fates – Lorelei responds dismissively. 'If I found out they were,' she says, 'I could toss them over my left shoulder into the Hudson river some night when there was a new moon, and it would take away the curse.'[1]

In the real world of the 1920s, similarly sanguine reactions to the mass expropriation of Tsarist and Russian aristocratic wealth were commonplace, and probably inevitably so. So many awful things had happened after the Bolshevik seizure of power

– both inside Russia and beyond its borders – that the loss of the country's most ostentatious finery could only be treated by most as a glittering footnote to the greater carnage. But, since the seized jewels were used to fund Bolshevik activities abroad, their significance could not be ignored. In addition, although little attention has been paid to the fact, an important connection exists between this apparently isolated catastrophe and the new global fashion for Art Deco jewellery in the 1920s. Many individual stones ended up adorning modernist pieces after being prised from much older settings in Russian brooches, necklaces, bracelets and tiaras – the majority of them stolen. Once they had been recut to appeal to the latest tastes, it became all but impossible to see these objects' grim provenance.

The story of how Russian pieces entered the West is intimately connected with Bolshevik espionage and subversion, including against Great Britain, and is therefore covered in unexpectedly great depth in the MI5 archives. When contemplating the kinds of things that spies typically try to smuggle across borders, it is natural to focus on secret documents, arms or people. Yet first and foremost spies have always needed money, because money is the most versatile and empowering of weapons. In the early 1920s, to smuggle secret Soviet money actually meant smuggling stolen jewellery, precious metals or works of fine art, and not just occasionally or opportunistically, but in huge quantities, month after month, through underground networks which became both extensive and elaborate.

The scale of Soviet smuggling is surprising given the economic hardships inside Russia itself. Yet, over the seven decades of its existence, the Soviet state persistently showed a willingness to spend funds it could ill afford to stoke foreign revolution. No definitive total has ever been, or probably can ever be, calculated. But at the USSR's collapse in the early 1990s an official Russian court investigation tracked down more than seven hundred foreign bank accounts belonging to the Soviet

Communist Party, and found balances in them exceeding $100 billion.[2] Although not all this money was intended for nefarious purposes, the vast majority would probably have been spent propping up foreign communist parties and other groups that owed their viability to Moscow.

The process of paying to try to recolour the global political map Soviet red started remarkably quickly following the Bolsheviks' rise to power. The need to engage in international work was mentioned by senior Bolsheviks in the very first hours after the storming of Petrograd's Winter Palace on 7 November 1917, and was then reiterated frequently, even at moments of domestic defeat. From 8 October 1918, an international bureau existed inside the Russian Communist Party with responsibility for coordinating overseas liaison with revolutionary groups. Then, from March 1919, a much grander and better-funded Communist International, or Comintern, took on the job. The Comintern's explicit goal was to found 'an international Soviet republic'.[3] Over the decades it employed all manner of tactics, both overt and underhand, to try to make this goal a reality, and the United Kingdom featured perennially as one of its prime targets.

The first Bolshevik arrivals in Britain were not routinely searched when entering the country. To have frisked them all and rifled through their luggage would, it was thought, have jeopardised the treaty, by instantly signalling bad faith on the part of the British government. Nevertheless, British security personnel longed to know what was inside the unwanted visitors' bags and what they had sewn into their suit linings and skirt hems. Evidence seeped out over the months of negotiations, including suggestions of hidden precious metals and caches of diamonds. But, even though the intelligence community felt certain this flow would only expand after the treaty was signed, the talks could not be derailed.

The Bolshevik Nikolai Klyshko was particularly lucky to

avoid personal censure during the negotiating period. Klyshko had brought two suitcases filled with platinum bars into the country on the *Iris* (they had probably been taken from the vaults of some Tsarist-era bank); he had also issued instructions to many others to carry out similar acts. Among the most outlandish were the journeys of a Briton called Francis Meynell, who travelled to the new Baltic states of Estonia, Latvia and Lithuania to collect expropriated Russian jewellery. In a later memoir, Meynell recounted how he had hidden some of these jewels inside pats of butter and put others into the middle of soft-centred chocolates, from which he and his wife had later sucked them. Meynell said he disposed of the booty through 'unorthodox but honest' dealers in Hatton Garden, London's jewellery quarter, with the proceeds going to left-wing projects.[4]

While the ink was still wet on the Anglo-Russian treaty, Klyshko had already begun repaying his hosts' extended hospitality by expanding subversive Soviet activities against the British Empire, including a much more formal operation to move stolen Tsarist jewels westwards into Holland, the world centre of gemstone cutting and distribution. Klyshko was, of course, well known to Britain's intelligence authorities, but he worked extremely hard to hide his connection to various Bolshevik intrigues, maintaining a conspicuous show of legitimate busyness.

After the treaty was signed, Klyshko remained Krasin's second-in-command and appeared to immerse himself in establishing Soviet Russia's permanent commercial and diplomatic presence in Britain. He sought out new premises for the Russian Trade Delegation and ARCOS and held a steady stream of meetings with businessmen who were interested in buying from or selling to the Soviet state. He also had numerous bilateral discussions with Foreign Office officials following on from the conclusion of the treaty, for instance to arrange the transfer to Russia of property that had been impounded by the British at the time of the revolution. This included, during the summer of 1921, the restitution of an icebreaker, the *St Alexander Nevsky*; at the dramatic handover ceremony in Leith, Edinburgh's port, the vessel was renamed the *Lenin!*[5] (Had Leonid Krasin, the official chargé d'affaires, been present in Britain more often, he might have led on such matters, but during 1921 and 1922 he was frequently absent at talks in other countries.)

Beneath Nikolai Klyshko's unobjectionable and industrious facade, British Intelligence could still detect much to dislike in his activities. He was thought to socialise far too often with British communists and others on the British left; his relationship with H. G. Wells, for instance, was seen as very unwelcome (Wells was known to speak up for the Soviet government in the British media and to British government ministers).[6] Klyshko's own meetings with journalists also continued and British spy chiefs could only surmise that his intent was propagandistic. Finally, and most alarming of all – because it was connected with money – there was the great murkiness of Klyshko's personal and professional banking affairs.

Bank accounts, then as now, were prerequisites for international trade. Special Branch and MI5 discovered that the Russian Trade Delegation had opened an enormous number in the period during and immediately after the negotiations. As they monitored Klyshko's accounts with special care – including ordering his bank managers to report every transaction, however innocuous it seemed – they found numerous large-value deposits and withdrawals that could not be explained by the overt and legitimate business of ARCOS and the delegation.

From the start the authorities suspected that these transactions were connected to the funding of revolutionary movements. By May 1921, Special Branch had established that Klyshko was in charge of seven bank accounts, which gave him 'absolute personal control of no less than £1,650,000', a huge sum equivalent to at least £66 million today.[7] These accounts were held at various institutions, including the London Joint City and Midland Bank, Lloyd's Bank and the Guaranty Trust Company of New York's London branch. Special Branch watchers detected large volumes of high-value credits into some of these accounts from a pair of 'shady financiers' called Sam and Max Rabinoff, brothers who divided their time between London, the United States and Estonia.[8] Sam Rabinoff was in the habit of paying £25,000 a week (£1 million today) into the accounts during much of 1921, via an American Express office on Pall Mall. And he was also spotted withdrawing amounts of up to £1,000 a time (£40,000 today) in cash, specifically requesting that the money be paid in 'old Treasury Notes' – 'no doubt,' as Special Branch's Basil Thomson put it, 'in order that tracing may be increasingly difficult'.[9]

From mid-1921 until the second half of 1922, British Intelligence laboured ceaselessly to try to pin down exactly where Rabinoff was getting this money from and what he and Klyshko were doing with it. Officers suspected that the Rabinoffs were selling something very valuable on the black market and funnelling the proceeds to radical left-wing groups. Yet the intelligence agencies knew that if they were to level such accusations successfully, they would need full details.

For many months little of substance was learned. All of Klyshko's postal and telegraphic communications were being tracked but, unsurprisingly, Special Branch discovered only a minimal amount from them. Klyshko must have presumed, or known, that such surveillance was going on and thus almost always communicated sensitive matters through untraceable routes. For a period, the Rabinoffs went to ground also. But then in late September 1922, SIS's French bureau suddenly produced a lead. Word had reached the French government's *Section de Centralisation du Renseignement* (Central Intelligence Section) that the forever-travelling Leonid Krasin had recently done a deal involving jewels with an Amsterdam merchant.

Somehow SIS in France came to know of this (it does not appear to have been through any formal intelligence-sharing arrangement with the French), and after a few weeks' sleuthing the merchant in question was provisionally identified as Gronik Papazian.

Papazian then became further linked to the Russian presence in Britain when he and a group of men he employed were tracked to Poland, where British Intelligence operatives found them staying at Warsaw's most exclusive hotel, the Bristol, along with 'an individual who signs himself "Sam" and who is in correspondence with Klishko of the Soviet delegation in London'.[10] 'Sam', it seems, had slipped up by assuming that so far from London no one would be able to identify him. Before long the British were able to confirm that he was Sam Rabinoff.

There followed several weeks of intensive detective work in and around Warsaw, and then across mainland Europe, as British Intelligence avidly searched for the evidence to tie the Polish group to ARCOS and the Russian Trade Delegation. The case is recorded in papers that Special Branch later transferred to the MI5 archives.[11] The level of detail is exhaustive, even by the standards of these detail-obsessed files, but this is an indication of how hard intelligence officers worked to keep one another informed about progress on the operation (a rare occurrence at the time), and also, it would seem, of their pride in a successful investigation.

Initially, local Polish sources told British Intelligence only that they knew of certain 'goods' arriving in the country in 'parcels' from Moscow, 'parcels' that were 'submitted to "Sam" and the GP Group [i.e. the Gronik Papazian group], whose people [were] at work on them from 9.30 in the morning till 3 p.m. without stopping for lunch'.[12] Fairly soon, however, hints were dropped of the 'large sums' of money involved. $500,000 ($7 million today) was rumoured to have been paid for the contents of the first 'parcel' alone and it was said that without careful handling the cargo – whatever it was – was of sufficient size to 'spoil the market' globally. Intelligence chiefs became convinced that what was being moved was jewels.[13] 'This all looks very like either Crown Jewels or pictures,' Captain H. M. Miller of Special Branch wrote to colleagues on 26 October 1922, 'and I think the recurrent use of the word "parcels" as well as the other peculiarities of the deal indicate jewels.''My presumption,' he continued, 'is that the goods [. . .] are to come to England for sale and that Klishko has a finger in the pie.'[14]

Further despatches from Poland exposed more about the conspiracy. It was established that the Polish government was likely to be in on the act, getting a cut of the proceeds in exchange for turning a blind eye (the monies most probably being part-settlement for reparations that Moscow had agreed to pay Poland at the conclusion of the Russian Civil War). A key conduit for the jewels was revealed as the wife of a middle-ranking Soviet diplomat, a Madame Kaganowski, who used her diplomatic immunity to smuggle the jewellery (presumably by the trunk-load) over the Soviet-Polish border whenever she travelled. Special Branch's Captain Miller briefly considered trying to get an injunction on the enterprise via the Polish courts, but the futility of such a gesture, given the likely involvement of the Poles themselves, swiftly impressed itself upon him. Instead, British Intelligence settled on a watching brief as first Rabinoff and Papazian, and then the jewels themselves, began to leave Warsaw for Western Europe.

During November 1922, the authorities somehow managed to intercept a letter that Rabinoff had sent to Klyshko. Given the care Klyshko had earlier taken, this was a key development. It seems most likely that someone in Warsaw saw the letter before it was sent; hotel porters and receptionists were sometimes paid to do such prying. 'The situation as it now stands is as follows,' the letter began, before helpfully outlining many of the elements of the operation that had previously been opaque to British spies.[15] The Bolsheviks and the jewellery valuers were definitely in cahoots. And it was also now clear that each side did not entirely trust the other. Rabinoff emphasised in particular how great the risks were for his valuation team, saying that this was 'without a doubt the largest deal of its kind in the history of the trade', and also adding that team members urgently wanted more certainty as to Soviet intentions.[16]

'It being a matter of only a few weeks more before the examination will be completed,' Sam wrote, 'it becomes necessary to take the next step, namely, a heart to heart talk with whoever is going to have the final arrangements for the Soviet Government.'[17] Rabinoff was not beyond issuing a thinly veiled threat. 'It is well worth bearing in mind,' he continued, 'that everybody in the trade knows that the GP Group are here estimating the goods and their standing in the trade is such that, if they do not undertake the deal, not another soul or group of souls will come within a hundred miles to look at the goods with any serious intention.'[18] While this was almost certainly untrue, Klyshko was being reminded that the valuers, and presumably Rabinoff himself, expected to be treated with respect, and that their fees would have to be commensurate with the risks they had taken.

For some time, the British authorities had assumed that the vast consignments of Russian gems would start turning up in Britain – indeed, they assumed that previous 'parcels' of jewels had been arriving in the country throughout Klyshko's tenure but that they had failed to track them down. 'My presumption is that the goods are to come to England,' Captain Miller wrote.[19] And with this in mind, both Special Branch and SIS officers kept a keen watch for signs of British citizens being drawn into the business. At times, the spies got quite jumpy. Mention of someone called Lawrence, for instance – a man the informants had spotted working alongside the valuation team in Warsaw – led to some wild speculation that a former British MP named Laurance Lyon had become one of the co-conspirators. (Lyon, a Conservative, had been declared bankrupt in 1921 and had resigned his parliamentary seat; he was known, perhaps uniquely among Tory MPs, as an enthusiast for Russia's new rulers; however, the Lawrence in Warsaw actually turned out to be a local official called Lorenz.)

Eventually, SIS discovered that the gems were destined for Amsterdam, where they were apparently providing a much-needed injection of work for Dutch jewellers. A report in March 1923 listed one of the many enterprises to benefit as F. Friedmann's Diamond Trading Company on Tulpstraat. It had recently received 'a very large quantity of diamonds from the Russian Government', all of which had been 'removed from jewellery', though it was 'impossible to ascertain from what jewellery'.[20] Friedmann's was expected to keep only one per cent of the diamonds it was taking in. These it would refashion and resell itself. But the rest had already gone to other 'large diamond firms' that would recut them in their factories. The original 'diamonds had not been cut in the modern way,' an SIS officer in Holland explained for the benefit of less-knowledgeable colleagues, 'and for this reason there is only a small demand for them in their original state'. The process of re-cutting, he added, was assisting 'in somewhat reducing the unemployment in the Diamond Industry'.[21]

As the jewels themselves helped to prop up the Dutch economy, much of the proceeds from sales came straight to London: money in the form of Dutch florins and French francs flooded into the Russians' British bank accounts every few days during the first months of 1923. By this point, the authorities already understood a great deal about where such money subsequently ended up. Nevertheless, it was horrifying to contemplate that reality afresh with each new boost to Klyshko's, and the Comintern's, resources. Brown envelope after brown envelope had been traced going into the headquarters of the

Communist Party of Great Britain, at 16 King Street in Covent Garden. An estimated £55,000 of Soviet funding (£2.2 million today) had been received by the British communists by the end of 1921, with a further £20,000 (£1 million today) coming during 1922, according to research by Professor Kevin Morgan.[22] Klyshko referred to himself on more than one occasion as British Communism's 'cash box'.[23] Allegedly his money enabled the fledgling, and not very popular, movement to pay newsagents to stock its papers and also gave salaries, often quite hefty ones, to many comrades who would not otherwise have been paid.

For British Intelligence, this was more than enough to justify the expulsion of the Russian Trade Delegation in a trice, yet this was just one aspect of Soviet financial wrongdoing. The *Daily Herald* newspaper, much criticised for accepting jewel money back in 1920, decided not to take further Soviet largesse during the 1920s. In its place, however, a host of other groups queued up to access the Bolsheviks' loot. As an internal Special Branch history of the period set out in 1930, this was 'the hectic time' when 'the principal slogan of the Soviet Government [. . .] was "Come to me, all ye discontented Britishers, and I will give you sinecures with fat salaries".'[24] So great was the demand, apparently, that on 9 November 1922 the Comintern's central executive passed a resolution to expand the programme of jewel sales in order to support its global funding agenda.

Although Klyshko typically requested used banknotes, his bank managers, acting on specific instructions from the government, recorded the serial numbers of any notes they paid him. This meant that on occasion intelligence agencies were able to piece together exactly where particular bundles of notes ended up. One such breakthrough, startling because of the distances involved, came at the end of 1922, the very moment when other aspects of the Papazian–Rabinoff jigsaw were slotting into place.

One portion of the jewel money suddenly turned up

thousands of miles to the east of Warsaw, in the Punjab region of India, and thereby helped to confirm all Churchill and Lord Curzon's worst fears. These were years when a large number of anti-British movements were flourishing in the sub-continent, some peacefully, some not. Historians now agree that Britain's imperial authorities tended to draw insufficient distinction between these movements, classing each as equally unwelcome and equally likely to be susceptible to extremist ideologies such as Bolshevism. The Indian authorities were permanently on guard for Soviet interference during the early 1920s, alerted by the unrest of the immediate post-war period as well as by the clear signs from Moscow that it wanted to play an active role in India's future.

Indian separatists and independence campaigners had already been caught attending training camps at a Comintern-funded school for revolution in Tashkent and quantities of propaganda arriving by ship and over the mountains from Afghanistan had also been seized. Then, during the second half of 1922, a routine arrest in a Punjab bank provided dramatic evidence of the reach of Soviet financial tentacles. An Indian man, described in the archives as a Punjabi separatist, was detained by police when attempting to convert a large number of British banknotes, each worth £100, into local currency. Presumably the man must have been watched as he approached the bank, and the initial purpose of his arrest seems only to have been to remove the funds from his hands. After several months of investigations, however, the banknotes' serial numbers were sent to London and the authorities quickly discovered that they corresponded exactly with those of a batch of notes issued to Klyshko back in June 1921, at the same branch of Lloyd's Bank that was holding his jewel money.[25]

Here, then, was a forensic, worked example of the way that expropriated Tsarist jewels could end up in subversive hands in the farthest reaches of the empire, with a Soviet agent operating from London as the lynchpin. It helps to explain why British Intelligence devoted so much time to tracking cash as it moved from Soviet coffers to Britain's enemies. A princess's tiara, glimpsed at a ball in 1916, really could turn into sticks of dynamite or machine guns in the hands of violent rebels who wished Britain ill.

After the stockpile of Tsarist jewels had been exhausted, later generations of Soviet planners would take to selling the nation's corn and oil to the West instead, but in other respects the model would remain the same. They too would use a significant amount of the country's hard currency to fund foreign radicals (leading to all those healthy bank balances at the moment when the Iron Curtain fell). Before 1917, the world's left-wing groups had frequently perished for want of money. The Bolsheviks saw it as their duty, and indeed their destiny, to use whatever means they could to further hard-line left-wing politics. To British Intelligence's immense frustration, London-based Klyshko, ARCOS and the Russian Trade Delegation were in the vanguard of that effort.

Jewels and other precious objects from the Petrograd palace of Prince Felix Yusupov being inventoried by Bolshevik officials. Thousands of gems like these would come to the West during the 1920s. Some items ended up adorning the necks and wrists of real-life Lorelei Lees, while the proceeds of sales went to pay for Communist Party of Great Britain propaganda or even anti-British attacks in India.

4

DEAR MAMA!

'Ideas have their place, undoubtedly. We need to draw upon them. But the statesman's task is the accommodation of stubborn fact to shifting circumstance [. . .] Look at the Russian Revolution . . . look at the Chinese Revolution . . . look at India . . . look at Poplar. We live in dangerous times.'

Harley Granville Barker, *Waste*, 1927

If there was ever to be a revolution in Britain, money on its own, indispensable as it was, was not going to man the barricades and storm the bastions of bourgeois-imperial power. To achieve that, it would also take people – people and, according to Bolshevik theories of how to run a successful revolution, a party. The Communist Party of Great Britain was Soviet Russia's principal vehicle for revolutionary agitation in the United Kingdom from its inception in the middle of 1920 until the USSR's demise, even though relations between the two entities were frequently strained and constantly underpinned by varying levels of mutual disappointment and distrust.

The CPGB, as the British version of the Communist Party was typically known, would often be described as Moscow's puppet. But while the Bolsheviks undoubtedly acted as the CPGB's puppet *masters*, they were not entirely the puppet's *makers*. Communism was not an external imposition on British political life in the 1920s in the way that many contemporary adversaries alleged, because there had been enthusiastic would-be revolutionaries and left-wing hard-liners in the country long before Lenin took over in Russia.[1] Karl Marx, along with most of his followers before 1917 – Lenin included – had tended to predict that the proletarian revolution would come first to Britain and only later to Russia.

The going had been tough before the Great War, however, and most of the ten thousand or so radical socialists who belonged to the precursors of the CPGB (the largest being the British Socialist Party and the National Socialist Party) felt galvanised by events in Petrograd during 1917, determining that they, too, must now get better at inspiring the masses and organising meaningful agitation. British Intelligence already knew these people, having tracked them to some degree before the war (in an attempt to reduce strike activity) and with much greater intensity during the conflict (because so many radical socialists were also pacifists). Intelligence moles, informants and officers were, thus, quick to pick up on renewed zeal within the movements and saw with their own eyes how guidance and financial support began flowing from Moscow. They instantly judged that this new CPGB would be much more troublesome than any of the radical groups that had come before it.

More troublesome but not necessarily more impressive. One notable fact that jumps out of many intelligence files from this era is that British Intelligence seldom gave British Communists the respect it accorded their Soviet counterparts. While memoranda and minutes fairly often depict Soviet spies as clever, masterly and experienced, the same documents are likely to point out the preposterous and delusional aspects of British Communism. Sometimes British comrades were characterised as little more than freaks and obsessives. And yet, simultaneously, Britain's spies understood that these freaks were capable of causing great harm. Derision and fear, thus, coexisted in the intelligence agencies' appraisals of Britain's far left.

A huge number of the files so far declassified by MI5 relate to CPGB members. All the party's leaders were under surveillance at one time or another, most permanently, and many rank and file members were tracked as well. In plenty of cases, files had been opened before the CPGB existed, but as the composition of the movement changed so the web of surveillance spread. Each week, CPGB members took to the streets to agitate in marketplaces and halls across Britain, campaigning against unemployment and the many other evils of modern life. In strike after strike, they attempted to organise the most radical workers in ways that would prolong, deepen and spread unrest. And in editorials in Communist newspapers they tried to whip up anti-establishment feeling and civil disobedience, including within the armed forces. With each new incident, with each new article, fresh names came to the notice of the intelligence agencies and were added to the list of suspects who had to be tracked and worried about.

Among the people under the most active surveillance were Albert Inkpin, the CPGB's General Secretary for most of the 1920s, and Harry Pollitt, his charismatic Central Committee colleague who would later succeed him as leader. Inkpin and Pollitt were bona fide members of the working class, the former a clerk, the latter a boilermaker, and still young men at the point when the CPGB was created – Inkpin was in his mid-thirties and Pollitt was just twenty-nine. Many other suspects fitted the same template. But the files also reveal others with less proletarian credentials. These included Rajani Palme Dutt, a Cambridge-born, Oxford-educated youth whose father was a Bengali doctor and whose mother was from an upper-class Swedish family; Eva Reckitt, the heiress to the enormous Reckitt's laundry detergent fortune; Ivor Montagu, youngest son of Lord Swaythling, the proprietor of the merchant bank Samuel Montagu and Co.; and Andrew Rothstein, who in the summer of 1920 was just completing an undergraduate degree at Balliol College.

On any given day, Britain's intelligence agencies received hundreds of separate items of information relating to the personal and political lives of these and other CPGB members. This constant flow of new material was the harvest of scores of warrants which the agencies maintained on individuals' post, telegrams and, with increasing frequency as the decade wore on, telephones. To get a warrant was the easy bit; the Home Secretary was supposed to sign off each one but in practice the agreement of senior officers usually seems to have been enough to allow surveillance to commence. What was harder was finding time to sift through all the resulting material; filling in the inevitable blanks with hypotheses that were logical, not fanciful; and separating the irrelevant and innocuous from the dangerous. It was also invariably difficult to know when – given the system's limited resources – an agency ought to stop concentrating on one suspect and switch to another.

The files on Andrew Rothstein – Edith Lunn's lover, whom we met in the prologue – illustrate both the scale of the challenge that British Intelligence faced and its varying degrees of success. Rothstein, the Balliol student, was an obvious target for surveillance because his father was an exiled Russian revolutionary. Theodore Rothstein had fled Russia in 1891 and taken up residence in London. His son Andrew was born in 1898 and grew up in a north London household that regularly played host to other exiled revolutionaries and radicals. From the early 1900s, Rothstein-*père* identified himself with Bolshevism and over time became one of the movement's key overseas supporters. Following the Russian Revolution, he increasingly found himself unwelcome in Britain, and when he left in 1920, on what he believed was just a short trip to Moscow, the British government took the opportunity of banning him forever from re-entering the country.

No sooner had the authorities rid themselves of Theodore, however, than his son Andrew came of age and presented a fresh cause for concern. The close and enduring relationship that Theodore maintained with the British-born,

British-passport-holding Andrew was, of course, one reason for this. In the years after his father's exit, their relationship may be seen as a microcosm of the wider bonds between Soviet Russia and British Communism – familial closeness and a father-son hierarchy that was hard for outsiders to penetrate. But Andrew also became a threat in his own right.

Andrew Rothstein, as we know, would be tracked to such a degree that in 1925 even his partner's summer holidays in Devon and her miscarriage were chronicled exhaustively. The invasion of his privacy started immediately after his father's exclusion. A warrant was taken out by Special Branch at the three addresses where he had been known to live – Balliol College, Whitehall Park in Highgate and Well Walk in Hampstead – on the grounds that 'Rothstein junior', as he was then described, was 'now being used by his father, who is [. . .] abroad and has recently been forbidden to enter the United Kingdom'. Additionally, the warrant referred to Andrew's own roles as 'leader of the Communist set at Oxford' and 'an extremely active propagator of intellectual BOLSHEVISM'.[2]

Every piece of Rothstein's mail was now photographed for the secret services before it reached him. Over the years, this emerging chronicle would throw up many red herrings and false leads, along the lines of the Devon miscarriage: innocent letters from friends and family; facts about where he ate and who he socialised with; mundane bills and invoices that initially seemed important; and even an incident – almost certainly a Communist prank – in which Rothstein's subscription to the Soviet newspaper *Pravda* was redirected to the War Office.[3] Yet from an early stage British Intelligence felt that its enormous interest in the man was justified. Not only did Andrew Rothstein rapidly graduate from student Communism to the upper echelons of the CPGB, he also travelled to Russia at the earliest opportunity, partly to visit his father but also to forge his own ties with the new Russian regime.

The intercepted despatches from this trip, which happened late in 1920, were the first confirmation that Rothstein was fully dedicated to Bolshevik political methods and also that he had become trusted by the Comintern and other parts of Soviet officialdom. Perhaps some would have seen little to be concerned about in a cursory read of his letters back home: Andrew's keenness to come across as older than his twenty-two years led ironically to the opposite impression being created. He appeared callow and inexperienced, and more than a little susceptible to exaggeration. 'Dear Mama! . . . What will they think of me in Oxford!' he boasted as he prepared to return home in November 1920 at the conclusion of his two-month odyssey.[4] (The university authorities were to think enough of him to exclude him from college altogether, thus preventing him from embarking on postgraduate study.)[5] From other sources, the authorities learned that he liked to call himself the mastermind of a recent Oxford bus strike – in fact his part had been minimal – and that he had asserted, at a dinner party, that it was 'primarily' he who would be 'responsible for the preparation of the list of persons to be shot in England when the revolution dawns'.[6]

Hyperbole? Absolutely. But, on closer inspection, Rothstein's letters to his mother show a remarkably cold-blooded response to revolutionary violence, and a total willingness to parrot official Bolshevik explanations for injustices and barbarities. Among his descriptions of trips to the ballet and a concert by the famous singer Chaliapin, Andrew casually dropped in mentions of operations by the Soviet Cheka, the notorious internal secret police (predecessor of the KGB). 'We read of rumours doing the rounds in England and France to the effect that there has been an uprising or some sort of disturbance in Moscow,' he wrote. But 'of course, there has been nothing of the kind. The Cheka [. . .] has merely been unearthing the latest in a long line of conspiracies [. . .] and is taking extreme measures to deal with it. Life in Moscow goes on as normal – a bit dirty [. . .] a bit hungry, but so contemporary and new all the same.'[7] After he had written something similar to his uncle in Poland, the uncle replied with a stern critique. 'It seems to me,' he said, 'that you have seen life in Russia with the eyes of a fanatical credulous man [. . .] you ought to go to another town [i.e. not Moscow] and there talk with the people and see there the poverty and depression of spirits and miserable conditions. Do you think all newspapers and travellers tell lies?'[8] British Intelligence officers reading this must surely have smiled to witness the youth being so upbraided.

Following his return and expulsion from Oxford, Rothstein busied himself with the development of the CPGB, serving as a high-ranking member and relentlessly imposing Moscow's will on independently minded comrades. To ease communications with Russia, and as a sign that some senior Bolsheviks trusted him personally, Moscow officials gave him a range of roles in London's Soviet bodies. A Russian Trade Delegation staff list from the middle of 1921 already describes Rothstein as the 'Assistant to KLISHKO' without specifying exactly what kind of assistance he was providing (it later emerged that he was considered Klyshko's number two in secret matters).[9] Six months on and another version of the same list described him as the 'Editor of the Information Bureau', a propaganda post that he would hold for many years, partly in conjunction with a job at the *Daily Herald*.[10]

At the end of 1920, an MI5 officer had written that Rothstein was 'reported to be the most dangerous and active agent of the Soviet Government in this country'.[11] A few months later, intelligence information caused a senior Foreign Office official, Esmond Ovey (later the British ambassador to Russia), to state in an internal document that Andrew 'appear[ed] to be the worst of the family', Ovey having already made it clear that the Rothsteins as a whole were a thoroughly bad bunch.[12]

Other damning superlatives from the British authorities included calling Rothstein 'the chief official apologist of the Soviet in this country' and accusing his staff at the Information Bureau – later renamed ROSTA and later still TASS – of being 'some of the worst elements' of the Soviet group in London.[13]

Just as with Klyshko, however, certain aspects of Rothstein's life were more easily tracked than others. His public activities within the CPGB and in the press were recorded in what appeared to be their totality – right down, for instance, to his participation in an anodyne end-of-year dinner of the Hampstead branch of the Communist Party. This was held at Pinoli's in Soho, a famous Jazz-Age haunt. Full details of the event, including menu choices, were circulated across Whitehall and to members of the cabinet (who thus got to read of *hors d'oeuvre variés*; tomato soup; fried fillet of whiting; lamb cutlets; chicken au chasserole; salads; ices; and cheese, and a rousing rendition of 'The Red Flag') as if the safety of the nation depended on it.[14] Examples of Rothstein's journalism were also minutely inspected, and when he was discovered sometimes using the alias C. M. Roebuck, the coordinates of a second life emerged to be tracked.

Yet, while there were persistent rumours that Rothstein was Moscow's principal recruiting sergeant for informants and secret agents in Britain, evidence of this crucial activity proved hard to come by. He was also suspected of spearheading an initiative to force all British employees of the Russian Trade Delegation and ARCOS to join the CPGB. Many of these people were just ordinary clerical and manual labourers drawn from the greater London area but it was said that he occasionally resorted to outright aggression in pressuring them to support the cause. British officials would have taken a very dim view of such coercion, but the evidence for this was largely anecdotal. By the middle of the decade, British Intelligence had been forced to accept that Rothstein carefully curated his public persona and otherwise tried to 'avoid coming too prominently into the limelight'.[15]

Through the signals traffic they decoded, and from other sources, intelligence officers were aware that Moscow put great store by Rothstein's analysis of British politics. This naturally led them to wonder if the young Communist had any access to privileged sources. At the end of 1921, they discovered that in at least one case he had. Rothstein was found to have tapped up an old friend from Balliol days, a fellow Communist called Tom Wintringham, to glean sensitive gossip from the man's aunt, the Liberal MP Margaret Wintringham. She was only the second woman to sit in the House of Commons and the gossip was said to relate to recent personnel changes at Special Branch, most obviously the mysterious resignation of Sir Basil Thomson.[16] Despite continually watching both Rothstein and the Wintringhams, however, no further leaks from this direction could be traced and officials were left anxious and uncertain.

It was to be the same story, time after time, throughout the ranks of the CPGB family. Of course, very few comrades could claim the quality of connections or the pedigree of Andrew Rothstein, but a great many showed identical enthusiasm and willingness to spend time on secret work, flirting with sundry forms of illegality in the process. The paths from CPGB head office in Covent Garden to ARCOS and the Russian Trade Delegation in New Bond Street and (from 1922) Moorgate were exceedingly well-worn. Whenever they had the resources, Special Branch and MI5 liked to watch people shuttling between these addresses carrying packages replete with money, propaganda, instructions or other unknown materials. Whether or not such people were actually breaking the law was a moot point, but the intelligence agencies treated their movements as proof of the continued illegal meddling of a foreign power. The British were particularly struck by the variety and number of people involved – everyone from top party officials and delegation directors to typists, errand-boys and fresh recruits. Could the authorities really expect to keep track of them all?

Below the level of the national CPGB there was plenty of activity as well, with infiltration frequently the name of the game – infiltration of the Labour Party, trade unions, and the armed forces. However, once again, the proof that these organisations were being infiltrated was tricky to come by. A report in August 1922 told Special Branch of around '300–400 communists (members of the Party)' who had infiltrated 'the South Wales Miners' Federation', as well as of 'similar attempts [at] establishing communist nuclei [. . .] in other sections of the Miners' Federation of Great Britain, [and] in all other trade unions where they can possibly gain a foothold'.[17] But this was unusually specific.

The same notion, of establishing nuclei, was clearly in Tom Bell's mind when he gave a speech to a Communist meeting at West Islington Library on 4 March 1923, unwittingly watched over by a Special Branch mole. His speech raised the authorities' hackles, yet he said nothing precise enough to warrant immediate action. Bell described how the Red Army had been vital to Bolshevism's triumph in Russia and added that, in this context, British comrades needed to 'sow [. . .] the seeds of discontent in the rank and file of the naval and military forces, who were all sprung from the ranks of the workers', and hope 'at the opportune moment to win over sufficient of these [sailors and soldiers] to form the nucleus of the armed forces of the Communist state'.[18]

Parliament was yet another place to infiltrate, even though in theory it was meant to be irrelevant to Communists, who denied the validity of bourgeois democracy. Getting in touch with serving MPs, like Margaret Wintringham, was one tactic, but having one's own representatives in the legislature was for a time thought to be even better. The 1920s Comintern acknowledged the potential importance of electoral success as a means of giving comrades influential platforms from which to speak and other stepping stones to real power. At the highest level, the CPGB sought to affiliate with the Labour Party on numerous occasions but was rebuffed each time. However, in the 1922 general election two Communist MPs were elected, both for vibrant working-class constituencies: Shapurji Saklatvala in London's North Battersea; and Walton Newbold in Motherwell in Scotland. In his maiden speech to the House of Commons, Saklatvala exploited this tribune to full effect, saying that his election showed how his constituents 'now require[d] that the people's matters [should] be talked [of] in the people's voice', and adding that 'neither this Ministry nor any other Ministry' (referring to the new Conservative government of Andrew Bonar Law) would be able to 'cure the evil' of 'traditions', 'family interest', 'class privileges' and 'private enterprise' without wider social transformation.[19] The London MP had already been under British Intelligence surveillance for years. Perhaps shockingly, or perhaps not, the surveillance continued on him throughout his time in office.[20] (While no files on Newbold have been released to date, it is hard to imagine he escaped the spies' gaze either.)

Alongside infiltration, British Intelligence also detected increasing CPGB involvement in so-called front organisations, a development that worried the authorities especially because Communist influence deployed in this way could be kept almost completely hidden from view. Most significantly, the CPGB established the National Unemployed Workers' Movement (NUWM) in April 1921, a group that went on to have huge success shaping public debate about unemployment and unsettling mainstream politicians and the wider establishment. On the day that Shapurji Saklatvala first spoke in the House of Commons, 23 November 1922, a demonstration of fifty thousand unemployed men and women had gathered nearby, under the auspices of the NUWM, to petition the government at the end of a nationwide 'hunger march'.

During the preceding year and a half, Special Branch had been keeping close tabs on the NUWM and its leader Wal Hannington, a founding CPGB member. Among the more eye-catching details it had observed was a demonstration in Newcastle-upon-Tyne which had taken place beneath a banner 'bearing skull and cross bones' and another, in Sunderland, where the slogan 'Starving in the Richest Country in the World' had been chanted.[21] Attempting to sum up the NUWM's and the CPGB's impact on the workless, one intelligence officer made it sound as if unemployment was a hardship that could be endured silently and without negative consequences if only the affected individuals were left in peace. 'The Communists are again devoting a good deal of attention to the unemployed, whom they keep in a state of perpetual ferment,' this gentleman wrote in mid-1921.[22]

Taken together, these activities confirmed to British Intelligence that the CPGB now presented a very real threat to domestic stability. Spy chiefs could see that, unlike in the past, the CPGB had much greater financial resources at its disposal – and that it was able to call on the help of experienced Bolsheviks whenever it wanted. Indeed, more often than not, it appeared to act simply as a Bolshevik subsidiary in Britain, with little or no interest in setting an independent agenda of its own.

As well as Rothstein's 1920 trip, top CPGB members crisscrossed Europe constantly to attend Comintern meetings. Harry Pollitt, for instance, made no fewer than four journeys to Moscow between the middle of 1921 and the start of 1924, which implies he saw the place as something like head office. The rhetoric of British Communism could be every bit as bloody as its Soviet counterpart's, too, conjuring up images of gory chaos and retaliation against anyone with an alternative point of view. The CPGB chairman, Arthur MacManus, clearly thought that violence would be unavoidable at some future date when he spoke at a special conference of the party in April 1921:

> If the working class wishes to get into the saddle, it must be prepared for the eventuality of the use of violence. We are realists. We have our minds made up that the one solution of the problem is revolution, and nothing else. Capital is going to have to resort to any method in order to prevent it. We shall have to resort to all the essential methods to achieve it. Already the working class have got the capital class so tottering that its members are leaning against each other to prop each other up. In its final attempt to kill the working class capitalism will find on the other side a fortified, relentless organisation.[23]

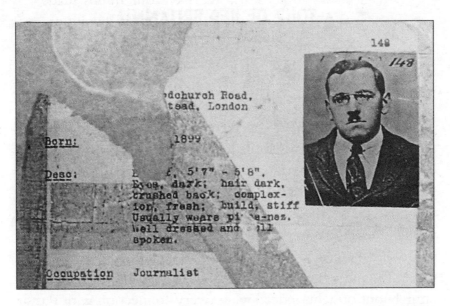

148

148

dchurch Road,
tead, London

Born: 1899

Desc: L £. 5'7" - 5'8".
               Eyes, dark; hair dark,
               brushed back; complex-
               ion, fresh; build, stiff
               Usually wears pi 'e-nez.
               Well dressed and ;ll
               spoken.

Occupation   Journalist

Andrew Rothstein looks more like a bank teller than a top-ranking Anglo-Russian revolutionary in this early-1920s MI5 identification document, but British Intelligence amassed tens of thousands of pages of information on him over several decades and, in the early years, the Soviets trusted him as one of their own. From the perspective of the British authorities, he was an eccentric young man who could not be respected but had to be feared.

5

A TOUR OF RED BRITANNIA

The Soviet government expected many of those employed by ARCOS and the Russian Trade Delegation to perform both overt and covert roles during their time in Britain. In exactly the same way, it expected CPGB members to work both publicly and in secret for the good of the revolution, slipping in and out of the limelight whenever necessary. But there was a third type of Bolshevik agent who resided in the United Kingdom during the 1920s and whose work for Moscow was supposed to occur entirely out of sight, indeed whose very connection with Russia was meant to be concealed from Britain's authorities. These were the undercover agents whom the Kremlin sent illegally into the country in order to try to influence events, with an explicit expectation that they would leave no official trace behind.

Truly undercover agents are the most celebrated type of spy. Theirs is usually believed to be the most dangerous of espionage jobs, entailing the biggest risks and the most sensitive missions. An undercover agent often has no way of communicating with his bosses once he or she is in the field and may not have anyone else to trust in the vicinity. The penalty for getting caught may be disownment by one's own side and harsh punishment by one's captors.

It had been fear of undercover German agents that had partly led to the creation of MI5 and SIS in 1909. Many Britons, egged on by right-wing newspapers, politicians and writers, had become convinced that their country was overrun by the Kaiser's spies – men whom they thought could be hiding in their local neighbourhoods, posing as music teachers or watercolourists or pursuing any number of other innocuous-seeming occupations. During the 1920s, similar fears continued to grip significant elements within British society, including the intelligence agencies, although now they were directed against the Soviets. As the intelligence archives show, these worries resulted from a combination of concrete facts and near-irrefutable fictions. The fictional dimension is important: a big problem with undercover agents was that, until you found them, you simply didn't know whether they existed or not. The Cold War cliché of 'Reds under the bed', which in time would give rise to McCarthyism and other witch hunts, was durable precisely because it was so hard to disprove.

In this context, British Intelligence in the 1920s became convinced that, at any given time, Britain was playing host to a sizeable number of undercover Soviet agents. The British agencies had objected to the Anglo–Russian trade deal precisely on the grounds that, even if the Soviet government appeared to adhere to the 1921 treaty, many Bolshevik spies might still be doing Moscow's bidding in secret and it might take years to root them out. Sure enough, this was what happened. Although the numbers never quite lived up to British officers' worst fears, the presence of undercover agents did come to symbolise the worst of the Soviet Union's meddling in British affairs.

When they thought of undercover agents, British Intelligence chiefs' default assumption was that these individuals had been sent to Britain to undermine the British state – and in a sense this was always true, irrespective of what the agents actually got up to. Yet this also ignored an important nuance of Bolshevik strategy – a nuance that it took the agencies a long time to appreciate – namely that in the early decades of

Soviet rule, Moscow only sent undercover agents to Britain when it doubted the ability of trade delegation employees or CPGB members to realise its goals. Sometimes this happened when a particular mission looked too complex, but more often than not it was because Moscow had lost patience with some or all of its local emissaries and wanted a fresh pair of eyes or hands on the ground. On many occasions, it could be argued, Soviet residents in London and members of the CPGB had considerably more to fear from the arrival of an undercover Russian than did the British authorities or the wider British public.

The most significant undercover spy case during the early 1920s began in March 1922, when a mysterious figure called George Brown suddenly popped up and started to attend CPGB meetings across Britain. This individual, a tall, dark-haired, thickset man in his late thirties, spoke English with a not-quite-American accent and moved round the country challenging comrades about their commitment to the Marxist cause and their application of revolutionary theory and technique. Brown materialised in the United Kingdom as if from nowhere and on his round-Britain travels always affected the same behaviour, entering meetings at the last possible moment and leaving before anyone else.

Brown had been sent direct from Comintern headquarters in Moscow with specific orders to provide detailed and unvarnished feedback on the CPGB and to change its direction of travel. Since its creation, the party had toiled diligently to try to get its message across to British workers, but it had not yet had the level or speed of success that Moscow expected. Brown's arrival signalled both the Bolsheviks' frustration with their British brethren and their determination to bring about a change. As far as we know, some members of the British party had encouraged the Comintern to send someone like Brown, but others saw his presence as both a slight and a threat. Significantly, just a few weeks before the secret agent's arrival, Arthur MacManus, the CPGB chairman, had stood before senior Bolsheviks inside the Kremlin's walls and painted 'a glowing picture' of the British party as one that already had 'very great political influence'.[1] It was already 'a centralised and disciplined party', he had said, aware that the role it had to play was 'of historical importance'.[2] His bosses had clearly not been persuaded.

In fact, Moscow's analysis of recent events was starkly at variance with the story MacManus told. While the infiltration of certain mainstream left-wing organisations in Britain had been advancing steadily under CPGB auspices, and the National Unemployed Workers' Movement had met with early popularity, the Comintern had become fixated by the British party's failure to capitalise on a supposedly revolutionary situation that had emerged in Britain during 1921. In the early months of that year, British unemployment had almost doubled, from 8 per cent to over 15 per cent, and there was unrest in most of the country's heavy industries.[3] When coal miners planned a strike, they did so fully expecting that railwaymen and other transport workers would join them under the terms of the Triple Alliance that had been agreed in 1914. On Black Friday (15 April 1921), however, these miners were deserted by their so-called brothers and left to strike alone.

Moscow felt this should have been the CPGB's signal to embark on a full-scale mobilisation – an opportunity to expose the narrowness and selfishness of moderate socialism and to expand the party's campaigning activities enormously. As a minimum, Bolsheviks had expected the CPGB to sign up thousands of disgruntled miners and other workers who wanted their unions to show greater solidarity, but there was also talk of a potential once-in-a-generation opportunity to channel worker anger into a more thoroughgoing attack on the state. The fact that the CPGB's tactics had remained broadly unchanged throughout the crisis, while party membership actually declined, was, therefore, desperately disappointing. At one point, membership fell to just 2,500, less than at the party's foundation.

It was George Brown's job to fix these problems.[4] Under a string of different identities (George Brown was only an alias), he had already spent almost twenty years in the revolutionary movement and was seen by the Comintern as something of an international troubleshooter. Brown's real name was Mikhail Borodin (though even this was a change from his birth name of Mikhail Gruzenberg) and he had come from a poor Jewish family in what is now Belarus. Before the revolution, he had spent a decade in the United States, learning to speak English fluently, including during a period at Valparaiso University in Indiana. He became renowned for both his toughness and his ability to interpret Marxist theory, and he had already been employed as the Comintern's main roving underground ambassador in the years up to 1922. He also attained a place in Bolshevik lore for his ability to go unnoticed for long periods of time, switching seamlessly between aliases and disguises and crossing continents seemingly with a cloak of invisibility. Capable of great charm and wit, he was nonetheless ruthless and cold. 'He is like the others,' a British woman who met him around this time observed. 'One feels instinctively that however much they may like one as a woman, they would sacrifice one in a minute if it was necessary for the cause.'[5]

Borodin had done his homework ahead of the trip to Britain. His thoughts on the Black Friday disaster were published in a book which appeared in Russia under the resonant title *The History of the Great Betrayal*.[6] From afar he was perplexed by the CPGB's supine reaction to the events of 1921. Once in the country, however, he quickly began to understand how a fragmented and insufficiently centralised party had framed such a pathetic response. Supported by Rothstein, Klyshko and the small circle of others who knew of his mission, Borodin proceeded to demand that comrades show greater obedience to the will of the Central Committee and the Comintern, and allow much stronger coordination of key messages and propaganda. In interviews that he set up, he would typically listen for a long time before responding decisively with his own vision of what needed to happen. At speaker meetings, he would similarly allow questions from the floor but would then respond ferociously if a question implied a divergence of opinion from his own, and therefore the Comintern's, perspective. His critiques could be coruscating, his putdowns memorable.

For most of the time from his arrival in March 1922 until the end of the summer, he moved around Britain without British Intelligence having any idea he was there. Borodin most likely entered the country by bribing Dutch fishermen to bring him across from Holland and drop him on a secluded beach somewhere on England's east coast. From Special Branch's retrospective investigations, among other sources, we now know that he managed to address gatherings of CPGB members and radical trade unionists in London, Cardiff and Blackpool, and we can safely assume that he met activists in other locations as well. On 18 March, just days after his arrival, he attended the fourth congress of the CPGB at St Pancras Town Hall in central London. None of British Intelligence's moles within the CPGB reported back on the man's existence; none of the letters and telegrams that were written and received by Communists under surveillance mentioned him either. His tradecraft was good enough so that, for a long time, the inner circle of Communist trust remained unbroken.

Eventually, however, a tip-off did come Special Branch's way. This happened on 7 July 1922. The archives do not reveal the source, but it seems to have amounted to little more than a suspicion that George Brown was not who he said he was, which led Special Branch to watch him more closely. Over the next six weeks or so, the organisation worked to establish both who Brown was and where he would turn up next. While his identity as Borodin remained elusive until August, officers quickly realised that they were dealing with an undercover spy who had come to Britain from Russia – a discovery that obviously increased pressure on them to run him to ground.

In early August, word that Brown was Borodin came to Special Branch via an 'exceptionally well-informed correspondent'.[7] This was followed, almost immediately, by news from a telephone and telegram warrant that Glasgow Communists expected the agent to arrive later that month for a meeting at the Scottish Labour College, a night school for workers. One local activist was mentioned as Brown's key contact: Freda Cohen, whom Special Branch already knew to be an 'anarchist and communist'.[8] As the day of the agent's arrival neared, the authorities placed a physical watch on Cohen, shadowing her every move.

Finally, at 6.50 p.m. on 22 August, a showery Tuesday evening, Cohen left her home to go to the college, apparently unaware of the police detail moving across the city behind her. Just fifteen minutes after she entered the college building, she and nineteen other Communists (the rest of whom were men) got a huge shock when fifty-three police detectives burst into their incipient meeting and detained them. According to officers' subsequent reports, eighteen of the attendees had been sitting in a horseshoe formation at the moment the meeting was broken up, facing two others, one of whom was a Scottish socialist leader, while the other was Brown/Borodin. The Russian had been preparing to make his speech.

While this was clearly the end of his mission to Britain, the Soviet agent appeared calm at the moment of his arrest and subsequently. He had been caught plenty of times before, and in considerably less hospitable surroundings than Scotland. According to Dan Jacobs, Borodin's biographer, at the moment of his capture he even managed to crack a joke. When an officer demanded to see his passport and documents, Borodin had knowingly tapped his trouser pocket, making clear that money had been the only passport he needed.

Days of intense questioning followed, yet Borodin remained

unbroken, returning each night to his cell in Duke Street prison in Glasgow with the key secrets of his identity and citizenship intact. Sometimes he pretended to police that he was Czech, sometimes Austrian, and sometimes Yugoslavian. Even though the authorities knew both who he was and where he was from, Borodin understood the importance of maintaining silence on these matters, so as to limit the British government's ability to capitalise on the case. During the course of Special Branch's inquiries, it discovered no fewer than sixteen suspected aliases for its culprit: fictitious identities that he had used across the globe. When he refused to confess, he was tried in early September on charges of being an illegal alien and convicted with a minimum of fuss, being moved to the larger Barlinnie prison to serve out his six-month sentence prior to deportation. He was eventually ejected from Britain on 22 February 1923, almost a year after his initial, secret arrival. Carrying papers that declared him a stateless person, he was taken in handcuffs to the port of Blyth in Northumberland, and put on the SS Loos bound for Petrograd.

The conclusion of Borodin's case clearly gave British Intelligence some grounds to view the debacle as a success. The operation in Glasgow had demonstrated how the intelligence agencies could function on a nationwide basis, in spite of budget cuts, and also how they could sometimes maintain the element of surprise (attendees at the Scottish Labour College event evidently had had no idea that they were about to be raided). But the reasons for optimism were limited. As with the uncovering of Klyshko's jewel network and the tracking of Rothstein and other British Communists, the episode was yet another indication of how Britain's security services perennially came late to the party, identifying problems long after they had arisen and, in spite of attempts to be systematic, discovering important information in a worryingly haphazard way.

To what extent had Borodin been able to boost the CPGB's fortunes during his five months at large in the United Kingdom?

Certain indications during late 1922 and 1923 suggested that he had managed to do quite some harm before he was caught. A fundamental reorganisation of the CPGB's structures and discipline was agreed at a congress in Battersea in October 1922 – very much in line with the changes Borodin had been calling for – and in 1923 the party's official newspaper, the *Communist*, underwent a major overhaul, reopening as the *Workers' Weekly*, and seeing its readership rise rapidly from 19,000 to 51,000 in the space of just eight weeks.[9] And it remained to be seen how many British workers Borodin might have recruited as Comintern agents or similar.

If all this made Borodin's imprisonment in some ways akin to shutting the stable door after the horse had bolted, the authorities also had to worry that there wasn't in fact a door to shut. Borodin's case, and in particular how he had entered the country, without legal travel documents and avoiding formal ports, was a sharp reminder of Britain's porous and poorly defended borders. With its island setting, the United Kingdom had traditionally relied on natural rather than manmade barriers to keep undesirables out, but men like Borodin exposed the inadequacy of such an approach. After his arrest, intelligence officers and other officials naturally wondered how many more Borodins there were. Each successful case tended to end like this, with higher estimates being made of the number of secret agents still at large. In reality, there were probably no more than a dozen or so undercover Soviet spies in Britain throughout the 1920s (with perhaps a dozen more operating around the empire). But British counterespionage agencies persistently behaved as though the country was playing host to scores of such individuals at any one time.

Just as concerning was what the Borodin case said about the assistance such people could expect upon arrival in Britain. Special Branch surmised that the Russian had received help at each stage of his visit from employees of ARCOS and the

Russian Trade Delegation (a fact that would be corroborated years later by evidence collected from another undercover spy).[10] This assistance included passing money to the secret agent in order to enable him to live, and allowing him access to the privileged and untouchable diplomatic bag, through which he was able to communicate securely with the Comintern in Moscow. While Borodin ended up in Barlinnie, the bosses of the official Soviet bodies in London – Klyshko, Krasin and others – got away without any punishment or censure for their contribution to his operation, and they continued to be free to do exactly the same again with future undercover agents, thanks to the British Prime Minister's seemingly unshakeable support for the controversial Anglo-Russian deal.

№ 26 (222)   Пятый год издания.   Цена в Москве, провинц. и на ст. ж. д. 10 коп.

Огонек

КТО ТАКОЙ БОРОДИН?

Upon returning from his British sojourn Borodin was not punished by his Soviet bosses, as many who got captured in later years were. Instead, he found himself promoted. Here, pictured with his son on the cover of a Soviet magazine in 1927, he had risen to be the Soviet representative in China. It was another role in which he would create headaches for the British.

PART 2

THE TRUTH ABOUT 'INTELLIGENCE'

The limitations and inadequacies of intelligence work are inherent in its make-up. As the renowned writer on intelligence matters James Rusbridger stated in a brilliant exposé at the end of the Cold War, *The Intelligence Game: The Illusions and Delusions of International Espionage*, 'it is frequently said about advertising that half the money spent is wasted but no one knows which half, [and] much the same can be said about intelligence services'.[1] Some problems have already been hinted at in the early chapters of this book: the risk of ignoring big leads; the risk of following completely insignificant ones; making incorrect connections; handling too many cases at once; and the threat of being disregarded, or even countermanded, by one's political masters. But it is now time to consider these problems in more detail, because a key revelation of the MI5 archives is the extent to which error and omission, and coping with their aftereffects, defined British Intelligence's work in the decade after 1920.

If doctors, nurses or engineers erred as often as spies, we would talk of little other than their mistakes. But spying, it is widely accepted, is unlike other highly skilled professions. It may best be thought of as akin to prospecting for gold, in which everything, from the decision to start, to the choice of where to look and how long to go on searching, is underpinned by large doses of faith and hope. Success itself is largely a matter of luck, and remains so even for those who have experienced good fortune before. But the gold glitters and is valuable, and so when it finally turns up the enormous effort expended to find it is easily justified in the minds of prospectors, and they are prepared to invest still more in future. In fact, just like a gold rush, spikes in intelligence activity, such as that experienced in the West throughout the USSR's existence, are almost always an interaction of tangible reality on the ground and a certain intangible mania in the air.

If this seems obvious, it is nonetheless something that intelligence chiefs have never found easy to admit. Today's leaders of MI5, SIS and GCHQ make intermittent public statements about the care they take when conducting their business and their commitment to accuracy, all the while remaining silent about how accurate it is possible for them to be or how the care they take makes a difference. When occasionally they do admit to problems, it is almost always as a precursor to requesting extra powers, extra money or extra people – the reasoning being that if these had been available in the first place, the mistakes would not have occurred.

Very similar paradigms existed in the 1920s. Although public statements were much less common because so few details about the secret services had been divulged, public discourses about British Intelligence did exist and state spies had at least some role in trying to shape and steer them. In particular, in the years after the Great War, a clutch of non-fiction books alluded to the role that secret intelligence had played in Britain's victory over Germany. A smaller number of titles also mentioned the secret dimension of Britain's new fight against Bolshevism, but since this was a live operation commentary was much more limited. In each instance, the intelligence organisations' competence and cool-headedness were emphasised, and little if any space was given to discussing errors or inherent limitations. A key text was Sir Paul Dukes's memoir *Red Dusk and the Morrow* about a

British Intelligence operative's exploits in Russia between 1917 and 1919. Dukes, a former SIS officer, helped to give credence to the view that British spies were dispassionate protectors of the common good, who saw the world clearly for what it was, and who were therefore immune to delusion and distortion. In what would become a stereotypical contrast, Dukes compared this with 'the phenomenon of Red Russia', which represented the 'supreme example of the triumph over reason'.[2]

In a similar vein, when Sir Basil Thomson wrote a series of articles for *The Times* shortly after standing down as head of Special Branch in late 1921, he too implied that British intelligence agencies were invariably right, except when they lacked sufficient power. Thomson had left his post unwillingly, yet, rather than use the newspaper to run down his internal rivals, he chose to wax lyrical about his own excellent work over the years and to pay tribute to the secret workers among the rank and file who had toiled alongside him. Errors were not inevitable, he said at the end of his thirteen-week serialisation in the paper, but the intelligence community was being hobbled by Britain's weak laws:

> The ordinary law, the legal procedure against sedition, is archaic and ponderous, and it provides no penalty for the introduction of money or valuable property from abroad to subsidise the advocates of violent revolution in this country [. . .] It is only a question of time [before] something will happen which forces the Government of the day into panic legislation [. . .] I vacate office with the feeling that the temporary lull in revolutionary activity is like the centre of a cyclonic disturbance, which is always followed by the strongest gale of all [. . .] we are no better prepared for it than the man who goes out to face a hurricane with an umbrella as his only protection.[3]

Historians of espionage have often played down the importance of routine mistakes, too, implying that, because secret service work is difficult, the truly surprising thing is that more gaffes did not occur. Blunders are most likely to be mentioned when evidence exists that they were spotted quickly and corrected or when they can be shown to have been the result of an opponent's brilliance – the most obvious example of the latter in British espionage is the story of the Cambridge Five.

Ordinary everyday miscalculations tend to be left out. But to my mind such mistakes are part of the main story. The MI5 archives show that error and confusion contributed greatly to the atmosphere of agitated uncertainty that prevailed in the intelligence community throughout the interwar period, while also fuelling the high levels of unproductive rage that British Intelligence directed towards its enemies, particularly Soviet Russia. Mistakes also fanned the flames of the paranoia that British spies and others came to feel. And, of course, there is no doubt that a greater number of genuine wrongdoers could have been identified if fewer innocent people had been tracked and trailed.

Learning from errors is always difficult in contexts where errors are not readily owned up to – and this was definitely true of British Intelligence in the 1920s. In the episodes that follow we look at some of the problems that Thomson, Dukes and others excluded from their own accounts, problems that were also mostly hidden from politicians and senior civil servants at the time. Many of these shortcomings are forgivable in context, but others are harder to explain, even after adjusting for hindsight. There are omissions, examples of wasted effort, misinterpretations and overreactions – evidence aplenty of how a fragmented intelligence community struggled to adapt to new threats at a time of falling budgets, but also of how officers followed too many leads indiscriminately, without pausing to assess whether they represented the most productive use of their time.

Gut instinct or, to put it less flatteringly, prejudice drove many decisions. Officers' over-estimation of the scale of the Bolshevik threat led to the conviction that the number of suspects must be very, very large, and since the number of suspects was typically the main proxy for measuring the scale of the threat, this easily turned into a self-reinforcing paradigm. The more suspects who were unearthed, the bigger the problem. The bigger the problem, the more suspects there were still to be found.

Though much of the information collected by British Intelligence would prove completely irrelevant in terms of its own work against Bolshevism, it is ironically of value to the present day for the way in which it shines an unusual light on the 1920s as a whole. In addition to recording the routines and rhythms of spies and secret agents, some parts of MI5's archives now resemble a catalogue of the habits and fashions of 1920s Britain more generally. There are, for instance, rendezvous in nightclubs, extramarital affairs and accounts of the lives of society artists. Details that turned out to be false leads or distracting ephemera for the intelligence officers at the time now offer us an unanticipated new perspective on the Jazz Age.

6

GETTING AWAY WITH IT

Before Borodin landed on some British beach masquerading as George Brown, we know of at least one other Soviet agent who had entered Britain undercover and worked there undetected during the early 1920s. Of all the cases British Intelligence dealt with in these years, this one – the Johnnie Walker case, as it became known – may well have left the deepest scars, because Walker travelled with a wife, a duo who ought to have been a lot easier to catch than a lone agent like Brown, and yet both Walker and his wife succeeded in leaving Britain at the end of their first mission, uncaught and able to re-enter the country again.

Long acknowledged as a low point for the intelligence services, the Johnnie Walker affair had a protracted and unpleasant afterlife, as many of its nastiest surprises were revealed only after Walker's final departure. Most stunning of all was to be the revelation in the early 1950s that Walker had in fact been no clandestine mastermind, but just a novice when he left Moscow in September 1920 – a novice who nonetheless managed to test the patience and effectiveness of Britain's leading intelligence officers to breaking point.

'Johnnie Walker' is certainly the kind of alias that a novice would choose. It is everything that 'George Brown' is not: eye-catching, a little arch and knowing, and, above all, very memorable – that is to say, a terrible name for a spy. Undoubtedly the name was connected with the scotch whisky that is still drunk today. The man who selected it, whose real name was Jacob Kirchenstein, may well have chosen it on the spur of the moment (the first thing he saw when he needed a name), or he may have felt it resonated in some way. Perhaps he found the brand's famous image of the 'striding man', which was used on bottles and in advertising from 1908 onwards, to be emblematic of his own intrepid life.

What we know for certain is that Kirchenstein was yet another Soviet agent whose life of peregrination had started early, in the aftermath of the failed Russian revolution of 1905. A young telegraph operator in the Baltic port of Riga at the beginning of the uprising, Kirchenstein was sentenced to exile in Siberia for his part in the strikes and violence. Aged just eighteen when he first manned the barricades, he must have been terrified as he faced transportation thousands of miles to the east. But he quickly discovered a means to escape and made his way back to Russia's west coast, where he boarded a ship for England. The young Kirchenstein then moved almost immediately from the United Kingdom to the eastern seaboard of America, where he worked for a number of years on commercial steamships, before eventually settling in New York, to use his skills as a telegrapher on the local railways.

While some exiled veterans of 1905 stayed in contact with revolutionary politics throughout their lives (including the most senior Bolsheviks whose biographies are best known), Kirchenstein followed what was the commoner path for survivors and initially tried to put the traumatic events behind him. He established a home among the Latvian community of the Bronx, marrying a Latvian girl, Vallie Waldman, in 1915 and becoming an American citizen. As he was to tell an FBI interrogator many decades later, Kirchenstein kept in touch with other Latvian socialists after arriving in America but mainly for social purposes. It is likely he would never have known the excitements of the radical life again had it not been for two separate events that occurred in quick succession at the start of 1917. Following the first Russian Revolution of March 1917 and the United States's entry into the Great War on 6 April, he and Vallie started to think that a return to their homeland, and a re-engagement with left-wing politics, might be a good idea.

This was for both positive and negative reasons. Progressives and proletarians across the globe were thrilled at the news that the despotic Nicholas II was no longer in power, none more so than the hundreds of thousands of former Tsarist subjects who had been driven from the country. For people with left-wing inclinations, in particular anyone who belonged to a minority ethnic group, there was now hope that events would bring a fairer future, including self-determination for ordinary men and women. Jacob and Vallie later admitted that they were caught up in this moment of fervour: 'The picture [. . .] painted of a new Russia where the rights and privileges of human beings would be recognised and respected after hundreds of years of Tsarist oppression convinced me,' Jacob confessed in the early 1950s.[1] But there was another significant factor behind the couple's decision to leave that they were not so quick to acknowledge. Compulsory military conscription began in the United States in May 1917, and, as a man who was not yet thirty, Jacob was liable to be drafted. He must have felt that he was now destined to return to Europe one way or another.

Jacob and Vallie decided that it was better to go of their own volition, crossing the American continent by rail and then sailing from San Francisco to Vladivostok with $3,000 of savings sewn into their clothing. At some point during the summer of 1917, as they made their way from Russia's far east to Petrograd on the Trans-Siberian railway, Jacob inadvertently completed a circumnavigation of the globe when he passed the place where Nicholas II had imprisoned him twelve years earlier. Back in the capital, he and Vallie were frequently to regret their decision to repatriate. 'From the first day of arrival in Petrograd we were highly disillusioned,' Jacob recalled. 'The streets were filled with deserting Russian soldiers [. . .] hunger and starvation were all about us. This was not the Russia we had envisioned back in the United States.'[2]

Importantly, Jacob had not left America a Bolshevik, though he had known and held discussions with Bolshevik exiles in New York, including the future Soviet leader Nikolai Bukharin. On reaching Russia, he only became a Bolshevik after Lenin's party clearly emerged as the dominant socialist movement, and the one to which it was increasingly dangerous not to belong. Kirchenstein's background as a survivor of 1905 along with his Latvian connections gave him a certain protection among the new rulers – something that was otherwise in short supply. At the end of 1918, with the civil war raging, he enlisted in the Red Army and succeeded in rising rapidly through its ranks to become an important and respected communications and transport expert, mainly based near the front at Smolensk.

As the war gave way to an uneasy peace, however, Jacob suddenly found himself transferred to Moscow to work at the heart of Trotsky's new railways commissariat, and rather than prospering by this promotion, he discovered that greater proximity to the centre of power brought greater risks. Before long, he had fallen out with top members of the commissariat after they questioned his professional judgement, and he began to fear for his and Vallie's safety. Jacob turned to old contacts from American days and called in a favour – a common activity in the factionalised, backbiting atmosphere of early Soviet politics. He asked if anyone knew of other positions in the burgeoning Soviet bureaucracy where he would be safe. Midway through the summer of 1920, someone found him a post – albeit a temporary one – on the staff of the Second World Congress of the Comintern.

Whatever Jacob had hoped to gain by this move (and prob-ably it was just to buy time), it changed his life utterly. The second Comintern congress in Moscow is widely seen as a key moment in the development of global Communism.[3] It was at this meeting that the CPGB formally came into existence. But even more fundamentally, this was the Soviet state's first opportunity to showcase itself to a watching world; it sought to use the gathering to assert its primacy and impose its will on the radical left of every other country. Jacob and Vallie played a crucial role, being put in joint charge of a special train service to convey important foreign delegates around the new country's highlights (model factories, model schools and model communities) as well as showing the worst of the devastation caused by the enemy Whites and their foreign backers. No country had moved so far towards true socialism, nor suffered so much in the process, was the message that visiting Marxists were supposed to take away.

After the trip, Jacob was judged to have done a good job, but it required quick thinking to prevent a return to Trotsky's bureaucratic empire. Fortunately he had some ideas about what to do next. He later described this as the moment at which he saw 'an opportunity [. . .] to escape Russia'.[4] Having discovered from other Comintern cadres that the Allied naval blockade was still causing enormous problems for the Bolshevik economy, starving Russia of basic foodstuffs and other supplies to a far greater extent than was publicly admitted (the blockade would last until the British and the Russians signed the trade treaty in March 1921), Kirchenstein offered to work as an undercover agent in Britain to try to frustrate it in any way he could. Through the congress he had also discovered that most foreign Communist groups were in grave need of material and political assistance; and he said he would use any secret position he established to help with this too.

He left it to Comintern bosses to thrash out the details of

his new role, and he admitted years later that he had had little confidence that they would back him. Surely they would think his proposals far-fetched. Yet they actually saw merit in them (while, quite possibly, also feeling that Kirchenstein was expendable). Had diplomats in the Soviet foreign office got wind of his proposal, it is highly likely they would have vetoed it, given its potential to jeopardise the ongoing Anglo-Russian talks. But they were kept in the dark and so, almost out of nowhere, Jacob and Vallie – for he insisted on taking her with him – found themselves on the road once more.[5]

It took six weeks for the Kirchensteins to make it from central Moscow to Britain. Their route lay via Murmansk and the Arctic Circle, where they made a dangerous sea crossing during which the boat in front of them capsized with the loss of all on board, and on down the western coast of Norway to Bergen, where they boarded a steamer bound for Newcastle-upon-Tyne. At each stage they were assisted by local socialists whom the Comintern was paying, including, according to Kirchenstein, a young journalist called Trygve Lie, who would later become Secretary-General of the United Nations.[6] As they were leaving Bergen, Vallie and Jacob stowed away in the cabin of a fire officer on board the ship, the *SS Sterling*. This man, whose name was Anker Petersen, was to become their main contact with the outside world during their first months in Britain. He instructed the couple to stay in his cabin throughout the voyage and until after dark on the day they berthed in Newcastle. At that point he helped them to escape into the dockyard. As Jacob would later recall, 'the only Passport Control and search was conducted for those legitimate passengers who left the steamer in Newcastle [but] we remained aboard until twilight'.[7]

Following their escape from the docks, Jacob could not believe his luck and was understandably jumpy. He and Vallie soon travelled from the north-east of England to Aberdeen, looking over their shoulders all the way and fully expecting to be apprehended at any moment. At breakfast on their first morning at Aberdeen's Temperance Hotel, Jacob – or Johnnie Walker as he was now to become – 'noticed sitting opposite us a very big man, who by his manner could not be mistaken for [anyone] but a police officer or detective'.[8] They promptly checked out. In reality, however, they had no need to worry since no one in the authorities knew they were there. Even if the man was a policeman, he was not watching Jacob. But the realisation that they were safe – safer in fact than they had been in Moscow – would dawn only slowly on the Kirchensteins in the weeks and months ahead.

Gradually they developed a thriving clandestine operation in Britain, suggesting that although Jacob had wanted an excuse to get out of Russia, he nonetheless remained committed to the Bolshevik cause (perhaps his loyalty was aided by the generous Comintern salary he now received in dollars). The ostensible purpose of his mission was not a success, as he failed to make any progress with his plan to break the Allied naval blockade. A fanciful notion of purchasing a British fishing trawler and sailing it back to Russia in secret, laden with supplies, unsurprisingly came to nought. Fortunately for him, however, this did not matter, as the positive outcome of the trade negotiations made the blockade an irrelevance and instead his bosses back in Moscow began to value Jacob for the other things he did.

First and foremost, he proved himself a reliable pair of hands when it came to conveying money, propaganda and instructions to British comrades, particularly in the north of England and Scotland, at a time when the reach of ARCOS and the Russian Trade Delegation was still limited, and some other Comintern middlemen had fallen under suspicion for misappropriating funds.[9] Soon, he also began passing messages from Moscow to Comintern agents in other countries, and passing their messages back to Moscow, effectively turning Britain into a kind of clandestine sorting office for worldwide Bolshevism. He also started to tell his Comintern bosses what he described as the frank truth about British Communism – exactly the kind of thing they loved to hear from their undercover agents. Some reports he sent back on the true strength of the CPGB in Glasgow, Edinburgh and the industrial heartlands of northern England almost certainly helped to persuade the Comintern that the picture painted by British Communist leaders was excessively rosy.

In the midst of all this activity, however, British Intelligence got only one real clue as to Jacob Kirchenstein's existence and whereabouts and its officers were unable to capitalise on it. This would later be seen as a significant failure, not only because of the length of time that Kirchenstein operated in the country but also because, coming as it did just before the Anglo-Russian treaty was signed, it could have added extra force to attempts to get Lloyd George to abandon the talks. The episode unfolded in December 1920, at which point Jacob and Vallie were living in Edinburgh but still using Newcastle as their main port for communication with Russia.

Late one night, in the vicinity of Newcastle docks, a patrolling policeman caught two British men and a Norwegian sailor hauling a pair of heavy suitcases away from a ship. Upon inspection, the officer discovered that the suitcases contained large amounts of illegal Communist propaganda, including pamphlets that called on British workers, soldiers and sailors to mount armed insurrections against the elected government.

The three men were arrested on the spot and tried. The Norwegian turned out to be none other than Anker Petersen, Jacob and Vallie's helper on their voyage from Bergen, while the two British workers were John Bell and Thomas Scott, men whom Kirchenstein had hired as couriers and fixers. Jacob later accused them of having 'bungled' their orders, but it was almost certainly just bad luck that got them caught.[10] His anger was understandable, however, since their capture brought the authorities closer to him than they had ever been before. A search of Petersen's cabin on the *SS Sterling* revealed a stash of letters that included one Jacob had written and signed with his alias, 'Johnnie Walker'. When news of Petersen's arrest reached the Kirchensteins in Edinburgh, they assumed that the authorities would now have this letter and that Jacob's alias had been blown. For a short time, Jacob expected the police to track him down. Lying low in the Scottish capital, he communicated with other British accomplices by dead letter drop only. In the event, however, none of the defendants revealed any more information about their boss (a favour for which Jacob would later reward them). Petersen, Bell and Scott ended up serving several months' hard labour in English prisons, but the trail on Johnnie Walker himself went cold.[11]

This passing reference to Johnnie Walker may seem like just a fragmentary clue, yet some of Special Branch's and MI5's behaviour with regard to the letter is hard to understand. Jacob had written in Latvian, but it appears the authorities may not have got hold of an English translation of his words until the second half of 1921, long after the trial of the three Newcastle men had ended. The letter clearly showed Johnnie Walker to be a top Comintern man and also indicated that his presence in Britain was part of an active and on-going operation – to have known its contents sooner would, therefore, have been invaluable, but we can only speculate about what caused the delay. Perhaps Newcastle police withheld the document from British Intelligence for some time after the initial arrests (such holdups, both deliberate and accidental, were fairly common) or maybe someone received it in Special Branch or MI5 but initially overlooked its importance.

In any event, even when the content of the letter was known, it did not lead to much in the way of concerted action. 'Johnnie Walker' is first mentioned in the intelligence archives in a report on 'Foreign Support of Communist Agitators' from October 1921, almost a full year after Petersen *et al* were apprehended.

He is described as 'the Third International [i.e. the Comintern] representative in the United Kingdom', responsible for distributing propaganda through 'stations' at 'South Shields, Hull, Grimsby and Cardiff', and it is also clear from the text that the authorities had identified his chosen name as an alias (though they incorrectly connected this alias with another Soviet citizen, a man called Fachers, who, as far as we know, never came to Britain).[12] The main British Intelligence response to Walker's presence appeared to be to bemoan the end of wartime border restrictions, with little in the way of remedial action thought possible. 'The control at the ports in this country has been perceptibly weakened by the lapse of the Defence of the Realm Act,' the report's writer concluded, in effect saying that now 'Johnnie Walker' had got in, he would be able to stay for as long as he liked.[13]

Jacob Kirchenstein alleged in his 1951 confession that Sir Basil Thomson's resignation at the end of 1921 was somehow connected to government anger about the failure to catch him, but no other evidence to corroborate this has come to light.[14] The next mention of the 'striding man' in British Intelligence archives came only in March 1922, long after Thomson had vacated the stage. On this occasion it was a report of an operation by police in Libau, Latvia, in which a consignment of Communist letters had been seized as they were about to leave the country. One of the letters, written on 8 February 1922 and signed by someone who styled himself the 'Deputy Director of the Department of the Worldwide Socialist International of Communist Germ Cells', mentioned Johnnie Walker and said that he was continuing his work for the Comintern in Britain.[15] The letter included a tantalising detail: that Walker had received £700 (about £35,000 today) to distribute to his left-wing dependants in Britain since the start of the year alone. This information must have dismayed the British authorities, because they still had no leads on Johnnie Walker (a name Kirchenstein had in fact long since dropped), and no operations under way to fill the gaps in their knowledge.

Jacob and Vallie left Britain invisibly later that same year and returned shortly afterwards under their own names. Their method of escape was a further humiliation for the British, though they would not realise it for several years. At some point in 1921, Jacob decided to procure a fake British passport, and succeeded in doing so without difficulty. The idea had occurred to him, he later said, when a clerk in a Thomas Cook bureau heard him speaking and mistook him for a British citizen. Shortly afterwards, Jacob acquired a passport application and filled it in using the details of a certain Cornelius Stormonth, an entirely innocent employee of the Scottish Workers Committee. Jacob passed off his own photograph as Stormonth's and went on to name Vallie as the Scotsman's wife, Anne. He had the application signed by two responsible men, a high-ranking Glasgow labour activist and a clergyman, and submitted it. After only 'six or seven days' the finished passport came back from what Kirchenstein described as 'the Liverpool Branch of the British Foreign Office', presumably the Liverpool passport office.[16]

The Stormonth passport would allow Jacob and Vallie to travel from Britain to the United States whenever they wanted without compromising their true identities as the Kirchensteins. It was a measure of Jacob's growing maturity as an agent that, before planning any such trip, he decided to send the passport back to the Foreign Office to get endorsements (similar to visas today) for travel to a number of European countries which he did not actually wish to visit. At the time, hundreds of individuals who lived in Britain were banned from travelling abroad, mostly because of their connections with Communism or Irish Republicanism. Had any of these individuals requested the same endorsements, their applications would immediately have been refused. As Jacob put it, 'I requested and obtained endorsements on the passport for travel to Germany, Holland, Belgium, France, and Switzerland. I did this in order to test the safety of the passport. The requested endorsements were made and I knew then that no suspicion was attached to the passport.'[17]

Jacob would later assert that the Stormonth passport was intended as a means for him and Vallie to escape the grip of the Comintern altogether. In the event, however, he ended up using it at the end of 1922 in order to deepen and regularise his connection with the Soviets.[18] For a variety of reasons – mainly because of ARCOS's success as a cover for clandestine activity – Jacob's Comintern bosses decided to transfer him from Scotland to London, and to have him take up a cover job at the trading company under his own name while continuing to engage, almost full-time, in illegal activities. To prepare for the change, Jacob held meetings with some of Britain's highest-ranking Soviet agents, including Andrew Rothstein, Nikolai Klyshko and the visiting Mikhail Borodin. British Intelligence failed to pick up on any of these meetings, just as it had missed the illegal Stormonth passport, so that during September 1922, Jacob was able to board one of the great transatlantic liners, the *SS Carmania*, and pose successfully as the thirty-one-year-old Stormonth travelling to America.[19]

Jacob's immigration to the United States on the fake passport went smoothly and he then destroyed the document (probably thinking that he could always get another one if need be). He and Vallie now reassumed their own names and, after spending a couple of months in New York, returned to Britain. To get back they used their own American passports, travelling aboard the White Star Line's *Majestic* service, departing on 3 November 1922. In the ship's manifest Jacob gave as the couple's proposed address the exclusive Savoy Hotel in London, home to the iconic Savoy Havana Band, which was just starting to make its mark as one of the hottest jazz acts in town. Jacob had clearly decided on anything but an undercover entrance to London, whether to signal publicly his new status as a highly skilled American whom the Bolsheviks had hired for his professional abilities (rather than an ideological commitment to Communism) or simply to treat himself and his wife before they settled into their new life.

In all the surviving documentation about him, one thing that continuously comes across is Jacob's heartfelt surprise that he was able to evade the British authorities for so long. Soviet agents typically emphasised the extraordinary lengths they had to go to in order to remain at large. But to Jacob, what was remarkable was the patchy and confused performance of his British adversaries. Having initially feared policemen at a hotel breakfast, by the time he re-entered the country for a second tour of duty and took up his post at ARCOS, he had learned that he could stay at the Savoy and take the entire British security apparatus in his stride, just as any real-life Johnnie Walker would.

Description of "Johnnie Walker" from Scotland
House.

Born 27.7.87. Height 6ft.   forehead high.

Eyes brown.   Nose retroussé - broad nostrils.

Mouth full. Chin round. Hair brown.   Complexion

dark.

Johnnie Walker whisky was advertised in the early twentieth century using a picture of a striding man. Was this what encouraged the intrepid Jacob Kirchenstein to adopt the name as his first alias during an illegal stay in Britain? By then, he had already travelled tens of thousands of miles around the globe, including escaping from Tsarist exile in Siberia and sailing through the Arctic Circle. Aged thirty-three in November 1920, he still had many more miles to travel, and many years of deception ahead.

Name of Ship ___ "MAJESTIC" ___

Steamship Line ___ WHITE STAR LINE. ___ Date of Arrival ___ 3rd November 1922.

NAMES AND DESCRIPTIONS OF ALIEN PASSENGER

(2) Port at which Passengers have been landed	(3) NAMES OF PASSENGERS		(4) Proposed Address in the United Kingdom.?	(5) Class (Whether 1st, 2nd or 3rd.)	(6) Profession, Occupation, or Calling of Passengers	(7) AGES OF PASSENGER					
						Adults of 12 yrs. and upwards				Children between 1 and 12.	
						Accompanied by Husband or Wife.		Not accompanied by Husband or Wife.			
						M	F	M	F	M	F
Southampton.											
39.	Blyth.	John.	2 Crystal Terrace. Upper Norwood London.	2nd	Merchant.			72.			
40.	Barrello.	Luigi.	280 Park Road. Liverpool		Barber.			32.			
41.	Brown.	Dudley.V.	Castlebank-Annieland Dye Works. Castlebank.		Engineer.	46.					
42.	"	Julia.	"		Housewife.		41.				
43.	"	Jack.	"		Student.			19.			
44.	Brown.	Robert.	Gatehouse of Fleet. Rockend.		Engineer.			61.			
45.	Chiba.	Makioki.	Japanese Consulate London.		Teacher.			35.			
46.	Grossbard.	Henry.	In transit to Ostend.		Broker.			37.			
47.	Grenbar.	Blanche.	London Joint City & Mid Bank King St. Manchester.		Teacher.				35.		
48.	Gorevan.	Bernard.	2 Camden St. Dublin.		Farmer.			48.			
49.	Hayashi.	Fukuo.	Japanese Consulate London.		Student.			26.			
50.	Ito.	Seiya.	"		Professor			39.			
51.	Jowett.	Harriett.	Baildon Bradford.		Widow.				42.		
52.	Kantsook.	Alice E.	48 Merton Road. Wandsworth. London.	.	Housewife.				40.		
53.	Koga.	Yukiyoshi.	c/o Japanese Consul London.		Teacher.			30.			
54.	Ito.	Koji.	London. E.C.2. c/o Yokohama Bank Bishops Gate.		Merchant.			35.			
55.	Klein.	Florence.	34 Bell Band Lane. Spitlefields London.		Forewoman.				26.		
56.	Kirchenstein.	Jacob.	Hotel Savoy London.		Agent.	35.					
57.	"	Vallie.	"		Housewife.		34.				
58.	Maloop.	James.B.	In transit to Spain.		Merchant.			21.			
59.	Laderman.	Moses.	58 Bedford St. London.		Manufactr.			45.			

Who would have guessed that when he gave his occupation as 'agent' Jacob Kirchenstein meant 'secret agent'? Here is the relevant page of the Majestic's manifest for November 1922. Jacob and Vallie would stay at the Savoy Hotel before resuming their lives as successful Soviet spies.

7

FROM MAYFAIR TO MOSCOW

'Difficulties add to the zest of Life. Endeavouring to overcome difficulties is like battling up hill against the wind on an autumn day. One comes out of it with a sense of health and glow.'

Clare Sheridan, *Mayfair to Moscow – Clare Sheridan's Diary*, 1921

There were many reasons why British Intelligence took as long as it did to identify Johnnie Walker. In their defence, intelligence chiefs would, as we have seen, mention the legal and security weaknesses that had allowed the man and his wife to come to the country in the first place, as well as the fact that their own teams were short-staffed and overworked. But at least some of the scarce resources that might have gone into a more thorough pursuit of Jacob Kirchenstein during 1920 and 1921 were tied up in inquiries into another individual who never became a spy, but who had an uncanny knack of attracting attention from real spies and convincing them that she might be one of their number.

Clare Sheridan, sculptor, author, pioneering working mother, and socialite, acquired a large MI5 file in the early 1920s (one that is almost certainly matched by equally large dossiers in other intelligence archives that remain closed). As an early British visitor to Soviet Russia, a public sympathiser with the Soviet cause, and a cousin of the senior cabinet minister Winston Churchill, she understandably came under official scrutiny at a time of heightened Anglo-Russian tension. But her story is ultimately a cautionary one, because all her suspicious behaviour turned out to be nothing more than a red herring.

Clare Sheridan was one of the earliest in a long line of British society figures who became enchanted by the Soviet state. Bolsheviks primarily wanted to win the hearts and minds of the workers of Britain, but their ideology also appealed to a subset of the country's upper and upper-middle classes, in particular, a large number of people who were involved in cultural and artistic professions – people who tended to dislike their own country's innate conservatism, small 'c' as much as big 'c'. As the years went by, Moscow increasingly sought to curry favour with such individuals, ignoring the fact that the Soviet regime would most likely have despised them, and even killed them, had they lived in Russia. Among early supporters from such backgrounds were H. G. Wells (who, as we know, was a friend of Nikolai Klyshko), E. M. Forster and Virginia Woolf. None, however, provoked the same level of obsession within British Intelligence as Clare Sheridan.

She was born Clare Frewen in 1885, the child of a British father and an American mother (Clarita Jerome, Churchill's maternal aunt).[1] Displaying a contrarian streak from childhood, she always sought to kick against the foreordained life of a society debutante, relishing new ideas rather than conformity and showing a strong desire to work for a living rather than be a kept woman. Her biographer, Anita Leslie, describes her as 'a restless, artistic girl [who] did not take to the round of balls and country-house parties', but instead tried 'to educate herself by serious reading [and] attempt[ing] to write novels'.[2]

Clare Sheridan only turned to sculpture after a great personal tragedy. One of her two infant daughters died suddenly in 1914 and she was moved to create a stone angel for the graveside; the sense of fulfilment that this gave her was unlike anything she had experienced before. When further tragedy followed in quick succession – in September 1915, her husband, Wilfred, was killed at the Battle of Loos – she was left to bring up her remaining daughter and a newborn son alone. Rather than retreat into full-time motherhood or allow herself to be overwhelmed by grief, Clare resolved to make her mark on the world at large. Entrusting the care of her children to her parents, she enrolled with a master sculptor in London and learned sculpture, before using her many contacts and considerable persuasive powers to win commissions.

Sheridan's unusual career brought surprisingly rapid results during the immediate post-war years. She first made a name for herself through an exhibition for the National Portrait Society and immediately moved on to sculpting the heads of senior politicians, including the former Prime Minister, Herbert Asquith, F. E. Smith (later known as Lord Birkenhead), and her illustrious cousin, Winston. She was popular with gallery visitors and owners, even though she received mixed reviews from critics. In one article in the *Observer* in 1920, she was admitted to be 'a modeller of no mean ability' but also someone who was still 'groping for the right convention' and who could be prone to 'flabby vagueness' and 'a curious looseness of touch'.[3]

Out of the blue in the summer of 1920 Clare found herself approached by an acquaintance and asked if she would be willing to meet the chief Soviet negotiator Lev Kamenev, while he was in London for the Anglo-Russian talks. She was told that he wanted to have a bust of himself made and, although she was never clear how he had come to discover her, that he had specifically selected her to make it. (Paradoxically, the apparent randomness of the meeting was one of the facts that would set alarm bells ringing for British Intelligence.) Clare agreed to the commission and met the senior Bolshevik several times during the month of August. In the course of these meetings, she fashioned his head and also talked to him about everything under the sun (they conversed in French). Somewhere along the way, they struck up what had many of the hallmarks of a romantic friendship.

Kamenev was already under official surveillance, so British Intelligence learned of the assignations almost at once. Kamenev himself knew he was being watched, while Sheridan was also aware that representatives of her government were most likely monitoring their encounters. Nevertheless, this seems to have done nothing to impede the burgeoning relationship. Kamenev sent Clare a bunch of roses just a few days after meeting her; he asked her to place them at the base of an anti-war sculpture she had made, but she clearly took them to be a token of personal affection as well. One Saturday evening, they also dined together at the Café Royal in Piccadilly before heading off to see a revue. Clare recalled how during the show 'the audience laughed a good deal [but] Kamenev wondered at their childish appreciation of rubbish'; an example in miniature, perhaps, of the fundamental clash of cultures between Bolshevism and mainstream Western culture.[4] On another occasion, the pair lunched at Claridge's and took a taxi to the Tate Gallery to look at British art, before driving to Hampton Court to tour the house and gardens.

There were many aspects of these encounters for intelligence officers to marvel at. Kamenev's un-proletarian act of vanity in wanting a bust made in the first place was surely one – an early example of the narcissistic bug that would infect many Soviet leaders during the seventy-five years of the state's existence. The rapid progress of Kamenev's and Clare's fling was another (he was married to a senior Soviet luminary who had stayed behind in Moscow). But what concerned British Intelligence most were signs that Kamenev was hatching a plan to bring Sheridan to Moscow – ostensibly so she could fashion busts of other top Bolsheviks, but, the British instantly suspected, actually for more nefarious purposes. The mooted trip was particularly disturbing because of Sheridan's blood relationship with Winston Churchill and the likelihood that Kamenev would be expelled from Britain sooner rather than later due to his unwelcome contact with British Communists. Sheridan, for her part, declared herself wildly excited at the prospect of visiting the new Soviet state, probably sensing that any trip she made, and any artwork that resulted from it, would be of international interest. She told Kamenev that visiting his country would also be the fulfilment of a long-term personal fascination. 'All my life,' she said, she had had 'a love of Russian literature, Russian music, Russian dancing [and] Russian art'.[5] 'Let me know when you are going to start,' she added, 'I will be ready in half an hour.'[6]

During the British phase of their relationship, the sculptor and the Bolshevik occasionally corresponded in letters and notes but their most significant exchanges always occurred face to face, sometimes with surveillance officers nearby but frustratingly unable to make out what was being said. In ordinary circumstances, Britain's spies might just have endured this state of affairs, hoping that something of importance would eventually crop up in the pair's written communications. But this time a different course of action presented itself – as a direct result of Clare's social status – and the authorities seized it with enthusiasm.

Sheridan had far more connections within the British establishment than most people whom British Intelligence placed under surveillance in the early 1920s. Even men who had studied at Oxford or Cambridge, like Rothstein, tended to have been solidly committed to socialism from early adulthood, so that they had thoroughly socialist circles of friends. Sheridan, however, was a well-known member of Britain's upper middle class, the granddaughter and cousin of MPs and the widow of a man who was directly descended from the playwright Richard Brinsley Sheridan. Unbeknownst to Clare, one of her close friends also happened to be a recent employee of MI5, and it was through him that the authorities found a way to pry further into what she and her Soviet lover were up to.

Sidney Russell Cooke had officially left the employment

of the British state at the end of 1919 or early in 1920, just a few months before Lev Kamenev and Clare Sheridan met. He had become a stockbroker in the City of London, but was still maintaining close contact with his former intelligence colleagues. Most notably, he was in touch with MI5's Oswald Harker, the man in charge of most of the organisation's anti-Soviet work (in late 1920, Harker was to marry Cooke's sister).[7] Cooke was also lifelong friends with Clare Sheridan, a connection that seems to have come about through mutual family acquaintance.

Around the time Clare and Kamenev visited Hampton Court, Cooke was asked by MI5 – almost certainly by Harker personally – to make contact with his old chum and find out as much as possible about what she was up to. Quite possibly, Cooke's relationship with Sheridan was already known to Harker, but equally it might have come up in conversation as the MI5 officer gossiped with Cooke about the agency's current caseload. In any event, with supreme nonchalance, Cooke presented himself at Clare's studio on the evening of Thursday 26 August 1920, and chatted to her about life in general and her new Russian acquaintance in particular. 'Sidney came to see me after dinner, and we talked fantastically about Russia, and what it might or might not lead to,' Clare wrote in her diary afterwards. 'He is terribly interested,' she added, without apparent irony.[8]

To say that Cooke was interested was an understatement. In the days that followed, he stuck to Sheridan and Kamenev like glue, first arranging to join them for lunch at Claridge's on Friday 27 August, and then inviting them to spend the weekend with him at his country house, Bellecroft, on the Isle of Wight. Sheridan, in her diary, takes up the story of this peculiar mini-break at the point when she and Kamenev boarded a train for the south coast:

We caught a 12.50 from Waterloo to Portsmouth. Sidney met us at the Harbour, and escorted us to his house on the Isle of Wight, near Newport [. . .] On arrival we flung ourselves down in the sun on the grass of the tennis-court. And after tea, as we lay full length on rugs, our heads leaning on the grassy bank behind us, and the sun gradually sinking lower and lower, Kamenev for over an hour told us the history of the Russian Revolution [. . .] We sat silent and spell-bound. He began as far back as twenty years ago, with the first efforts of himself and Lenin, Trotsky and Krassin. He described their secret organisations, their discoveries, their arrests, his months and years of prison, first in cells, then in Siberia [. . .] He described to us shortly but vividly the individuality and psychology of Lenin. There were others also, the president of the Extraordinary Commission [the Cheka] [. . .] an ascetic and a fanatic, whom the Soviet selected as organiser and head of 'La Terreur' [. . . But] it is useless to try to tell any of Kamenev's stories, they require his individuality and would lose in the repeating. I only felt that it was a great waste that his audience consisted only of us two, when so many might have been enthralled.[9]

But of course more than two people would be enthralled by Kamenev's words on this holiday. Cooke, we can be certain, had invited the Russian to his home with advance permission from MI5, and he must subsequently have fed back everything that Kamenev said in his presence, as well as his own impressions of the Bolshevik's relationship with Sheridan. He would have recounted, for instance, how, during the visit's second day, the trio had gone to a beach on the south of the island, and, while Sidney and Clare paddled, Kamenev had written for the sculptor a love poem on the back of a five pound note.[10]

Perhaps Sidney was under instructions to dissuade his friend from going to Russia, but if so he was unsuccessful. The small number of others whom she took into her confidence about the trip tried to warn her off but also failed. Ignoring them and her own concerns – including, as she put it, that she might end up making orphans of her children – she decided to go, departing London for Newcastle on 11 September 1920 accompanied by Kamenev and boarding a steamship for Sweden. 'There was something indescribably exciting and clandestine about slipping away without anyone knowing,' Sheridan wrote in her diary, a clear indication of how much she enjoyed the secrecy.[11] 'For some time Kamenev and I stood on deck to see the last of England, with her Turner sky. Kamenev said, "It looks mysterious, the land, doesn't it?" But to me it was just the old world wrapt in a shroud. Mystery lay ahead of us in the new world that is our destination.'[12]

For the two months she was in Russia, Sheridan was out of British Intelligence's reach and officers could only speculate about what she was getting up to. No sooner did she get back, however, than Sidney Russell Cooke was again despatched to see her. He quickly discovered – because she freely revealed it – that she had kept a diary throughout her time in Moscow. Cooke asked to borrow the diary, so as, he said, to read it at his leisure. Clare assented, though by now she must have suspected that something more than personal curiosity lay behind his extraordinary level of interest. Cooke held on to the diary for several days, enough time to read it at his leisure and also to share it with MI5. Both he and his former colleagues were now able to peruse Sheridan's descriptions of Lenin, Trotsky, Zinoviev, Dzerzhinsky, Litvinov and Chicherin, men who had done so much to unsettle Britain and the rest of the world, and her thoughts about the Soviet experiment in general.

According to the diary, Sheridan was wide-eyed with enthusiasm about all the top Bolsheviks she had met, including the dreaded chief of the Cheka, Feliks Dzerzhinsky, a man who, for her, was 'bathed in tears of eternal sorrow' with a mouth that 'smiled an indulgent kindness'.[13] Her account of the entire trip was filled with giddy excitement. On walking through the grounds of the Kremlin, she described 'feeling that I am staying at Versailles just after Louis XVI. My emotions and impressions are too deep, too many, and too bewildering to be measured in words'.[14] As for her art, she declared that she 'love[d] the bedrock of things here, and the vital energy. If I had no children I would remain and work. There may be no food for the body, but there is plenty of food for the soul, and I would rather live in discomfort in an atmosphere of gigantic effort, than in luxury among the purposeless.'[15]

From this point onwards, Sheridan was seen as a serious and dangerous Soviet sympathiser by British Intelligence; officers considered her likely to be involved in secret work of some sort. But in reaching this conclusion, they seem to have assumed that her warm feelings towards the Soviet regime were now a permanent feature of her personality. They also seem to have dismissed several entries in her diary where Sheridan clearly stated that she did *not* see herself as one of Lenin's followers and did not agree with every aspect of Bolshevism. 'My stay in Russia is nearing its end,' she wrote in the entry for 2 November 1920, for instance; 'Already I see my departure in the near distance. People at home will think I am a Bolshevist, on account of my associations, but I am much too humble to pretend I understand anything about it [. . .] I am not a Bolshevist.'[16]

In any case, the idea that Sheridan could have functioned effectively as a secret agent is laughable, given her addiction to the limelight. Although her talent for self-publicity was noted by British counterespionage agencies, they did not see that it might conflict with her being a spy: Sheridan could supposedly be thoroughly indiscreet and worryingly secretive at the same time. Once her diary was returned to her, she immediately sought and accepted a lucrative offer to publish it in both

Britain and the United States, but even this did not seem to rule her out as a dangerous individual. What Cooke and his former colleagues at MI5 treated as private revelations, Sheridan was in fact willing to share with every customer of W. H. Smith.

Cooke's surveillance of Clare Sheridan lessened after her trip to Moscow, as the authorities adopted a more conventional, on-the-books approach. Despite lacking evidence that she was involved in illegal activity, however, British Intelligence watched her extremely closely for years following the Russia visit. Her post was intercepted, her movements tracked, and her financial affairs investigated, while at times her journeys to other countries were subject to restrictions. Even when she was allowed to travel, secret tip-offs about her imminent arrival were sent to British missions in the relevant cities.

Sheridan's impulsivity and flightiness were sometimes presented as risks in themselves; diplomats were often warned to have nothing to do with her simply because she was a blabbermouth. But sometimes these qualities were dismissed as merely the cover for her work as a Soviet agent; on these occasions, the advice from spy agencies suggested that she was nowhere near as scatty as she made out. In 1922, Sheridan's MI5 file noted that colleagues in Turkey should be informed that she was about to turn up there. 'Perhaps it might be as well if [the British Embassy in] Constantinople do not know it already,' Oswald Harker wrote, 'to warn them that she is not the kind of person to be trusted with any information [. . .] and has a passion for international mischief-making'; a letter to this effect was duly dispatched.[17] A year later, an anonymous note from a British Intelligence informant in Munich recorded a conversation in which she had said that she was heading for Konigsberg, the scene of recent riots and demonstrations. 'In view of the present situation,' the informant wrote, 'she is anxious to be in the thick of any trouble and she thinks there is going to be considerable trouble in the near future.'[18]

MI5 was never able to produce concrete evidence of specific operations Sheridan had been involved in, yet in report after report it insinuated that she was doing Moscow's bidding. In November 1922, in Rome, she was said to have made 'a bit of a splash in a social sense' and to be aspiring 'to sculpture [*sic*] Mussolini'. But she was also detected 'advertis[ing] her presence' in the country (whatever that meant) and 'preach[ing] Bolshevism in private circles'. In Turkey on another visit in 1925, she was observed by an SIS officer who described her as 'a very attractive person of a most facile disposition'. Facile as she was, however, this officer also said that she was using 'her energies [. . .] in every way for the furtherance of Soviet schemes'.[19] She was then banned from visiting Egypt without the express permission of the Egyptian High Commissioner, and on the rest of the trip she took through North Africa in the mid-1920s was said to be 'undoubtedly in the pay of the Russians', albeit for purposes unknown – purposes that might include getting 'in touch with the local situation' or acting 'either as a reporting agent or possibly a forwarding agent'.[20] When Oswald Harker wrote to SIS about Clare in 1925, he said 'MI5 have never suggested Mrs Sheridan's inclusion in any Black List [to ban her from some countries altogether]'; he added that this was not for want of evidence but rather because the organisation feared 'to arouse her suspicions or those of her supposed employers'.[21]

In reality, Sheridan had become less and less interested in Bolshevism as time went on and more and more attracted by Europe's other Bohemian sub-cultures. She wrote articles on these new Europeans for a number of newspapers, eventually taking herself off to live among a fashionable emigré set in Algiers and taking her children with her. MI5 had picked up on this change of mood as early as 1923 but seemed not to factor it into its broader analysis. A note initialled by Harker on 14 November that year went as far as to say that Sheridan was now 'entirely disillusioned about the present regime in Russia'.[22]

Nonetheless, every contact she had with British Communists or Soviet citizens continued to be treated as evidence of her ongoing status as an agent – a status she almost certainly never possessed.

Having Churchill for a relative did not help Sheridan in her dealings with British Intelligence. If ever moments arose when MI5 and Special Branch might have considered calling off their costly surveillance of the sculptor, it was this connection that prevented them, especially after Churchill became Chancellor of the Exchequer in 1924. From time to time, Clare was overheard to repeat to strangers things that her cousin had said in private, either to her personally or, more often, to mutual acquaintances: comments about matters of state, but nothing particularly sensitive. Sheridan was blamed for these indiscretions, even though the leaks had actually come from the equally loose-tongued Churchill.

At the very end of 1925, Churchill's name cropped up in a letter that the journalist W. N. Ewer wrote to a colleague. Ewer was known to be a Soviet secret agent by this time, and therefore under British Intelligence surveillance in his own right. He wrote that Clare had heard from 'Winston' that he was unsure about whether the French would be able to hold on to their new colony in Syria. Although hardly privileged information – political unrest in Syria was common knowledge at the time – the fact that the snippet could be attributed directly to Churchill, via Sheridan, and had been shared with a known Soviet agent was enough to send the MI5 chief, Sir Vernon Kell, round to interview Churchill and remind him of the danger his relative posed. In Sheridan's MI5 file, Harker noted the outcome of the meeting:

[The] CSI [Chief of Secret Intelligence] today interviewed 'Winston'. Winston informed him, in answer to his question as to what he thought of Clare, that he was not prepared to go bail for her, that in fact he was prepared to believe anything CSI told him about her and also that he was prepared to take any action if and when CSI wished him to do so. He promised that he would do nothing unless CSI should ask him to do so.[23]

A later note on the file requested that Kell confirm whether further action was necessary. Kell at this point must have spoken to Churchill again, for the reply was: 'W. says no action'.[24]

Sheridan remained one of MI5's most important suspects for another year, but from the end of 1926, when she left Algeria to return to her parents' mansion, Brede Place in Sussex, the information in her files reduces to a trickle. The last entry from the most intense period of surveillance is, appropriately, as unrelated to espionage and sedition as could possibly be. In a letter to a friend, Clare bemoans an illness she contracted during a farewell trip into the Algerian desert. 'I went down south and got ill, *really* ill, a delirious fever and dysentery in a caravanserai, beyond the railway and far from a town [. . .] A military doctor who was an idiot [nursed me] and then food ran out and they put me – long before I should – into the driving seat of my car and told me to drive on [. . .] Half dead I reached the next place and collapsed again, and so on and on, until I got back.'[25]

The letter is typical of Sheridan's garrulousness and penchant for self-dramatisation. Similar tendencies persisted in the more intermittent additions that MI5 made to the file in later years. Usually, these entries coincided with Clare's public pronouncements about her exciting, dare-devil past. MI5 added material in 1936, for instance, when a series of newspaper articles about her relationship with Kamenev was published at the time of the disgraced Bolshevik's show trial.[26] There were further entries in every year but one between 1941 and 1946, and again in 1949; so that it was only in the 1950s that Sheridan finally managed to shake off Britain's secret services, three decades after their interest in her had begun.

Had British Intelligence's resources been greater and Clare's personal privacy of no importance, it might be easier to explain the level of attention she received. Certainly the authorities learned interesting things when they documented her movements with Kamenev in both Britain and Russia. The trip to Bellecroft even had the makings of a blackmail set-up, though British Intelligence chose not to use it in this way (probably because Kamenev was expelled so soon after returning from the Isle of Wight and possibly, too, because Cooke would not have allowed an old friend to be thus exploited). But the subsequent years of intrusion are harder to justify, both on the grounds that little useful intelligence was generated and as a violation of the sculptor's private life. The 1920s was a decade brimming with politically engaged, opinionated women who strongly advocated a variety of causes without ever seeking to provoke violent revolution or to sell, or give, secrets to a foreign power. Clare was one of these, a particularly luminous and captivating example, perhaps, but nothing more.

The most telling part of the Clare Sheridan case actually comes in an episode she recounted in the diary of her trip to Russia. During the visit, Clare was shocked to discover that certain senior Bolsheviks believed her to be a *British* spy – just as the British were assuming she was a Soviet one. It is a good indication of how the clandestine wings of both states made similar assumptions about her behaviour. On this occasion, however, it was the Russians who came to their senses more quickly, realising that she was beguiling but harmless. Ironically, what first gave the Russians cause for concern was Sidney Russell Cooke. Klyshko and the other secret agents who worked in the Russian Trade Delegation automatically suspected any non-Communists who wanted to spend time with Kamenev in London. They therefore made inquiries into Cooke's background and when the results came through (after Sheridan and Kamenev had set sail for Russia) they forwarded them to Moscow.

Clare recounts what she clearly experienced as a chilling moment during her visit, when the senior Soviet diplomat Maxim Litvinov suddenly asked her questions about Cooke. 'To-day [Litvinov] gave me furiously to think,' she wrote in her diary on 23 October 1920:

> Suddenly, without any warning, he sat back in his chair and fixed me with his small eyes: 'Do you know a man called Russel [sic] Cook?' he asked. It was a rather surprising question, and I admitted that I knew a very young man called Sidney Russell Cooke. Though why Litvinov should have ever heard of him I couldn't imagine. He went on to say that Kamenev knows him. I said yes, that Kamenev had met him through me. Litvinoff said: 'He is in the British Intelligence Service, isn't he?' I confess to a slight shiver down my spine when he said this; but I refuted the statement. I said that so far as I knew (and it hadn't interested me very much) Sidney Cooke was working in the city awaiting a propitious moment to plunge into rather liberal politics. Litvinoff gave a sort of grunt, which denoted nothing at all, and refused to be drawn on the subject. But something seems to be in the air, and I cannot tell what it is. Odd things happen, quite small things, but they give one a feeling of insecurity.[27]

Clare was right to be worried. So far from being welcome within the regime's inner sanctum, she was actually under a cloud of suspicion and may well have faced considerable danger. A few weeks later, when Litvinov came to wave her off at a Moscow railway station, he hinted as much but still refused to be explicit. 'Litvinoff, when he said good-bye to me, promised to send on my cases by courier,' Clare wrote. 'He then roused my curiosity by telling me that he had been a better friend to me than I should ever know. I begged him to explain, but he said I must wait ten years or so.'[28]

Perhaps Britain's secret services saw this element of Sheridan's story as nothing more than a tall tale, though it is fascinating to imagine what Cooke himself made of it when he read Clare's diary. Could he, Harker and Kell really have interpreted this revelation as a double bluff – a calculated attempt by Clare to throw sand in their eyes? Cooke was fully retired from anti-Soviet operations after Sheridan's return, suggesting that the authorities decided his cover really had been blown. But towards Clare British Intelligence applied the logic of 'once a suspect, always a suspect', so that she remained squarely in their sights. 'There is no privacy in Russian life,' she observed at one point in her diary.[29] In her case, the same was true in Britain.

MAYFAIR TO MOSCOW—
CLARE SHERIDAN'S DIARY

BONI AND LIVERIGHT
PUBLISHERS   NEW YORK

Clare Sheridan was close to spies, secret agents and revolutionaries on both sides of the East-West divide in the early 1920s, but that did not make her a spy. With British Intelligence always watching in the wings, she capitalised on the new Communist state's mysterious allure by publishing a spirited account of her visit there.

8

FROLICS

'Must be cracked, must be off her head. Or perhaps she took
drugs. That was more likely: that was much more likely. Most
of them did nowadays. Vicious young women. Lesbians, drug-
fiends, nymphomaniacs, dipsos – thoroughly vicious, nowadays,
thoroughly vicious.'

Aldous Huxley, *Antic Hay*, 1923

Women in general proved to be distracting, confusing and
periodically threatening creatures for British Intelligence in the
1920s. A male-dominated set of organisations, MI5, Special
Branch and SIS all had to have regular dealings with the opposite
sex, and yet the archives suggest that officers were frequently
perplexed by them – those strange entities who made up just
over half of the population! – and especially by their relationships
with men. The confusion was partly a reflection of the wide gulf
that still existed between men and women generally in interwar
society. But, whatever its cause, British Intelligence's 'woman
problem' proved a persistent challenge as the organisations tried
to pursue the right suspects for the right reasons.

The 1920s was a decade in which the battle of the sexes
raged. It was too soon for widespread campaigns to give rights
to homosexuals or non-white races, but by the end of the Great
War women's rights had moved decisively to the forefront of
political discourse across most of Europe and in most other
advanced states. In Britain in 1918, a large proportion of women
(those aged over thirty) was granted the right to vote, a victory

that was quickly followed by the election to parliament of the first women MPs (the very first, Countess Markiewicz, was a member of Sinn Fein and declined to take her seat, but the second, Nancy Astor, went on to become one of the most vocal and well-recognised backbenchers of the era, while the third, Margaret Wintringham, became – as we have already seen – a well-placed source of gossip for the CPGB). In 1920, women also got to sit on English juries for the first time and gained the right to work in the legal and accounting professions. In 1922, they became able, officially, at least, to petition for divorce on the same grounds as men.

Needless to say, such progress did not meet with universal enthusiasm. Large numbers of people, both men and women, expressed reservations about the fundamental shifts that were occurring in relations between the sexes, seeing them as a threat to the existing structure of society and, in many cases, a deviation from divine intentions. It did not help, as far as reactionaries were concerned, that some women used their new freedoms in ways that seemed distasteful. Women were now going unchaperoned to nightclubs; some wore trousers; and middle-class women increasingly chose to take up paid employment. Women of all backgrounds appeared to be more inclined to speak up in public about matters that had previously been the domain of men. Indeed, vocal groups of women were continuing their campaign for reform, despite what critics saw as the enormous changes they had already extracted from government and society. This led to charges that feminists were insatiable and unreasonably demanding. As additional staging posts on the road to equality, some women were now calling for suffrage on equal terms (which was granted in 1928), equal pay, and access to birth control, among a range of other measures. Where would it end?

Such developments were significant from British Intelligence's point of view for two reasons: first, because intelligence officers themselves were members of this rapidly changing society and held their own views about women, what they should do, and how they should behave, views that sometimes affected their work; and, secondly, because a significant number of emancipated women were attracted to the new Soviet state, which appeared to be moving much more quickly and enthusiastically towards full equality and a fundamental realignment of women's roles. The Soviet threat to Britain was, thus, seen by some to comprise a generalised threat to the traditional position of British women and a specific threat of Soviet women coming to Britain to be employed as secret agents.

The Bolsheviks certainly always talked a good game when it came to women's rights, and in their early years in power they actually came close to matching these words with actions. Tsarist Russia had been an extremely limiting environment for women who wanted to make their mark in public life. Tentative developments in the first decade of the twentieth century had given Russian feminists some cause for hope, but it was only with the edicts and decrees of 1917 and later that changes started to come rapidly, as first the Provisional Government and then Lenin sought to reimagine Russian society.

Full suffrage was granted to all Russian men and women on equal terms in 1917 (though the meaningfulness of this was later dented by the failure to hold free elections). Under Bolshevism, mothers were immediately entreated to work and use nurseries for childcare (admittedly, it took time for the nurseries to be set up), and the new Soviet state emphasised its indifference to age-old moral conundrums like the religious ban on sex outside marriage. During 1920, it even allowed pregnant women to ac-cess abortion on demand, the first country in the world to do so. And, as in other aspects of social affairs, Bolsheviks seemed happy to challenge pre-existing stereotypes, creating new hierarchies and laws of ownership, new family relationships, and even – and it would be wrong to minimise the importance of this – new styles of hair and clothing that were notably more androgynous and utilitarian than what had gone before. In government, a small number of women were to feature prominently in the Soviet state's early years: one, Aleksandra Kollontai, was made responsible for social welfare, and another, Anzhelika Balabanova, briefly became the first secretary of the Comintern.

Non-Communist Britons learned of Soviet sexual politics mostly through travelogues that foreigners penned and oral and written accounts by exiled White Russians, both of which received widespread coverage in the British media. While some reports were positive, most were not, presenting Bolshevik attitudes towards women as a distortion of the natural order and something that was being done to females against their will. This new breed of woman, it was frequently said, was less feminine and less maternal than her predecessors, and also more liable to be used, abused, controlled and brainwashed by the Communists' over-mighty state.

Unsympathetic British commentators got particularly agitated about how sexual liberation was working in practice inside Bolshevik Russia, with the most extreme voices presenting the new status quo as little more than a cover for rape. In early 1919, for instance, a British general was quoted in a House of Commons report as having witnessed the establishment of 'commissariats of free love' where 'respectable women [were] flogged for refusing to yield'. He also said that there had been 'several experiments to nationalise children', by which he meant that offspring had been removed from their parents to be raised *en masse* and indoctrinated with Bolshevik values.[1] In a similar vein, the Earl of Denbigh wrote to *The Times* to complain about 'Bolshevist ideas of sex relations and the position of women', based on conversations he had had with someone recently returned from Russia. 'It may be said that the position of a woman seems to be little different from that occupied by a breeding animal on a stud farm,' he asserted bluntly. Implying that this was just the logical extension of recent developments in Britain, he added that 'these facts should be published in every paper in the country and brought home to the mind of every woman,' including 'our newly enfranchised women voters'.[2]

For British Intelligence, the most evident effect of the Soviet government's woman policy was the employment by the Russian Trade Delegation and ARCOS of far more women than were working in equivalent British organisations. (Indeed, the British Trade Delegation to Moscow, which set out soon after the 1921 treaty was signed, contained no women whatsoever.) British spy chiefs seem to have assumed that a large proportion of Soviet women in London were secret agents, in the same mould as their male counterparts. While this turned out not to be true – because Soviet intelligence officials were actually much more chauvinist and traditionalist than was commonly thought – it led to a period of intense speculation as British Intelligence desperately tried to establish what Soviet women were up to.

Until recent decades, female spies have tended to be treated as less versatile then their male counterparts, their main role being to entrap men sexually.[3] In appraising the threat from Soviet women, therefore, British Intelligence mostly feared something akin to an invasion of Mata Haris. Mata Hari, whose real name was Margaretha Zelle, was the Dutch-born exotic dancer whom France had executed during the Great War on charges of spying for Germany. She was said to have been responsible for fifty thousand Allied deaths because of the vital secrets that she stole from the military personnel with whom she had affairs.[4] In the early 1920s, the memory of Mata Hari was still fresh in British minds – especially in Basil Thomson's: he had interviewed her at length during one of her visits to Britain but then decided to set her free.[5] Intelligence chiefs now worried that any Soviet women who came to Britain might turn out to be similar *femmes fatales*, setting honeytraps for unsuspecting British men to fall into, perhaps even men like themselves or their Whitehall colleagues.

Suspicion ran high during the first two years of ARCOS's and the Russian Trade Delegation's existence, although the evidence came almost entirely from rumours and hearsay provided by anti-Bolshevik Russian exiles. A frequent White Russian informant of the intelligence agencies got in touch with MI5 during March 1921, for instance, to warn suggestively that many female 'typists' in London's Soviet organisations were working 'under assumed names' with secret orders that were 'startling'.[6] A few months later, in October, additional clues emerged from a different informant. These caused MI5 to direct its attentions towards an organisation called the Russian Social Club, which met on Wednesdays and Fridays in rented rooms on Regent Street in central London. This tip-off, too, relied on the power of suggestion: 'Bolshevist sympathisers' were apparently using the club 'to recruit others to their cause' 'under the veil of [. . .] social entertainment'.[7] Investigations ensued but in the end MI5's Captain Phillips decided that the club was not a hub of debauchery after all. Members 'occupy themselves playing cards and drinking coffee,' he wrote in the file, after sending someone to make enquiries about the premises. It was 'hardly likely,' he concluded, 'that the Club constitute[d] any serious danger'.[8]

The vicinity of Regent Street remained in the frame, however. A year after the Russian Social Club allegations, in the autumn of 1922, another White Russian came forward, this time via a British army major, to share his worries. He began by noting that 'women employees both at Moorgate Street and Bond Street', where the Soviet government had its two main offices at that time, received 'salaries out of all proportion to their qualifications as clerks'.[9] Many, he asserted, took home as much as £10 a week (the equivalent of around £500 today). And his theory was that these funds were spent on intimate hospitality: 'this special pay [is] granted to enable them to get into touch with British officers and young men of good social standing for the purposes of carrying on pro-Soviet propaganda'.[10]

The informant knew that such activities had been occurring in different places all over the capital, he said, but he singled out one venue that was the favourite 'night haunt' of 'girls employed at the Delegation', Frolics.[11] Frolics nightclub was situated just a short walk from the Russian Social Club, on the corner of Regent's Place and Warwick Street, and its stock in trade was much racier than cards and coffee. It sprang into existence suddenly, around 1920, and enjoyed great popularity until its closure in 1923. During the brief time that it was in the limelight, the club hosted jazz bands, employed cocktail makers, and – like all nightclubs in central London in the 1920s – welcomed a wide mix of society.

At various points, Frolics' owners faced criminal charges for admitting 'non-members', allowing 'unlicensed public dancing' and 'supplying whisky and champagne after permitted hours'.[12] A bottle of champagne set thirsty punters back an extortionate 35 shillings (about £90 today).[13] But the club's most valued clients were easily able to afford such extravagance. Many were what MI5's informant called 'officers and young men of good social standing', a fact that is confirmed by a list of defendants from a 1923 court case. These included army officers and residents of exclusive addresses in Mayfair and Kensington, all of them charged, following a police raid, with 'consuming intoxicating liquor' out of hours.[14]

But were the Soviet habituées of Frolics really going there to entrap these men? The possibility cannot be excluded, yet MI5's subsequent investigations failed to produce concrete proof, neither there, nor at any other West End nightspot; nor did British counterespionage officers come across any government officials who had been recruited by the Russians in this way. Could it be, therefore, that the White Russian informants who made so much of this matter were lying or exaggerating – or simply allowing their prejudices about the new Soviet woman to get the better of them? Evidence from non-intelligence sources indicates that ARCOS and Russian Trade Delegation employees did frequently go on drinking binges in central London during the early 1920s. But these seem to have involved both men and women and to have been fuelled by a combination of the staff's outsized pay cheques and the typical exuberance that expats display when far from home. Perhaps White Russians who witnessed these events or heard about them jumped to the wrong conclusions in their eagerness to make trouble for the Soviets.

In a memoir published in 1930, Georgii Solomon, a high-ranking ARCOS official in the early 1920s (who later deserted from the Soviet state), recalled parties in London drinking establishments where 'some people [. . .] drank themselves into a dead state and at the end [. . .] – at 5 a.m. or so – remained to sleep the night'.[15] These could well have been the events at Frolics that MI5's informant was also describing. Solomon felt deeply unhappy about what he saw, believing that, far from creating an opportunity for Soviet espionage, this behaviour exposed the Soviet delegation to considerable risks by 'compromis[ing] us in the eyes of the English'.[16]

Solomon attended just one such session himself and describes it in vivid, horrified detail. 'I looked around the battle site,' he wrote:

> The assembly was spread across three rooms [. . .] In the big room there was a table, laid with bottles, and glasses, some full, some empty. The tablecloth was covered in wine already. There were some snacks. Employees were sitting behind the table in informal poses. Everyone was talking loudly, over one another, in clearly drunken voices [. . . One of them said to me] 'Here, nothing is not allowed. Here, everything is possible. Drink. Dance if you want to. If you want a girl, please yourself.'[17]

Solomon departed the club as soon as he could and later insisted to both Krasin and Klyshko that such antics must end. There is no record to indicate whether they did or not, but he later remembers another colleague labelling him 'Savonarola', after the 15th-century Florentine firebrand and preacher, and accusing him of wanting 'to turn real life into a monastery'.[18] MI5's archives record no attempt by British intelligence officers to exploit the opportunity that Solomon saw in this roomful of drunk Bolsheviks – no attempt, that is, to lay honeytraps of their own.

When considering the cases of individual women, British Intelligence also seems to have been frequently baffled and misled. The Clare Sheridan debacle illustrated how such mis-understandings could occur (the dogged insistence that she had to be a spy when, in fact, she was just a highly opinionated woman who enjoyed controversy); at one point, indeed, it was specifically her opinions on Soviet 'free love' that were cited as the cause for concern.[19] A more forgivable and frequent error was to mix up a bona fide suspect's intimate and secret lives. We saw this in the surveillance and commentary on Edith Lunn's miscarriage in Devon, and it was also to be a key flaw in the authorities' handling of the top Bolshevik Leonid Krasin.

After the Anglo-Russian treaty was signed in 1921, Krasin re-mained the official head of the Russian Trade Delegation until 1924, although he was frequently away from the country on other Soviet business. With an explicit remit to show that the Bolshevik regime could behave pragmatically, Krasin strived to appear as a man of commercial sensibilities who was content to leave the revolutionary politics to others. He frequently cited his experience as head of the German company Siemens's branch in St Petersburg during the 1910s, and it was clear to those he negotiated with that he really did understand the way the capitalist world worked (something that could not be said of many Bolsheviks).

Despite this, it would have been remiss of British Intelligence to leave Krasin unmonitored after the talks ended. Intelligence officers could not know that he was increasingly sidelined by Bolshevik colleagues, and not rated at all by the regime's spymasters. Instead, they gave due weight to the way he had lived before he worked for Siemens. (Following the 1905 revolution, Krasin had masterminded a series of bank robberies and bomb attacks, including one particularly deadly attack on Russia's Prime Minister, Peter Stolypin, in which Stolypin himself survived but twenty-eight others were killed.)[20] As they tried to keep close tabs on Krasin throughout the 1920s, Special Branch, MI5 and SIS all discovered him to be extremely secretive in his movements and communications, a fact that naturally increased their suspicion but which, in reality, seems to have had little to do with the Marxist cause.

One of the first supposed breakthroughs revealed only that Krasin was probably stealing from the Soviet regime. The contents of a safety deposit box he kept in Selfridges department store on Oxford Street intrigued the British authorities so much that, during the summer of 1921, they broke into it, only to discover not state secrets or plans to subvert the British Empire but architectural designs 'for a grand new house' and 'a large number of shares'.[21] It took the British much longer to work out that Krasin's many female acquaintances were not secret agents in their own right but mistresses. (He was, as a 1990s biographer put it, 'exceedingly popular with women'.[22])

While Krasin's wife Lyubov and their three children resided first in London and then Paris, Leonid himself travelled across the continent, seemingly maintaining a girl in every port. During 1921, Special Branch and MI5 became aware of a particularly close connection with a Russian emigré called Marussia; it took them considerable time to decide that she was a sexual partner and not a spy. Then in 1922, Krasin began a new relationship with a Russian artist he met in Berlin, Tamara Miklashevskaya.

More than twenty years his junior, she fell instantly and wildly in love with him, and he reciprocated. She became pregnant and over the next year, as Krasin continued to travel the length and breadth of the continent, they corresponded frequently, trying to work out what their joint future would hold. (Perhaps the shares and the architectural plans were part of it.)

Tamara's relationship with Krasin first caused concern to Germany's intelligence agencies – which, like the British, mistook the couple's sexual connection for espionage. British Intelligence became involved in 1923 after managing to intercept some of Tamara's correspondence with Krasin. Several weeks of inquiries followed, with all three agencies showing what one officer described as a 'lively interest' in the young woman, despite clear indications in the letters that she was not a spy, only an isolated, and evidently quite frightened, single parent missing her lover.[23] 'I don't like this business,' Tamara wrote in October 1923:

> Supposing they [the German secret police] wanted to worry me and drag me to be cross-examined. You see how it is and you wouldn't believe what I wrote to you. These fools think that I am a spy and an agitator, however stupid this may seem. I urgently beg you will come here. I am very cross with you and am afraid I shall get used to treating you badly. I am very dissatisfied with you. You can't love me a bit if you can behave so indifferently to me and Tatarochka [the couple's newborn daughter].[24]

There would be many other trips down romantic and sexual cul-de-sacs in the years ahead. In 1925, for instance, the authorities would struggle to work out whether or not a 'fashionable demi-mondaine' called Irma Mikhailova was a courier whom the Bolsheviks were using to transport money around Europe.[25] And in 1927, thousands of personal adverts in the national press were suddenly pored over in the course of an investigation into a woman called Kate Gussfeldt. For those on the lookout for espionage subtexts, such 'lonely hearts' notices and other short messages appeared deliberately designed to confuse and mystify. But, once again, no conclusive trail to particular spies was ever found:

> 'Teth. – Swans are supposed to sing sweet songs of farewell – but not in Arcady – C.'
> *Morning Post*, 26 April 1927.
> 'I. I. – "Stormy Actress" probable 29. Scrap awaits, more preparing.'
> *Morning Post*, 26 April 1927.
> 'Ruby. You can always rely upon me – G.'
> *The Times*, 28 April 1927.
> 'L. Rc'd yrs. Long'g to see you ag'n, am OK Love V.'
> *Daily Mail*, 28 April 1927.
> 'Darling, am under a cloud and all I can do is send you my love – Ever your devoted – G.'
> *The Times*, 30 April 1927.[26]

In fact the only 1920s 'lonely heart' who definitely led a double life as a spy was the former Special Branch head Sir Basil Thomson, who was caught in London's Hyde Park in December 1925 having sex with a prostitute, Thelma de Lava. Despite trying to argue that he was actually consulting Miss de Lava on the subject of 'vice conditions in the West End', the retired Thomson was found guilty of violating public decency and fined £5.[27] It is interesting to speculate whether, and in what way, this public shaming of one of Britain's top intelligence officers and his connection with de Lava are covered in the still-secret files of the Comintern and the KGB.

The Soviet state was accused by many overseas critics of nationalising the female body and exploiting women in various ways. In Britain, the authorities feared that Soviet women working at ARCOS might lead double lives as femmes fatales, *but in reality there is little evidence that this was the case. In this Soviet poster from the late 1920s a practically dressed Soviet woman confronts the social evil of prostitution and calls for it to stop.*

PART 3

WE CANNOT STAND IDLY BY

'Spying is waiting', wrote John le Carré in *The Russia House*, his classic thriller about Anglo–Soviet relations in the 1980s.[1] So it also was for British Intelligence during much of the 1920s: waiting for secret agents to reveal themselves among the members of the Russian Trade Delegation and the CPGB; waiting for the Papazian Group to slip up and divulge how exactly it was liquidating Tsarist-era jewels; waiting to discover who Johnnie Walker was. But whereas in the second half of the twentieth century British and other Western spy agencies came to see patience as a virtue – waiting, watching, learning, and, above all, giving the enemy as little indication as possible that they were doing so – 1920s British spies were typically impatient to act.

Had it been up to British Intelligence in the 1920s, Soviet negotiators would never have come to Britain in the first place. Instead, British military and undercover operations against the Bolsheviks would probably have continued inside Russia, and perhaps even been stepped up (a popular option in British military and security circles, despite the fact that most of the population wanted Britain to retreat from foreign wars).[2] It was only natural, therefore, that intelligence officers refused to accept the permanent Soviet presence in Britain, and remained anxious to crack down on, and ultimately rid themselves of, these troublemakers in their midst.

Of course, Britain's spies were limited in what they could achieve on their own: the real levers of change tended to be in the hands of the elected government or senior departmental officials. So a major part of British Intelligence's job was to brief the government and advise civil servants and politicians about how best to respond to hostile threats. It is clear that Special Branch, MI5 and SIS all briefed government officials and ministers frequently in the 1920s, arguing typically that the threat level in the country was too high, and that strong action was needed to reduce it – action against both the Bolshevism that had been exported from Russia and homegrown Communism.

Frustratingly for British intelligence chiefs, however, their words of advice often fell on deaf ears or otherwise led to no discernible action. This was particularly the case between 1920 and 1922, when David Lloyd George was still in power. As the principal architect of the Anglo-Soviet agreement, Lloyd George appeared to be permanently reluctant to punish the Soviets even for proven misdemeanours. The Borodin case was a rare example of an emissary from Moscow ending up in a British jail, but, in spite of catching the Bolshevik red-handed, the authorities were not allowed to take any broader action against the Russian Trade Delegation or ARCOS, both of which had facilitated his presence in the country. The Liberal Prime Minister was adamant that the best way to neutralise Bolshevism was to integrate it into world affairs and woo it back to the norms of international commerce. In pursuit of these goals, he was prepared to overlook a great deal.

Many in the British establishment (not just Britain's spies) disagreed with Lloyd George on this issue, seeing him as immoral and naive. More widely, there was growing consternation at his unscrupulousness and apparent tolerance for things that were generally held to be objectionable – not only Bolshevism but also Irish republicanism and the sale of honours. When he was finally forced to resign in late 1922, Britain got its first entirely

Conservative government for almost twenty years, and an immediate consequence was a much less conciliatory policy towards the Soviet state. This policy was overseen by Lloyd George's successor, Andrew Bonar Law, and supported by the new cabinet as a whole, but it was spearheaded by one politician in particular, the Foreign Secretary Lord Curzon. Thanks to him, British Intelligence now became more closely allied with the wider British government in the fight against Bolshevism than at any time since 1917.

There was considerable rejoicing in intelligence circles following this important turnaround. But, as we shall see, it was short-lived. Within months of coming to power, Bonar Law had to resign due to ill health. There then followed a year and a half of political turbulence, including three changes of prime minister and two complete reversals in the British state's approach to Russia. A febrile and sometimes paranoid mood developed in the establishment as a whole, and it was matched by a new willingness among the intelligence community to act, sometimes unilaterally, in defence of what officers saw as their country's best interests. In developments that would have seemed impossible just a short time earlier, members of British Intelligence even began to fear that people close to the elected government were taking their orders directly from Moscow. In such circumstances, they, the guardians of national security, were no longer prepared to stand idly by.

9

BULLETINS ON BOLSHEVISM

One of the greatest challenges for British Intelligence was to distil the massive amounts of material it gathered into clear, meaningful and usable nuggets of information for politicians. Deciding which particular suspects or suspicious activities to draw attention to was hard enough in itself, but proposing an official response was still more difficult. At a time when the ongoing shape and funding of the intelligence agencies was by no means assured, intelligence chiefs were often reluctant to incur the disapproval of their political masters, for instance by recommending actions that would seem too risky or controversial. Some elements in this tricky balancing act inevitably remain shrouded in mystery because so many conversations between spies and politicians took place informally, behind closed doors and without written records being made. Nevertheless, sufficient sources have come to light to give a good indication of the nature of these confidential exchanges, which were often sparked by or followed up with written briefings, some of which have survived and been declassified.

Intelligence chiefs in the interwar period had many ways to get in contact with senior civil servants, secretaries of state and prime ministers. Weekly set-piece briefings were complemented by standing invitations to interrupt the normal course of working life in an emergency. Myriad opportunities existed for impromptu meetings in the corridors of Whitehall or, perhaps still more frequently, in nearby Pall Mall, where all spy chiefs and the vast majority of government ministers belonged to at least one gentlemen's club.[1] Even if the secret doors and underground passageways of popular fiction were mostly absent from real-life 1920s espionage, other sorts of discreet and invisible connections abounded.

Sir Vernon Kell of MI5 knew that he could easily secure a confidential conversation with Winston Churchill on the subject of Clare Sheridan in 1925, for instance, because he had been in regular contact with the statesman for years. Churchill, who was particularly interested in intelligence work, also counted the senior SIS officer Desmond Morton among his personal friends – the pair ending up with country houses just a short walk from each other in Kent.[2] In Westminster, Basil Thomson and his successor at Special Branch, Sir Wyndham Childs, also had ongoing contact with successive home secretaries and prime ministers, while the heads of SIS could likewise see foreign secretaries and war secretaries at will.

Clearly, the quality of these relationships varied with the individual post holders, as some elected politicians and top civil servants felt more kindly disposed towards spy chiefs than others. In all cases, however, counterespionage experts knew they had to back up their advice with hard facts. They were also aware of the importance of keeping the general profile of intelligence work high on the government's agenda. This was why the regular intelligence bulletins that British Intelligence sent to the cabinet were so prized. They allowed the intelligence community to drip feed views about sedition and espionage straight to the government's heart. Initiated during the war, the weekly Special Branch reports on domestic threats to national security survived into peacetime, albeit with a narrower focus on supposedly revolutionary organisations. In 1919, they were joined by monthly bulletins written by the Foreign Office (with contributions from the main intelligence agencies) about revolutionary threats to British interests overseas. Every government between 1920 and 1924 received these compendia, which were sent to every cabinet member, not just those with a national-security portfolio, as would later be the norm.

While we do not know the extent to which each minister read the reports, they were clearly intended to be eye-catching. Front pages comprised short tables of contents and punchy summaries, and were typically followed by ten to fifteen sides of articles. In both series many entries took an episodic form, with fresh updates being provided weekly or monthly on emerging situations, many of which developed into long-running sagas. The dominant theme was always left-wing extremism, and the inferences and conclusions that British spies drew from the material presented ranged from pithy and ironic to histrionic and paranoid. 'Agitators' speeches are becoming more violent', one front-page headline ran in 1922. 'The lock-out of members of the Amalgamated Engineering Union, which came into force on Saturday, has produced a grave industrial situation, which all extremist organisations are endeavouring to exploit', exclaimed another in the same summary. And, further down on the same page: 'Details are given of the transmission of money from Moscow to Great Britain last month; minor officials in the Russian Trading Delegation are involved'.[3]

A notable feature of each report was the dizzying number of separate cases, activities, suspects and organisations that were covered. The overall impression was of a multitude of serious problems, any one of which might have the capacity to weaken Britain substantially. For those who already saw the country as being under Bolshevik attack, the reports were a key source of corroboration. Conversely, for anyone who felt sanguine about the nature and intensity of the Communist threat, they contained nothing to justify such complacency. Although reports sometimes paused to gloat at the far left's misfortunes or to poke fun at its failures, this was never done in such a way as to undermine the overall message about the danger of extreme socialism. To read just a single issue of the series, even now, is to get the sense of a country – and indeed an empire and a world – under relentless attack. To read every issue at the time must have felt like attending a grim and never-ending lecture.

This only makes it the more surprising that there was not more governmental action against Russia between 1920 and 1922. This, however, was entirely the result of the Prime Minister's personal intransigence. Frequently, cabinet members had tried to persuade Lloyd George of the need to react more aggressively to British Intelligence discoveries. Foreign Office documents show Lord Curzon, in particular, keeping up near-constant pressure on his boss to do more about Moscow. They also describe him defiantly taking action by himself, without prime ministerial approval, to try to limit the damage the Bolsheviks were causing.

Curzon initially refused to shake Kamenev's hand when the Bolsheviks arrived at the 1920 talks; thereafter, his Foreign Office proceeded to draft a string of memoranda cataloguing all that was wrong with the new *status quo* and setting out what ought to be done about it. In June 1921, for instance, diplomats issued a scathing minute describing how 'since the signing of the Trade Agreement on March 16 there has been little evidence of any sincere intention on the part of the Soviet Government to abandon their propaganda campaign'.[4] A few months later, in October, Curzon personally challenged the Russian Trade Delegation about its bloated staff numbers (based on evidence collected by British Intelligence), no doubt seeing this as a concrete way to limit the number of Soviet secret agents who were entering the country. 'In future,' the Foreign Office wrote to Leonid Krasin on 20 October 1921, 'applications for the admission of Russians to this country can only be considered, if the capacity in which the individual in question will be employed is stated together with full particulars of the nature of the work for which he is required'.[5]

It was a sensible plan but, without prime ministerial backing, Curzon was always going to find it difficult to implement, since both Krasin and Klyshko could appeal directly to Number 10 if any visa request was rejected. Only a few weeks later, Curzon held a conference at the Foreign Office to try to hammer out further details. By the end of the meeting, however, the proposal was in shreds, as attendees all agreed that it was not feasible to place numerical limits on the size of the trade delegation given current political circumstances. Still more depressingly, it had emerged during the course of preparations for the meeting that the total number of Soviet citizens at ARCOS and the Russian Trade Delegation was much higher than had originally been calculated – closer to two hundred than one hundred.[6]

Despite the persistently poor response they received, British intelligence officers never stopped trying to persuade the elected government to act against the Bolsheviks. Their patience was rewarded quite suddenly in September 1922, when a political crisis erupted that quickly swept the 'Welsh Wizard' from power. Lloyd George, supported by Churchill, had threatened to go to war against the new Republic of Turkey (the very thing he had steadfastly refused to do against Bolshevism). The Conservatives in the governing coalition, who held the majority, objected to such rashness and argued instead for peaceful relations with the Turks. When Lloyd George, as usual, overruled them, they met in secret and voted to withdraw their support. Consequently, on 19 October 1922 he was left with no choice but to resign allowing a new Conservative-only administration to take office, with the former Chancellor of the Exchequer, Andrew Bonar Law, as Prime Minister.

Among the first decisions Bonar Law's administration took was a tougher line on Russia. The intelligence community scented its best opportunity to date of getting rid of the

Bolsheviks and expanded and sharpened its reports accordingly, deliberately seeking to arm the new administration with every kind of hard-hitting ammunition against the Soviet enemy and to galvanise them into action. Special Branch reports for late 1922 and early 1923 were consequently even fuller than before. A representative example from 8 March 1923 (four months into the new administration) ran to eighteen pages, and dealt with no fewer than thirteen different suspect organisations and thirty-six named individuals.[7] The episodic nature of the briefings continued, but the ramifications of each storyline were now spelt out in full each time, with the clear aim of hammering home British Intelligence's overarching narrative. Problems that had been known about for years, but which had gone unaddressed, were rehearsed again, and with greater force, for the benefit of the new men in power.

The first item in the 8 March briefing provides a perfect illustration of this. Entitled 'The Communist International and Great Britain', it brought news of a Comintern resolution to get the CPGB to improve its work with the British proletariat. Scores of identical resolutions had been passed previously, but the implications of this one were explained in detail, the bulletin's authors assuming no prior knowledge. 'The Presidium of the Communist International in Russia has passed an important resolution on the "Parliamentary activity of the Communist Party of Great Britain",' the compilers stated, before going on to reproduce the document in full, including a list of issues that Moscow had instructed British Communists to campaign about:

a. Unemployment, and the attitude of the Government towards the economic position of the Working Class.
b. The Colonies & Ireland.
c. The Foreign policy of the Government, particularly in connection with the question of the Ruhr, reparations, etc.

  d. The policy towards Soviet Russia.
  e. Militarism.
  f. The Budget.
  g. The Bourgeois policy of the Labour Party.[8]

While there was nothing new in the list or in the Comintern ordering CPGB activists to follow it, setting it out in this way allowed Special Branch to raise anew the question of how long ministers would permit such interference in British life.

Other parts of the bulletin brought fresh evidence of Moscow's meddling in the dominions (on this occasion Australia); of British Communists using public meetings to advocate a British dictatorship of the proletariat; and of various instances of alleged incitement to mutiny. Again, such occurrences had been common enough in the past, but by describing them in detail Special Branch hoped to make unignorable the scale of the challenge Britain was facing. Intelligence analysts also gave weight to the Communist movement's own assessment of its success, even though, in other ways and at other times, they dismissed such CPGB analysis as entirely unreliable. In the 8 March bulletin, for instance, Special Branch quoted without further comment a view expressed in the *Communist Review*, that there was 'one point upon which the Communist Party has scored a most emphatic success, and that has been in its handling of the unemployed [. . .] With unerring revolutionary instinct the Party [has seen] in unemployment the greatest danger to capitalism; and it [has] concentrated upon it in order to make it the rallying centre of the discontented masses and of the whole Labour movement'.[9] Another quotation from a Scottish branch of the CPGB – 'No other Political Party has any influence in the Unemployed Movement [. . .] our members completely dominate the situation' – was also printed without challenge.[10]

The most anti-Communist members of the cabinet took this information and knew that, with Lloyd George gone, they could now hope to use it. Lord Curzon, in particular, had been readying himself for this moment for years. He had personally registered every major infringement of the Anglo-Russian treaty since its inception and, within weeks of the 1922 general election, was signalling to the Soviet Foreign Minister, Georgii Chicherin, that there would be a change in Britain's Soviet policy.

Chicherin met Curzon at an international conference in Lausanne in late 1922 and opened a brief bilateral conversation with what had long been the official Soviet Foreign Ministry line (so different from the *political* line pushed by the Comintern). He asked his British counterpart what the Soviet state needed to do in order to have better relations with Britain. Curzon replied in blistering tones, making it absolutely clear that the softly-softly diplomacy of the Lloyd George era had ended. According to his own, somewhat boastful, telegram back to the Foreign Office, the Foreign Secretary went on to say that no 'advance [could] be made' in Anglo-Russian relations until Russia met all of her obligations under the existing treaty.[11] He added that Britain's intelligence services had proved that wrongdoing was taking place in many different areas of the Soviet state's dealings with the United Kingdom. 'I [was] personally responsible for paragraphs in [the] trade agreement renouncing political propaganda against [the] British Empire', he had told Chicherin; 'Nevertheless, I [have] overwhelming evidence up till [the] present hour to show that [. . .] Soviet Russia [has] been persistently intriguing and spending large sums of money in anti-British policy and propaganda. How [can] we be expected to embrace a would-be friend who thus stab[s] us in the back? Until there [is] an absolute desistance from this pestilent activity, there [can] be no real reconciliation. [. . .] Where one of two parties [is] exclusively guilty,' he concluded, 'while the other [is] wholly innocent, no mid-way house or compromise appear[s] to be possible.'[12]

After this dramatic statement – word of which understandably did the rounds back in Whitehall – Curzon carefully and cautiously took stock. The language of his speech suggested that he wanted to lash out immediately, but in reality he knew that the circumstances for acting against Moscow had to be absolutely right. The briefings he received over the next few months, including the one from 8 March, he scrutinised with particular attention, and he stayed in close contact with the intelligence services while weighing his options. At some point in late March or early April, he finally decided what it was he wanted to do. The time had come, he judged, to issue Lenin's regime with a strong and unequivocal ultimatum. Finally, it looked as if British Intelligence was going to get its way.

342

13

Special Branch,

New Scotland Yard,

S.W.1.

No. 196

March 8th, 1923.

REPORT ON REVOLUTIONARY ORGANISATIONS
IN THE UNITED KINGDOM
--------------------oOo--------------------

S U M M A R Y

On February 26th the wholly unemployed on the live registers
called approximately 1,328,000, a decrease of 12,260 on the
previous week: on the same date the number working short time and
drawing benefit for intervals of unemployment was 54,500 as compared
with 55,524 on February 19th.

41 unemployed marchers are still in London.

The Communist Party is making careful arrangements in connection
with the national conference of the organised unemployed next
month: definite instructions regarding policy and resolutions
have been sent to the District Party Committees.

The Presidium of the Communist International in Russia has
passed an important resolution on the "Parliamentary activity of the
Communist Party of Great Britain", which is quoted in this report.

The Communist Party has renewed its application to the Labour
Party for affiliation.

The Communist Party and the Red International of Labour Unions
in this country have been instructed to send delegates to the
Conference which is to be held in Germany on March 17th in
connection with the occupation of the Ruhr.

The anti-militarist campaign of the Young Communist League
has led to the issue of literature which is intended to undermine
the discipline of His Majesty's Forces.

---

*For some government ministers between 1919 and 1924, the weekly reports
on revolutionary organisations in the United Kingdom were the most exciting
documents they received. Special Branch wrote each one hoping it would lead to
concrete action against the Soviets and their British supporters, but until Lord
Curzon seized the initiative in 1923 these hopes went largely unfulfilled.*

10

THE MARQUESS'S ULTIMATUM

The United Kingdom was the most powerful country in the world from the end of the Napoleonic Wars in 1815 until the 1930s, when the great dictators reached their zenith. Throughout this period, however, the country worked hard to avoid many of the overt displays of power that might be considered the very reason to achieve global pre-eminence. This included only sparing use of ultimata, which, as far as most Whitehall mandarins were concerned, came with a major risk of backfiring on those who issued them. Perfidious Albion – as many enemies came to think of Britain – typically preferred softer, less public means of coercion and inducement, which could more easily be rowed back from and might even be denied altogether should the circumstances require.

In the decades before 1923, only two major diplomatic ultimata were despatched from London. The first, in 1890, was sent to the Portuguese government, successfully ordering it to pull its troops out of certain parts of sub-Saharan Africa to which Britain already laid claim; these territories would subsequently become the British colonies of Northern and Southern Rhodesia. The second ultimatum, in 1914, demanded that the German army withdraw from Belgium; and the Kaiser's failure to comply with it led directly to Britain's entry into the Great War.

Suddenly, less than five years after the conclusion of that conflict, Lord Curzon proposed to use this rare diplomatic device once more, to signal the scale of Britain's displeasure with the Bolsheviks and its determination to put a stop to Soviet wrongdoing. Curzon selected the mode of complaint in full awareness of the serious consequences it could have. He was perhaps even quite complaisant about the prospect of Britain being backed into a corner on this subject, having had to bide his time and officially back a different policy for so long. He could be confident, of course, that British Intelligence and many other parts of the establishment supported the approach too.

Work on what would become the Curzon Ultimatum began around the turn of 1923, when Curzon instructed groups of civil servants, diplomats and intelligence officers to collaborate in assembling as convincing a case as possible against the Russians. The Marquess (as Curzon was also known after becoming Marquess of Kedleston in 1921) had his own views about what needed to be included: plenty on the threat the Soviets posed to British interests in the East (his own most pressing area of concern); plenty on Bolshevik underhand tactics, unwelcome propaganda and other forms of meddling in Britain's domestic affairs; and also – somewhat contradictorily – plenty on those aspects of *Soviet* domestic affairs that Curzon found particularly noxious, including issues of freedom of religion and freedom of conscience. The Foreign Secretary knew that the weight of evidence would have to be unassailable, so the dossier was subject to a painstaking sifting process: any material that contained flaws, however eye-catching it might otherwise be, was excised.

When the cabinet met on 25 April 1923, Curzon informed his fellow ministers of the details of his plan for the first time. He started by reassuring colleagues that the President of the Board of Trade, a fellow cabinet member, had already given his full backing to the proposal (an important consideration, since Anglo-Russian trade could soon come to an abrupt end because of the action). The discussions that day concluded with a formal request to Curzon to 'prepare for the consideration of the Cabinet, a draft despatch to the Soviet Government rehearsing the numerous recent incidents to show the unsatisfactory and discourteous attitude of the Russian Soviet Government, including [. . .] such matters as propaganda contrary to the Trade Agreement [. . .] and any other similar cases; insisting on satisfaction; and intimating that if no acceptable reply [was] received within an early period of time our present *de facto* relations would be severed.'[1]

The Foreign Secretary had been given the green light he required and he duly circulated a complete draft of the ultimatum just five days later (naturally, the 3,500-word letter had been substantially in existence ahead of the 25 April cabinet session). Signing himself 'C. of K.' (which stood for Curzon of Kedleston), as was his custom, the Marquess appended a note to the text warning colleagues that they must 'exercise special care that the draft does not pass out of their hands'; it would not have done to allow any early versions of such sensitive material to leak to the press or, worse still, to an overseas power.[2] When ministers gathered two days later, the Foreign Secretary fully expected a lively debate, but he could be almost certain that the ultimatum would eventually be approved – partly because of the quality of his preparations and partly because he now found himself in charge of the government as a whole, owing to the Prime Minister's absence through illness (Bonar Law was suffering from an advanced form of throat cancer and was urgently seeking treatment).

The ultimatum Curzon presented was made up of several parts, with an initial thunderous preamble being followed by dedicated sections on specific incidents and allegations. It opened with the assertion – directed as much at Lloyd George as at Moscow, we may assume – that Britain had already been too patient with the Bolshevik state: His Majesty's Government felt a duty, the letter stated, 'which has perhaps been already too long delayed, of considering carefully [. . .] whether it is desirable, or indeed possible, that the relations of the two Governments should remain any longer upon so anomalous and indeed unprecedented a footing and whether His Majesty's Government can with due self-respect continue to ignore the repeated challenges which the Soviet Government has thought fit with apparent deliberation to throw down'.[3]

Among the challenges then mentioned were flagrant violations of the trade treaty in India, Afghanistan and Persia, all areas where Britain saw itself as formally or informally in charge and about which Curzon himself cared deeply. A key example was the discovery that money withdrawn by Bolsheviks in London had ended up in the hands of revolutionaries in the Punjab, one of the aforementioned fruits of the Papazian–Rabinoff–Klyshko triangle:

> In [1922] a number of Bank Notes of 100 *l.* each, issued through Lloyd's Bank and the Russian Commercial and Industrial Bank in London to Nikolai Klishko, Assistant Official Agent of the Soviet Government in London in June 1921, were cashed in India on behalf of a revolutionary Panjabi in touch with other Indian seditionaries who are known to have been closely associated with the Russian representative in Kabul.

This showed, the ultimatum said, how the Soviet government had 'flouted and infringed' even 'the preliminary conditions upon which the Trade Agreement was signed'. And, far from being an isolated example, it was matched by 'many scores of similar incidents covering in their wide ambit Egypt, Turkey, the British Dominions and [. . .] Great Britain [itself]'.[4]

Curzon also singled out the Russian ambassador to Tehran

for criticism. Significantly, he was none other than Andrew Rothstein's father, Theodore. The elder Rothstein, the letter said, had 'housed Indian seditionists within his hospitable walls and had sped them on their mission to India'. The ultimatum also expressed anger about Bolshevik assistance to 'seven Indians who had been trained as Communist agitators at Tashkent' and who 'were arrested on their arrival in India from Moscow whence they had travelled [. . .] by a circuitous and very difficult route, in order to evade detection'.[5] This and many other incidents were held up as evidence of the close links between the Russian state and the Comintern, something the Soviet government always tried to deny. The latest secret proof, Curzon said, had come as recently as 25 November 1922, when 'a member of the Soviet Government [had attended] a meeting of the Financial Commission of the Fourth Congress of the Third International', a meeting at which 'sums of 80,000 *l* and 120,000 *l* [were allotted] to the British and Indian Communist parties respectively.'[6]

Curzon listed many other instances of illegal propaganda and attempts to roil the waters of Britain's domestic and imperial affairs before going on to set out, with equal fervour, his more humanitarian concerns. He raised a number of longstanding worries, including about the execution by the Bolsheviks of a British engineer, C. F. Davidson, and the false imprisonment of a British journalist, Mrs Stan Harding; both events that had occurred in 1920 and that the Foreign Secretary had always felt Lloyd George had disgracefully ignored. Davidson was shot in January 1920 on what the British said were trumped up charges of treason, while Mrs Harding, a British citizen who was working for the *New York World* newspaper, had been thrown into a Moscow prison after spurious claims of espionage were made against her.[7] She was then kept in solitary confinement for five months, being led to believe that she was on death row. In each case, the Marquess now wrote, 'His Majesty's Government are unable any longer to trifle [. . .] They must now require that the Soviet Government should admit their liability and should undertake to pay such equitable compensation as may be awarded by an arbitrator to be agreed upon.' British 'public opinion', he said, was 'at a loss to understand how such treatment as that accorded to these unfortunate and innocent persons should be meted out by a Government to which the British Government had gone out of its way to extend a friendly hand.'[8] Again, fingers were being pointed at both Moscow and the previous British administration.

On the subject of Bolshevik religious persecutions, Curzon was no less condemnatory. In 1922 and 1923 there had been an increase in state-sponsored measures against religious groups in Russia, including the murder of priests, renewed expropriations of church property, and (particularly controversial in Britain) the banning of Protestant groups, including the Salvation Army. Curzon wrote with shock of how 'no attempt [had been] made in Russia to deny that [these] persecutions and executions [were] part of a deliberate campaign [to] destroy [. . .] all religion in Russia, and enthron[e] the image of godlessness in its place'. He said that this had inevitably 'excited the profound consternation [and] indignant remonstrance of the civilised world'.[9]

Overall, the ultimatum was striking for two features: first, as in the passage just quoted, for the intemperateness of Curzon's language (a recapitulation and, indeed, intensification of his approach in the face-to-face discussion with Chicherin in December 1922) and, secondly, for the direct references to secretly gathered intelligence on Russian misdeeds. On the former point, the majority of the cabinet seemed happy to endorse the Foreign Secretary's approach. Indeed, some colleagues argued for critical passages to be made still more unequivocal, particularly a section at the ultimatum's end which outlined what the Bolsheviks could expect next if they did not comply. In the draft version, this ran as follows: 'it is not possible for [His Majesty's Government] to acquiesce in a continuance of the treatment which has been summarised in this Memorandum and which is incompatible alike with national dignity and with mutual respect'.[10] By the time ministers left Downing Street it had been strengthened into a more concrete threat: 'unless within ten days of the receipt of the above communication by the Commissariat for Foreign Affairs, the Soviet Government has undertaken to comply fully and unconditionally with the requests which it contains, His Majesty's Government will recognise that that Government does not wish the existing relations between them to be maintained. In that case, His Majesty's Government, on their part, will, in view of the manifest infringement of the Trade Agreement by the Soviet Government as set forth in the earlier part of the present memorandum, consider themselves immediately free from the obligation of that Agreement.'[11]

With regard to the Foreign Secretary's prodigious use of secret intelligence, however, there was considerably greater un-ease among ministers. This truly would be a first for the British government – exposing its clandestine surveillance of a foreign state for everyone, including that foreign state, to see. Curzon himself recognised the need for explicit cabinet approval on this point, not wishing to be personally exposed were there to be any negative consequences. The cabinet minutes, guarded as always, imply nonetheless that there was a robust exchange of views, before recording that the government eventually agreed with the Marquess that 'the advantages of basing the published British case on actual extracts from the despatches which had passed between the Soviet Government and its agents outweighed the disadvantages of the possible disclosure of the secret source from which these despatches had been obtained.'[12]

It seems likely that the force of Lord Curzon's personality, as well as a general appreciation of how deeply he felt about this issue, weighed heavily on cabinet members as they considered the draft ultimatum. Curzon's extra leverage as the acting head of the government must have helped too. As would become clear in the weeks ahead, at least some of those present that day – most notably the Chancellor of the Exchequer Stanley Baldwin – hoped dearly that the ultimate sanction which the ultimatum established would not need to be used.

Curzon himself was delighted with the outcome he achieved and made all haste to ready his document for despatch. Frustratingly, this was a process that took longer than it once would have, because governments in Britain's overseas dominions (Australia, Canada, New Zealand and South Africa) now had to be informed, and nominally consulted, ahead of this sort of major diplomatic manoeuvre. The Curzon Ultimatum was finally telegraphed to Soviet Foreign Minister Chicherin on 8 May, and the first public word of its existence broke in the newspapers of the Western world the following morning. It was to go on making headlines for weeks.

The letter's impact was electrifying. For a few days the British government did not discover how the Soviets would react, but across the British political spectrum the press and other commentators immediately agreed on the significance of the Foreign Secretary's intervention. 'A straightforward action' that 'will be heartily approved by the majority of the nation,' *The Times* said approvingly.[13] 'Lord Curzon has the country behind him,' cheered the *Sunday Times*, a sentiment echoed by all Britain's other right-wing publications.[14] Charles Hunter of the Association of British Creditors of Russia, an anti-Bolshevik pressure group, publicly stated that 'as business men [we desire] to tender our hearty support to Lord Curzon on the stand he has taken. In our opinion, it was high time that the rulers of Soviet Russia were called sharply to account for their bad faith and their deliberately anti-British line of conduct. Our Government has carried forbearance to a point where it might easily be misinterpreted as weakness'.[15]

Liberal and left-wing critics, meanwhile, concurred as to

the significance of Curzon's daring departure but saw it in a more negative light. The *Economist* wrote that 'the ultimatum which has just been dispatched [. . .] has produced a crisis', and, while admitting that 'the case against the Russian Government is undoubtedly a strong one', wondered whether it had been 'wise to couch the protest in terms so challenging and un-diplomatic'.[16] In the *Manchester Guardian*, a long and involved leading article went further, bemoaning 'an extremely grave step' which threatened to sever 'the slender thread which binds us diplomatically to Russia'. The writer of this piece worried about the return of a 'kind of antagonism which, shortly after the Armistice, impelled this country to squander its wealth in the vain effort to crush Bolshevism and all its work', that is to say, a return to war.[17]

Across the Atlantic, the *New York Times* referred to the ultimatum as a 'sharp British note' and predicted that it was certain to make 'a great impression' among the Bolsheviks.[18] Similarly, but in cheekier language, *Time* magazine (which was then just eleven issues old) foresaw an outbreak of 'Curzonophobia' across Soviet territory – and so it was to prove.[19]

On receiving the ultimatum, the Bolshevik leadership felt shocked and demoralised. Even if the text in many respects represented chickens coming home to roost, Curzon's language left Soviet leaders with almost no room to manoeuvre and seemed to presage the end of Anglo-Russian relations in under two weeks if they did not capitulate. After ruminating on the document for a couple of days, Moscow's government decided to reprint it in full in the state-controlled press. As intended, this led to a great surge of emotion among the general Soviet populace, including a spike in fears of an imminent British invasion and indignant reactions to Britain's misplaced imperiousness, seen as an unwelcome echo of bygone days.

Living in Moscow at the time was Arthur Ransome (a Russia expert, sometime contact of British Intelligence and later the author of *Swallows and Amazons*), who described for the *Manchester Guardian* how there were suddenly 'demonstrations all over town'.[20] Many of them were apparently headed by effigies of Lord Curzon, mostly made of cloth and cardboard, but in one case played by a human being, an individual who was 'unlucky because near the Art Theatre a number of real Hindoos pulled him down from the lorry and beat him with a certain amount of vim'.[21] The British Trade Mission, Ransome added, had been rushed at by a group of angry protesters. The celebrated novelist Mikhail Bulgakov told a similar tale in a Russian-language newspaper. 'At two o'clock in the afternoon,' he wrote, 'it was impossible to cross Tverskaya. In an unbroken flow, as far as the eye could see, a long ribbon of people slowly moved through, with a forest of banners and posters over their heads.' One of the banners read, 'Don't Play With Fire, Lord Curzon. We Have Kept Our Powder Dry.'[22]

It might have been tempting for British politicians to dismiss such public manifestations as confections of the Soviet state. The protests were definitely officially sanctioned (by this point large groups of people did not gather in the Soviet state unless permitted to do so) but, as we continue to observe today, long after Britain's international power has waned, hatred of the United Kingdom can still draw enthusiastic and organic crowds in many parts of the world. Whether synthetic or not, the mood of the mob mirrored the frustration and fury of the men at the Russian regime's centre. Bolsheviks made a point of never apologising for anything, not even tactically. Moreover, they had no intention of stopping the foreign propaganda and subversion campaigns that had become their hallmark. And yet now they were being confronted with evidence that their agent network and operations had been thoroughly mapped and monitored by British Intelligence for years – and, worse still, they were having to endure the washing of this dirty linen in public. The care that the Foreign Secretary had taken to ensure that all the material in the ultimatum was certifiably accurate really did increase the document's impact in Moscow. Had there been just one error or false accusation, the Russians would have felt on much safer ground.

A week of fierce deliberations in Moscow ensued. The letter's effect was magnified by a completely unrelated event that occurred on 10 May: the assassination in a hotel restaurant in Lausanne of the Soviet diplomat Vatslav Vorovsky. This sent shockwaves through the Bolshevik leadership and, when word reached the press, through the rest of Soviet society. People inevitably feared a connection between the British ultimatum and the Swiss assassination (which had in fact been carried out by a White Russian). As Karl Radek, a senior Bolshevik, reportedly said, the murder of Vorovsky could be seen as 'the outcome of British threats and British anti-Soviet propaganda'.[23] Curzon's sabre-rattling may have appeared more menacing than it really was.

In this confusing and unsettling context, the Soviet Politburo finally agreed an initial response to London on 13 May. The Russian note may be read as preserving Bolshevik dignity – just about – but also contained passages of significant self-abasement. The Foreign Affairs Commissariat indicated willingness to acknowledge that there had indeed been wrongdoing on the part of the Soviet state. Simultaneously, Soviet diplomats moved to withdraw Nikolai Klyshko from the United Kingdom, a development that was instantly noted in Whitehall, even though it did not get picked up by the British press for some months. In return, however, the Russians said they wanted a bilateral meeting between Curzon and Krasin to discuss mending relations. Russia could not 'submit to an ultimatum', they stated, though they also conceded that they might now pay compensation in the cases of Davidson and Harding (so long as similar compensation was payable to Soviet victims of British justice – though no names of such victims were provided). The note finally acknowledged the veracity of the various coded telegrams that Britain had secretly intercepted and reproduced, merely observing that these had been 'misleadingly edited'.[24]

It was a sign of Russia's relative weakness at this moment that its strongest card was to accuse Curzon of warmongering. The Bolsheviks played this card to the best of their ability, using, among other things, the recent protests and rallies to corroborate their assertion that Britain was pushing Russia to the brink. The Russian reply stated that while the Soviet government did 'not necessarily assume that there [would] be war [. . .] if a breach with England [became] definite', it felt absolutely certain that 'the British Government [was] responsible for having created an atmosphere in which war might be engendered'.[25]

Curzon definitely did not want war. But he was in no mood to meet the Bolsheviks halfway either. The Soviet reply represented a debasement and humbling along the lines that he had intended but not yet to the extent that he wanted. As a sign of good faith (or, perhaps, desperation), Soviet leaders sent Leonid Krasin back to London before even learning what the British government's response to their proposals would be. On arriving, Krasin still had no idea whether Anglo-Russian relations were salvageable, or indeed if Curzon would meet him. The Foreign Secretary himself probably did not want to speak to the Bolshevik again, seeing this as a concession too far. (As recently as 11 May, the Foreign Office had even held an internal meeting to discuss the possibility of taking hostages from among Britain's Soviet community should the diplomatic situation deteriorate rapidly.)[26] Curzon was prevailed upon, however, to meet Krasin so as to avoid the possibility of Britain being accused of unreasonableness.

In the course of a House of Commons debate on 15 May, a junior Foreign Office minister confirmed that 'Lord Curzon would be ready and glad to see Mr Krassin to go through the whole of our claims'. He hastily added that this was not in any way to be a negotiation in the normal sense. 'We have negotiated until we are sick of negotiating,' he said, 'and the Government are not to be drawn again into negotiations where all these trumped-up counter-claims can be put forward and where there is no intention of meeting our case. It must not be taken that we mean to be satisfied with anything less than compliance with our demands'.[27] This message reached Krasin instantly, because – with nothing better to do – he had decided to sit in the public gallery of the House to hear the minister with his own ears. (According to the *Manchester Guardian*, just a few seats away from him was the journalist Mrs Stan Harding, the Soviets' former death-row prisoner whose case had helped to make the ultimatum so compelling.)[28]

Krasin was received in the Foreign Office on the morning of 17 May, when he found the British to be as good as their word. Curzon treated the two-hour meeting as an opportunity to rehearse orally all the grave accusations that he had already set down on paper. The one compromise he was prepared to make was to extend the deadline in order to give the Soviets a final chance to satisfy the British demands. The original time limit had been 18 May, but Curzon now agreed to allow Krasin such time as was necessary to communicate with Moscow and receive one further reply from his bosses.

The reply did not come until six days later, on 23 May, which must have irritated the Foreign Secretary greatly. Perhaps recognising this, Krasin himself delivered the letter to the Foreign Office by hand. In it, there was additional movement towards Britain's position, both in material terms and rhetorically. 'The very fact of the extension of the time limit of the ultimatum gives ground for hope that there is a possibility of reaching an agreement and of avoiding the consequences of a break,' the text began emolliently, before trying to establish non-humiliating grounds for a further Soviet climbdown. 'The consequences to the general peace which might arise from a break between

England and Russia are causing the Russian Government serious apprehensions,' it said, and went on:

> In such an event great danger would threaten the pres-
> ervation of peace, and humanity would, as a result, be
> threatened with countless calamities [. . .] Not wishing
> to give anybody grounds for placing, even in the small-
> est degree, any responsibility for the possibility of such
> results – even indirectly – upon the Soviet Govern-
> ment, the latter is willing to make new concessions.[29]

These concessions amounted to an immediate granting of compensation in the Davidson and Harding cases, with no expectation of reciprocal compensation for the Soviet citizens (still unnamed) who had supposedly been incarcerated by Britain in like fashion; resolution in Britain's favour of the rights of British fishermen to fish near the Soviet coast; and willingness on Moscow's part to renew its anti-propaganda and anti-meddling vows, provided – and this was the document's only significant caveat – that Britain renewed similar vows not to act against the interests of the Soviet government. 'It is self-evident,' the letter added, turning to the hoped-for future, 'that if and when the British Government makes to the Russian Government friendly representations as to what it regards as infringements of the Trade Agreement, by any agents or officials of the Russian Government, the cases will be carefully investigated and the necessary measures will be taken.'[30]

Even if no one really expected the Russians to stop propa-ganda or attempts to spark revolutions around the world, this letter arguably represented the most that Curzon could reasonably have expected to achieve. Nevertheless, both he and his senior advisors reacted with extreme negativity to any notion of Britain repeating its pledge not to meddle in Soviet affairs just so the Soviets would recommit to theirs; Britain, they maintained, had steadfastly kept her promises and so no recommitment was necessary. While a growing number of people around Whitehall began to wonder if the time had not come to put an end to the Bolsheviks' humiliation, or at least to give them a chance to hang themselves with new promises, the Foreign Secretary remained against any compromise. As the Foreign Office's permanent secretary, Sir Eyre Crowe, wrote on the day the second Soviet reply came in, 'That the Soviet government think it necessary to give way on part of our case is, to my mind, evidence that they are really afraid of breaking with us. This should be an incitement to us to persist in our demands being fully met.'[31] Which was to say, Britain should not give an inch.

Although we cannot see into the minds of Britain's top spies during this episode, we may safely assume that their attitude was similar to Sir Eyre's, and that they felt increasingly hopeful that, with Curzon's intransigence, Anglo-Russian relations would soon end and London's most troublesome inhabitants would be sent home. A similar view was expressed in an interesting *Times* leader on 24 May, which stripped the Soviet problem back to its first principles, and looked beyond the emollience of the latest Soviet letter to what was described as the wider reality of Bolshevik behaviour:

> No one in this country is hostile to Russia. But the vast majority of Englishmen, seeing what Bolshevism has accomplished in Russia, have a profound repugnance for Bolshevism. They have become familiar now with Bolshevist methods and they do not regard the word of the Soviet Government as possessing the same value and the significance that would attach to the word of any normal national Government. At a moment when Bolshevist leaders in Moscow are declaiming against the British Government, when they are charging

our statesmen with responsibility for the murder of
Vorovsky, when gross caricatures of our Government
are being published in the Soviet Press, the British
public can hardly be expected to believe that the
Moscow Communists really cherish the pacific and
friendly feelings so laboriously expressed in the Note
delivered to Lord Curzon yesterday. The present is an
occasion for taking full account of the position created
by the Trade Agreement [. . .] The existence of a
Trade Delegation in London [. . .] gives the wavering
Communist regime a certain international prestige as
well as a remarkably useful centre for propaganda [. . .]
British national rights shall be respected and [. . .] no
countenance shall be given to alien and subversive
tendencies whose falsity has become a byword.
We have no doubt that the Government will insist
resolutely on the complete fulfilment of the demands
presented by Lord Curzon.[32]

Curzon himself wanted such 'complete fulfilment'. Yet by
the time people were reading this article over breakfast on 24
May a crucial shift had begun within the British government
that would affect both the outcome of the Curzon Ultimatum
and how the Foreign Secretary conceived of his own future in
public life.

Like many politicians who enter the Palace of Westminster,
Lord Curzon had long entertained the hope of becoming Prime
Minister. In the normal course of events such hope tends to
shrink with advanced age, but for Curzon it had grown –
indeed, quite spectacularly so during the course of 1923, as
Andrew Bonar Law's illness led the Prime Minister to hand over
the reins of power to the Foreign Secretary. On 22 May, Bonar
Law finally surrendered office altogether, after discovering that
his treatment for throat cancer would rob him permanently

of his voice (he was to die just a few months later). This left Lord Curzon fully expecting to ascend to the highest political position in the land. On 23 May, as he ruminated over the latest reply from Moscow, he was also eagerly awaiting a summons to Buckingham Palace, in the expectation that King George V would ask him to form the next government.

No such summons ever came, however. Lord Curzon had been lobbying behind the scenes for some time to be recognised as Bonar Law's rightful successor. He had even written to the terminally ill Prime Minister to press his case (though in his own mind this and other acts of self-promotion were no more than insurance policies, since he could see no contest between his credentials and those of other cabinet colleagues).[33] In practice, however, his assumptions were not shared by the King, who decided to summon Stanley Baldwin instead, having been advised by the elder statesman Lord Balfour, among others, that, in an age of mass suffrage, the political leader of the United Kingdom should come from the elected House of Commons rather than the unelected House of Lords. (He was, of course, right, and no subsequent prime minister has ever ruled from the hereditary chamber.)[34]

Curzon was devastated by the news, the more so because the King left the task of telling him to his private secretary, Lord Stamfordham − something the Foreign Secretary viewed as shameful cowardice. In gossip which spread quickly throughout the establishment, the Marquess was said to have broken down in tears after learning his fate. It was an extreme and memorable reaction from a man who came from the most reserved element of Victorian society. Stamfordham later confirmed that an indignant Curzon had described the decision not to promote him as 'the greatest blow and slur upon him and his public career, now at its summit, that he would ever have conceived'.[35] Privately, Curzon went still further, labelling Baldwin 'a man of no experience and of the utmost insignificance'.[36]

And yet this insignificant man was now, suddenly, Curzon's boss, because the Marquess (to the surprise of many) consented to remain at the Foreign Office when both Stamfordham and the new Prime Minister entreated him to do so. It is likely he felt motivated to stay at least in some part because of the Russian ultimatum debacle, which he wanted to see through to a successful conclusion, but it is also hard to imagine him, at his time of life (he was sixty-four), leaving the political stage to enjoy a happy retirement. Initially, Curzon expected to have freedom to continue to act as he saw fit in regard to Moscow; indeed, he felt this had been guaranteed. But quickly Baldwin started to impose Number 10's will on foreign affairs, including the ultimatum, yet another development that left Curzon feeling both frustrated and trammelled.

Stanley Baldwin came from a part of the Conservative Party that had been less preoccupied by the Soviet state during the latter's six-year existence, believing it to be less threatening than more right-wing Tories made out. Focussing on the demonstrable outcomes of Bolshevik meddling rather than the meddling itself or the rhetorical excesses of Bolshevik propaganda, Baldwin felt that a milder anti-Soviet policy could be justified, one which, although nowhere near as accommodating as Lloyd George's approach, did not require the total cessation of Anglo-Russian relations.

In a private conversation with the Labour MP C. P. Trevelyan just a couple of days after becoming leader, Baldwin described bringing the ultimatum crisis to a swift end as one of his main priorities; he said he still had 'hopes of avoiding a breach with Russia'.[37] (This can be read as the earliest sign of Baldwin's broader commitment to keeping Britain's international relations on an even keel, something that would become his hallmark in the many years he spent as premier, including his appeasement of Hitler in the 1930s.) As he was to reveal in the House of Commons at the end of May 1923, the new Prime Minister was acutely 'aware of the deep feeling in the country against being dragged into another war'.[38] More than anything else, this was what guided his thinking about how to treat the Bolsheviks.

Curzon and Sir Eyre Crowe were, therefore, able to continue their hard-line stance against Moscow only briefly after Baldwin took over. The wounded Curzon seems to have used this hiatus to insist even more adamantly than before that he would not budge in the standoff. But, in a matter of days, the new Prime Minister made clear that in his view the Soviets' humiliation, warranted though it might be, had gone on long enough.

Consequently, on 29 May, Curzon wrote back to Krasin to offer him the concession that Russia had asked for: a reciprocal promise from Britain that it would be well-behaved in respect of Soviet interests if the Soviets promised to be well-behaved in respect of British interests. Curzon drafted the concession as grudgingly as possible and it is quite likely that, had the Russians decided to push back, Baldwin would have ordered a further softening. But Moscow was perhaps unaware of the new Prime Minister's dovish attitude, and took the offer that was on the table, attempting to spin it as a victory for common sense and mutual cooperation, and, above all, for Soviet maturity and moderation.

The final 'formula respecting Propaganda for the Signature of the Soviet Government' that Curzon sent Krasin read as follows:

> [The Soviet Government undertakes] to refrain from hostile action or undertakings against Great Britain, and from conducting outside of its borders any official propaganda direct or indirect against the institutions of the British Empire and more particularly to refrain from any attempt by military or diplomatic or any other form of action or propaganda to encourage any of the peoples of Asia in any form of hostile action against British interests or the British Empire, especially

in India and in the Independent State of Afghanistan
[. . .] The Soviet Government [further] undertakes not
to support with funds or in any other form persons
or bodies or agencies or institutions whose aim is to
spread discontent or to foment rebellion in any part
of the British Empire, including therein all British
Protectorates, British-Protected States and territories
subject to a British Mandate, and to impress upon its
officers and officials the full and continuous observance
of these conditions.

The British Government gives a similar undertaking
to the Soviet Government to refrain from any similar
acts of propaganda in respect both of the territories and
institutions of the Soviet Republic and of the countries
which formed part of the former Russian Empire and
which have now become independent.[39]

The Bolsheviks signed the document on 4 June 1923,
and it did actually seem to lead to a short-term dip in Soviet
wrongdoing across most of the parts of the world where Britain
held sway. For Curzon, however, the episode's conclusion was
inherently unsatisfactory. He felt the concession had shown
Britain in a weak light and, given Moscow's obstinacy, would
gladly have burned Britain's bridges with Russia.

Nevertheless, Curzon knew that in the circumstances he
had got the best deal possible, and that no one else would
have been able to push the Bolsheviks further. In a letter to
his friend the British ambassador in Paris, Lord Crewe, in June
1923, the Foreign Secretary allowed himself a brief boast. 'I
think that I may claim to have won a considerable victory over
the Soviet Government,' he wrote, before expressing the hope
that Moscow might 'behave with more circumspection' in the
immediate time to come.[40] Curzon would have taken Anglo-
Soviet relations over the cliff edge in May 1923, doubtless

precipitating a world crisis, though not, in all likelihood, war. As it was, however, he had to content himself with clipping the Bolsheviks' wings and laying traps for them to fall into in future. Further attempts to slay the beast would now fall to his successors. What he could not know was how long it would be – and how much worse things would get – before the chance to remove the Soviets came again.

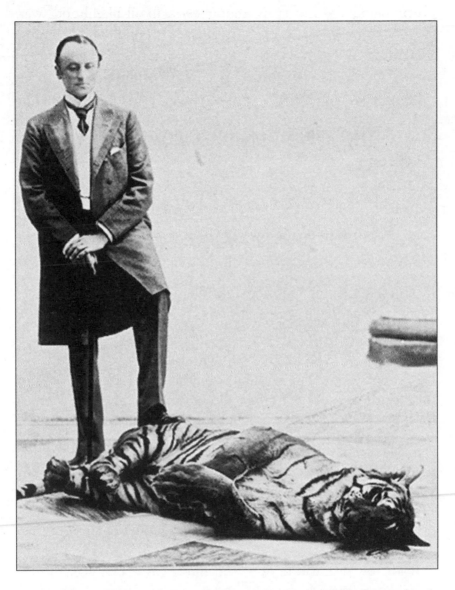

Lord Curzon's ultimatum seemed to prove that, by standing its ground and stating its demands, Britain could get the better of the Bolsheviks. In June 1923, anti-Communists, including many within British Intelligence, hoped that the day was not far off when the Red beast would be slain for good. In fact, it would be several years before someone as determined as Curzon decided to force matters to a head once again.

II

THE APPARITION OF A MONSTROSITY

'Today, twenty-three years ago, dear Grandmama died. I wonder what she would have thought of a Labour government.'

The diary of King George V, 22 January 1924

If Curzon's foreign policy machinations brought drama to British politics in the first half of 1923, this was at least matched by Stanley Baldwin's sudden decision to call a general election at the end of the year. In the November 1922 election, the Tories had swept to victory, winning by a large margin and holding seventy-three more seats than all the other parties put together. This gave the new Prime Minister a significant electoral and political safety blanket, with a fresh poll not required until 1927. No one expected Baldwin to squander such a golden opportunity by choosing to fight another general election as soon as the end of 1923, and certainly not on a controversial policy that had been deliberately excluded from the previous Tory manifesto.

Baldwin's decision has puzzled historians ever since, though it seems to have been a genuinely principled act. The new Prime Minister had long advocated Tariff Reform, a wide-ranging change to Britain's trade with the rest of the world which called for penalty fees to be levied on goods from outside the British Empire. In 1922, the Conservatives backed Free Trade (the opposite of selective tariffs) in their manifesto, so Baldwin felt a fresh mandate was needed in order to turn his longstanding ambition into reality. Having fundamentally misjudged the mood of the nation, however, he went on to lose the ensuing election on 6 December. The Conservatives haemorrhaged more than eighty seats, and, with them, their overall majority.

From the day after the election until the following November, Britain was pitched into one of the most frenzied chapters in her peacetime history. The consequences of Baldwin's rash act worked themselves out only slowly, beginning with the creation of the country's first-ever Labour government in January 1924 and culminating in one of the dirtiest and most hostile election campaigns that the country has ever seen, in October of that year. For over three hundred days, wildly divergent opinions flourished as to the state of the nation and its leaders – opinions far more polarised, both in the media and among the public, than those that had been expressed about any previous elected government. Soviet Russia was at the heart of the controversies that unfolded from month to month, and, along with British Intelligence, played a crucial role in Labour's premature downfall.

Labour was a moderate, social democratic party, which had considerably more in common with the British Liberal Party than with the Bolsheviks of Soviet Russia (indeed, it had much more overlap with the Tories than with the Bolsheviks). Nevertheless, ever since the movement's creation at the turn of the twentieth century, some on the right of British politics had advanced the view that Labour was dangerously extreme. That view hardened in the years after 1917, partly because some members of Labour made positive noises about the new Soviet state and voiced other hard-line attitudes, and partly because Labour's representation in parliament grew rapidly with each post-war election, causing great anxiety to its opponents. Labour started 1918 with just over forty seats in the House of Commons but ended 1923 with 191, an increase of almost

400 per cent. However moderate Labour was, its policies were aimed at weakening the power and wealth of Britain's elites, and so, as the time grew closer when those policies might be implemented, the elites grew uneasy.

Conservatives who did not share Baldwin's obsession with Tariff Reform (and even some who did) considered that the need to keep Labour out of government ought to have been the Prime Minister's uppermost priority at the end of 1923. When the disastrous election results came in, powerful voices within the party and in the right-wing press quickly blamed the premier for what they depicted as an outrageous act of folly and self-regard; many then went on to list the reasons why Labour must not now be allowed to take power. (It was still possible to hope that Labour would not take power because it lacked an outright majority, although, according to precedent, the Conservatives, who had called the election and lost, were duty-bound to leave office.) On the last day of the year, the *Daily Mail* wrote in an editorial about 'certain fussy people [who] during the past few days [have] been counselling the Conservatives and Liberals to give what they call "fair play" to the revolutionary Socialists [*sic*]'. But, the paper continued, the Labour Party was 'in sympathetic relations with the Russian Soviet Government – for all its infernal cruelty, tyranny and blasphemy' – and so should be locked out of government.[1]

Just a week later, on 7 January 1924, the *Mail* published the views of Lord Birkenhead, who at this point in his career was a bitter right-wing enemy of Baldwin's. Birkenhead, the former Lord Chancellor, wrote that appointing a Labour government in the coming days would be 'an event which [would] shake Europe and the world, and which may even destroy the position of the British people'. Other politicians, he said, were deluding themselves if they thought they could 'sleep soundly in their beds because of the sanity and sobriety of the Socialist leaders'. In fact, 'Britain would sink to the position of an outlaw State, like Soviet Russia, and would be viewed by all the free nations with well-deserved dislike and distrust'.[2]

Though extreme, these views were not isolated. In his private diary, the novelist and arch-right-winger H. Rider Haggard had written on 4 January of 'a kind of numbness [that had] fallen on England since the Election', explaining that 'the country is paralysed by the blow that has been dealt to it'.[3] Churchill, then still a member of the Liberal Party (though only just), confided to his friend Violet Bonham Carter that there seemed to be 'no possibility of averting the great misfortune of a Socialist government', which he described as 'the apparition of [a] monstrosity'.[4] Lord Curzon, soon to be the ex-Foreign Secretary, told supporters of the Conservative Party's mass membership Primrose League (of which he was Grand Master) that, irrespective of who ended up governing, they 'must use all [their] strength [. . .] to prevent policies from being forced upon the country' that would inevitably lead to socialism.[5] (Because Labour would have to rely on Liberal backing in order to stay in office, this argument about policies being *forced* on the country was energetically made by several reactionaries, the implication being that Labour in power somehow amounted to a sort of bloodless *coup d'état*.)

Some Conservatives – though not, of course, Curzon – took their worries directly to the man whom they saw as Britain's last bulwark against the rising Red tide: the King himself. In a seminal work, *The Impact of Labour*, the historian Maurice Cowling described how the Earl of Derby, who was Baldwin's Secretary of State for War, wrote to the monarch making 'hysterical demands [. . .] that he should not let Labour take office'. As Cowling explained, the King, although 'a reactionary' and 'with strong anti-socialist instincts and a real dislike for many aspects of the modern world', was not prepared to alienate the working class, which he now understood to be a 'powerful segment of popular opinion'.[6]

Acting under George V's direct instructions, therefore, Lord Stamfordham emphasised to petitioners like Derby that 'His Majesty [. . .] was not in the least alarmed [. . .] at the prospect of a Labour government [. . .] never doubted their loyalty or patriotism and felt that the best interests of the country would be the primary aim of their policy'.[7] Baldwin agreed with this analysis and, indeed, encouraged it, supporting George V in his eventual decision to transfer power to Ramsay MacDonald. Thus it was that, on 22 January 1924, the first Labour government in Britain came into being, leaving the King to wonder what his grandmama, Queen Victoria, would have made of it. Labour had a great deal to prove in the face of harsh criticism, not to mention much to do to ameliorate the lives of its core supporters.

As they then played out, however, Labour's ten months in office were variously depicted as a string of disappointing compromises or an endless and ever-more-perilous lurch to the left. For those who advanced the former analysis, it was the party's performance in domestic affairs that seemed to be key. Labour supporters initially accepted that, as the party did not have a majority, it would need to govern with tact and restraint, making progress where it could, particularly where it had Liberal support, and always ensuring that it had the necessary votes in place before bringing measures to parliament. That said, however, the heightened level of caution with which MacDonald acted was eventually viewed as a let-down by people who saw a unique chance to help Labour's electorate going to waste. Labour was able to soften some sharp edges of the previous government's austerity drive by making small increases to both the value and coverage of unemployment and child benefit and old-age pensions. It also passed legislation, known as the Wheatley Housing Act, to increase central government subsidies for council houses. Nevertheless, on the most daring measures in its election platform – the nationalisation of key industries, the expansion of the state's role in work creation, and the redistribution of the nation's wealth – the MacDonald administration was inactive and almost entirely silent.

Those who argued that Britain was in the grip of a hard-left cabal thus had a difficult job proving it on the basis of Labour's domestic agenda. While some tried, others took the easier route of asserting that this was all part of the socialists' secret long-term strategy of lulling voters into a false sense of security only to reveal their true colours at some later date. In either case, critics tended to move quickly to focus on the government's more controversial record in foreign affairs.

Ramsay MacDonald performed the roles of both Prime Minister and Foreign Secretary throughout Labour's first spell in office. When he looked back on this time, it was his achievements in Franco-German relations that made him most proud. A crisis-hit Germany had failed to keep up payments on war debts it owed to France and, consequently, Paris had ordered troops to occupy the German Ruhr. This dangerous deterioration in relations between Europe's main continental powers was seen as very undesirable. MacDonald, through a series of meetings in London and at the Prime Minister's official country residence, Chequers, played a major role in bringing the situation to a peaceful end. However, this was not what Labour's harshest critics focussed on. Their emphasis was the other main plank of the party's overseas policies: the British relationship with Soviet Russia, and in particular the government's decision, just days after coming to power, to invite Bolsheviks back to Britain for talks about a new Anglo-Russian treaty and closer trade ties.

This move was foreshadowed in Labour's manifesto, which had called for 'the resumption of free economic and diplomatic relations with Russia' as an alternative to the increasingly hostile approach of the previous year and also as an impetus to world disarmament – what the party believed was 'the only security for the nations'.[8] MacDonald himself explained that he was extending the hand of friendship to Moscow because it would be 'pompous folly' to stand 'aloof' from the Bolsheviks when aloofness in itself could not change the fact of their existence. [9] He did 'not [. . .] agree with what the Russian Government [had] done', he hastened to add. But he immediately accorded *de jure* recognition to the regime, meaning that Britain now accepted that the Bolsheviks were Russia's legal rulers (to date, the Lloyd George treaty had given them only *de facto* recognition) and he stated publicly his ambitious future priorities: 'I want trade; I want negotiations; I want a settlement from the coasts of Japan to the coasts of Ireland.'[10]

The Russians took a little time to assemble a fresh delegation to send to London, mainly because MacDonald's announcement coincided with the period of official mourning after Lenin's death on 21 January 1924. In the meantime, a stream of articles appeared in Britain's right-wing press, and dozens of speeches were made in both the Commons and the Lords, decrying Labour's plan. This might have been dismissed as Labour's enemies playing politics but, significantly, MacDonald and his ministers faced similar hostility from within the bureaucracy. Labour was now in charge of the civil service, the armed forces and the intelligence agencies, yet the government was to meet strong resistance to its Russia policy from each of these quarters every step of the way. High-ranking officials rallied round, with informal but energetic encouragement from the watching Conservative establishment, trying to protect what they saw as Britain's enduring interests from what they hoped would be a short-lived Labour government.

In the Foreign Office, MacDonald and his deputy, Arthur Ponsonby, quickly discovered that the Permanent Secretary, Sir Eyre Crowe, fundamentally disagreed with their approach. Crowe, as we saw, had staunchly supported Curzon in the ultimatum crisis a year before. He now refused to do the *volte face* that was constitutionally required of him, while also declining to resign, which would have been the principled response. 'I have put it formally and repeatedly on record that I entirely disapproved of and protested against the whole proceedings,' Crowe later said with pride, adding that he saw the Anglo–Soviet talks as nothing less than 'a ridiculous farce and a disgrace'.[11] As head of the Foreign Office, he ordered other officials to keep away from the latest round of Anglo-Soviet negotiations, too. 'The Foreign Office as a department [is] free from all responsibility,' he subsequently felt able to write. Blame rests 'entirely with Ponsonby', he added, who 'in the end [. . .] will suffer from his idiotic performance'.[12]

Still more dangerously, impartiality was in short supply at British Intelligence. Just a few months earlier, the heads of the intelligence agencies had looked forward to a future in which many of their worst enemies might be forced to return to Russia, humiliated and disempowered. Now the same chiefs had to face the threat of even more Soviet citizens arriving in Britain, and the possibility that these troublemakers and those already *in situ* might soon enjoy expanded rights and privileges. MI5 and other organisations had harboured growing doubts about the Labour Party for some time, mainly due to the CPGB's periodic attempts to infiltrate it and make common cause with moderate socialists. During the previous decade, Labour had proved its ability to govern in a reasonable and temperate manner in many local councils and in the national war cabinet. It had more than three million members. And yet the intelligence community, like others, still questioned the party's fitness to rule. They saw Labour as a kind of Trojan Horse – surreptitiously bringing a radical ideology into the country – and increasingly they felt justified in trying to frustrate it.[13]

It must be said that British Intelligence's relationship with Ramsay MacDonald got off to a spectacularly bad start. In line with normal protocol, the head of Special Branch, Sir Wyndham

Childs, had continued sending his organisation's weekly briefing about revolutionary organisations in the United Kingdom to the Prime Minister, expecting him to read it and circulate it to the rest of the cabinet. MacDonald, naturally, had had no idea that such briefings existed before taking up office and, upon reading the first one prepared for him, for the last week of January 1924, was shocked by its tendency to overstatement and by its one-sidedness. In a note to Childs, the new premier gave the senior police officer a dressing down. He criticised in particular the way that Special Branch had tried to pass off as secrets things that were actually common knowledge to anyone who chose to look (for instance, the CPGB's repeated attempts to affiliate with the Labour Party) and he also emphasised the unacceptable failure to include coverage of Britain's nascent fascist movements.

MacDonald furthermore declined to share this or any subsequent Special Branch briefing with his other ministers. He told Childs that 'in its present form' he doubted 'whether it would provide very edifying or interesting reading' for them.[14] News of the Labour leader's treatment of Childs quickly did the rounds at Whitehall. Some who heard of it doubtless just rolled their eyes, but others felt the discourtesy contrasted starkly with Labour's renewed determination to extend the hand of friendship to Moscow. So worried were both officers and officials that they did not even tell MacDonald for many months that GC&CS could decipher all the Soviet state's diplomatic telegrams.[15] They thought that if he learned of this, he might put a stop to it.

Very quickly, British Intelligence realised that it was not going to be able to influence the new government in the same way as its predecessors (albeit that then, too, it had achieved mixed results). Rather than adapt to the altered atmosphere, the intelligence agencies determined that they would wait for the Labour storm to pass and, in the intervening period, do their best to limit the damage that MacDonald and his colleagues could cause. Intelligence officers continued gathering information in much the same way as they had previously, but they now kept a particular eye out for things that could complicate Labour's plans or, indeed, that might be used to discredit the party. Britain's spies almost certainly expanded their direct contacts with Tory MPs and right-wing journalists during the course of 1924, well in advance of the moment in the autumn when these informal, and highly questionable, channels of communication became of pivotal importance.

Soviet subversion and espionage continued across the British Empire during 1924, at the somewhat reduced level that had been the norm since the Curzon Ultimatum. Propaganda and provocation remained commonplace too but, during the first half of the year in particular, they exhibited a half-heartedness that was perhaps the result of deliberate restraint during the new Anglo-Russian talks. The sale of Tsarist-era jewels to fund worldwide Communism came to prominence again briefly in May. But what looked like a plan to sell more jewels actually amounted to nothing, or, as a Special Branch memo to SIS dismissed it, a 'characteristic bit of Bolo bluff'.[16] Financial assistance still flowed to the CPGB but, whereas this had been worth £20,000 in 1922 (equivalent to £1.1 million today), estimates put it at only £5,000 (£275,000 today) in 1924.[17] In March, when the government discovered that the Bolsheviks wanted to send Andrew Rothstein's father to Britain as part of a twenty-five-strong negotiating team, Ramsay MacDonald requested that they did not and they agreed.

Around the negotiating table consensus proved harder to come by, as the differences between the two sides were both genuine and substantial. The turmoil caused by Lenin's death did not help, with a battle of competing egos and visions under way back in Moscow. The talks, once begun, ground on for months and during that time both the British press and MPs continually disputed the wisdom of the Labour approach. Voices on the right typically spoke of how desperate MacDonald and Ponsonby seemed to be to reach a deal, and also highlighted the still-plentiful examples of Soviet bad faith. CPGB statements, meanwhile, criticised Labour from the opposite side, and were, therefore, seized on by right-wingers as fresh evidence of Bolshevik meddling in British affairs; few people bothered to make the equally valid point that the Communists' anti-Labour statements also showed the distance that existed between the two parties.

In August 1924, the United Kingdom and Soviet governments finally agreed a pair of treaties that were meant to regulate their future political and commercial interactions, and to chart a way forward on a number of thorny issues. The treaties were fairly limited in their effect, since the talks had not covered as much ground as hoped. There was a promise to exchange ambassadors for the first time since the Tsarist era, an extension of the *de jure* recognition of earlier in the year. There was also an undertaking to appoint a six-person commission (with equal representation from each national government) to determine the scale of Russia's pre-existing debts to Britain. And, most controversially, if the commission's work could be brought to a successful conclusion, there was an agreement in principle that the British government would guarantee a loan to the Soviet state which would allow the Russians to buy British goods.[18]

The provisions provoked uproar. Almost everyone agreed that the loan was a stupid idea. The value of shares on the London Stock Exchange dipped after hearing of it, and the five major British banks issued clear warnings that they would not be providing any more money to Russia until she repaid her existing debts in full. Even the left-wing *New Statesman* magazine, which usually backed constructive approaches to Moscow, argued that any loan would mean 'an artificial prolongation in Russia of an economic system which is impracticable'.[19]

This, however, was just the beginning of the insults that rained down on Labour. Moderate critics spoke of a fudge. Sir Robert Horne MP, who had signed the 1921 Anglo-Soviet treaty on Lloyd George's behalf, called the new settlement 'a makeshift, a sham and a pretence'.[20] Militant anti-socialists, meanwhile, relentlessly used the language of conspiracy, depicting the treaties as acts of treachery. As far as they were concerned, the British government had effectively shown its approval of the Bolsheviks' actions since 1917, including all their crimes against Britain, and also invited them to do more and worse in future. Rumours that the talks had been on the point of collapse before a last-minute intervention by British trade unions (which had, it was said, ordered MacDonald to do a deal) were taken as positive proof of secret extremist forces at work.[21]

In a response that encapsulated these views, the hard-line Conservative MP Guy Kindersley wrote to *The Times* a few days after the deal, saying,

> The present Government has recognized as the Government of Russia, and signed Treaties with, an international revolutionary organisation which is seeking through its agents in this country [. . .] to overthrow the existing social and political order. I write this letter in the hope that some of those who were, and perhaps still are, deceived by the apparent moderation of the present Government may have their eyes opened, before it is too late, to the perils which confront the country and the Empire.[22]

Many others agreed. Evelyn Hubbard, a former Conservative MP who had had business interests in pre-revolutionary Russia, expressed incredulity in his own letter to *The Times*. 'Are we to grasp in friendship the hands that are covered in blood?' he wrote. 'The Soviet has no right or title to represent the Russian people [. . .] I pray that the crime of aiding and abetting this infamous tyranny may never be laid to our charge.'[23]

With summer holidays beginning, the temperature at Westminster rose still further when it emerged, in a separate development, that Labour's Attorney General, Sir Patrick Hastings, had instructed the Director of Public Prosecutions to drop criminal charges against a Communist journalist who had published an article suspected of being an incitement to mutiny. The article, which was undoubtedly hostile towards the state ('let it be known that, neither in the class war nor in a military war, will you turn your guns on your fellow workers'), had initially been thought sufficient grounds for a court case by Hastings. But he reconsidered after learning that the accused, John Ross Campbell, was a decorated war hero who had lost both feet at the front.[24]

Such magnanimity towards war veterans was not uncommon in criminal proceedings during the 1920s. Even with fears about the CPGB running at their highest, it is possible to imagine a Conservative minister showing similar leniency. But, whereas a Tory in this position might have got away with it, there was no escaping the negative backlash for a Labour attorney general. Together with the treaties, anti-socialists now had all the ammunition they needed to attempt to bring the Labour government down. When parliament resumed after the long recess, in September 1924, Ramsay MacDonald quickly found himself defeated on a vote of confidence and obliged to ask the King for a dissolution and a fresh general election.

The apparition of a monstrosity? Ramsay MacDonald, the United Kingdom's first Labour Prime Minister, was so cautious in his domestic policy during 1924 that even many of his moderate supporters were disappointed. A society figure, who felt comfortable mixing with the establishment, he was nevertheless accused of jeopardising Britain's national security by negotiating with the Bolsheviks. Key diplomats, civil servants and intelligence officers refused to cooperate.

12

THE BIG LIE

The run-up to 1924's general election was a tawdry affair. To a far greater extent than normal, voters were urged by non-Labour candidates to treat the poll as a referendum on the party's fitness to govern, despite the fact that it had had only a few short months of minority rule in which to produce results. For the duration of the election battle, leaders of both the Liberal and Conservative parties gave free rein to the wildest voices in their midst, backed up by a right-wing press, which daily accused MacDonald and his supporters of deliberately pushing Britain towards revolution. In a rare moment of hysteria in British political history, scores of influential people – some of whom were quite level-headed the rest of the time – appeared willing to exaggerate for short-term gain and, at least in part, came to believe their own exaggerations.[1]

It is now hard to judge the relative merits of mainstream British politicians' different approaches towards the early Soviet state. Hindsight almost inevitably leads to anachronism, particularly on an issue that was to have such enormous ramifications for the rest of the twentieth century. If we focus just on Russia, it is probably true to say that 1920s Conservatives tended to advocate what we would now consider an ethical foreign policy; their visceral reaction to the Bolsheviks seems close to the kind of response we would expect, given the scale of suffering that

Soviet Communism caused. The blithe fascination that a few left-wingers displayed towards the new Russia and the more widespread sense (dating from the nineteenth century) that Britain ought to trade with any state, irrespective of how badly it treated its citizens, now make us feel uncomfortable. Equally, Labour's more noble desire to prevent future world conflict has been eclipsed by future events: it is almost impossible to disentangle this from the later failure to respond adequately to Europe's great dictators.

In the circumstances of 1924 specifically, however, it is perhaps more important to consider whether there was anything exceptional about the way Labour approached the Soviet state. The party's fiercest critics alleged that Labour was behaving highly *unusually* with regard to Russia, in a manner likely to put the future of Britain in imminent jeopardy. But in fact, Labour's decision to intensify relations with the Russians in 1924 was seen as both timely and appropriate by a large number of other foreign powers. After MacDonald had granted *de jure* recognition at the start of the year, Mussolini's Italy followed suit on 7 February and there then ensued a string of others: Norway (13 February); Austria (20 February); Greece (8 March); the Free City of Danzig (13 March); Sweden (15 March); China (31 May); Denmark (18 June); Mexico (4 August); and France (28 October).[2]

In words penned shortly before taking office, the Labour Prime Minister had identified the exceptional double standard of right-wingers' demand that Russia be ostracised. This was not, he said, something that these people ever advocated for other regimes.

> It is true that the Russian Revolution has been marked by a ruthless dictatorship, by cruel repression, and by bloody events. And yet I cannot attribute to that the real reason for the hostility of other Governments.

Had there been a revolution of White Monarchists, it would have been just as tyrannical and quite as bloody, but in that case forgiveness would have been easy and recognition would not have been withheld. Let us be frank about this. It was the class that conducted the revolution [and] the class victimised by it [. . .] that determined the attitude of other Governments.[3]

In the maelstrom of the 1924 election campaign, Labour made these points frequently, and, as the subsequent results showed, they were accepted by a sizeable core of its supporters. More broadly in the country, however, the right-wing rhetoric proved more effective. It included a string of colourful interventions by one of the twentieth century's greatest demagogues, Winston Churchill, who was re-entering national politics after a couple of years in the wilderness, and who remained one of Britain's most outspoken anti-socialists. On 9 October 1924, Churchill made a widely reported speech at Woodford Memorial Hall in north-east London, referring to Labour as a kind of 'poison' and exhorting 'Britannia' to cast off all 'ridiculous and dishonourable disguises and rags [. . .] made in Russia [and] reveal herself once again, sedate, majestic on her throne, grasping the trident with determination, and displaying on her shield not the foul Red Flag of Communist revolution, but the Union Jack'.[4] Two days later, he accused Labour of being 'spellbound by the lure of Moscow' and 'wire-pulled through subterranean channels'.[5]

Others spoke similarly. William Joynson-Hicks, a Tory MP who was shortly to assume a central role in handling Anglo-Soviet relations, told Conservative supporters in Norfolk on 5 October that 'the one thing England demands in her statesmen is principle' and that this was something that MacDonald and other Labour MPs lacked. 'It would have been far better for Mr Ramsay MacDonald,' Joynson-Hicks continued, 'to have said that "I stand for certain definite Socialist principles; I hate capitalism; I loathe capitalists; I mean to destroy both. I am heart and soul in favour of union with Bolshevism [. . .] and I will not take office unless I can carry my principles into effect".'[6]

Hard-line Conservative MP Guy Kindersley strode yet further into the realm of conspiracy, giving public credence to White Russian newspaper reports, first published in Paris, which stated that Labour ministers had secretly received gifts from the Soviet government and thus found themselves blackmailed into signing the August treaties. On 9 October, the last sitting day before parliament was dissolved, Kindersley spoke in the House of Commons to demand a response from Ponsonby about what he said were 'serious allegations'. These included the fact that 'a large number of exceedingly beautiful Russian jewels [. . .] emeralds, diamonds, precious stones [and] pearls [had been] sent to six members of Mr MacDonald's cabinet [so that] when Moscow said, "Sign, or we shall give the names of your six comrades"' MacDonald had to sign.[7] In the House, Ponsonby denied the slur in the strongest possible terms and the Speaker reprimanded Kindersley for citing rumours from an unworthy source. Yet the damage was done: after Kindersley aired the story, it was widely reported in the following morning's press.

Historians and political scientists have long agreed that from the moment the 1924 general election was called, the Conservatives were destined to win. Sufficient mud had been slung at Labour during its brief stint in power, and it had acted with sufficient naivety, to leave a majority of the electorate wanting the return of strong, stable, traditional government. Britain was still fundamentally a Tory country at this time, despite changes to the franchise, as the sizeable Conservative majority in the 1922 election had shown. The defeat of 1923 was almost entirely caused by a single unpopular policy – a policy which Baldwin had been sure not to reinsert into his party's manifesto in 1924. Nevertheless, in an era before opinion polls, contemporary politicians had no idea in advance how their parties would fare on election day. With so many on the right believing that the alternative to a Conservative victory was catastrophe, anxiety as to the way the electorate would vote not only encouraged scare tactics and bombast, but also led to outright dirty tricks.

Towards the end of September 1924, the latest in a long line of communications purporting to come from the Comintern fell into the hands of SIS officers in Estonia, apparently *en route* from Russia to the CPGB headquarters in London. Like most such letters, it was signed by a number of top Comintern officials, including the organisation's president, Grigorii Zinoviev.[8] On 2 October, the SIS Baltic field office in Riga forwarded a translation of the document to London. It arrived at SIS head office on 9 October, the same day that the general election campaign started. SIS immediately shared the text with a wide range of colleagues in central government, including senior officers at MI5 and Special Branch, and also the Foreign Office, the War Office, the Air Ministry and the Admiralty. (As was normal practice, the document was not shared with ministers at this point, while its importance was still being assessed.)

The letter was in many respects very similar to others that had been intercepted previously, yet it would spark an unprecedented pan-Whitehall campaign for rapid retaliation against the Russians. 'Dear Comrades,' it began:

> The time is approaching for the Parliament of England to consider the Treaty concluded between the Governments of Great Britain and the SSSR [USSR] for the purpose of ratification. The fierce campaign raised by the British bourgeoisie around the question shows that the majority of the same, together with reactionary circles, are against the Treaty for the purpose of breaking off an agreement consolidating the ties between the proletariats of the two countries

leading to the restoration of normal relations between England and the SSSR.

The proletariat of Great Britain, which pronounced its weighty word when danger threatened of a break-off of the past negotiations, and compelled the Government of MacDonald to conclude the treaty, must show the greatest possible energy in the further struggle for ratification and against the endeavours of British capitalists to compel Parliament to annul it.

It is indispensable to stir up the masses of the British proletariat to bring into movement the army of unemployed proletarians, whose position can be improved only after a loan has been granted to the SSSR for the restoration of her economics and when business collaboration between the British and Russian proletariats has been put in order. It is imperative that the group in the Labour Party sympathising with the Treaty should bring increased pressure to bear upon the Government and parliamentary circles in favour of the ratification of the Treaty.

Keep close observation over the leaders of the Labour Party, because those may easily be found in the leading strings of the bourgeoisie. The foreign policy of the Labour Party as it is already represents an inferior copy of the policy of the Curzon Government [. . .]

A settlement of relations between the two countries will assist in the revolutionising of the international and British proletariat not less than a successful rising in any of the working districts of England, as the establishment of close contact between the British and Russian proletariat, the exchange of delegations and workers, etc., will make it possible for us to extend and develop the propaganda of Leninism in England and the Colonies. [. . .]

From your last report it is evident that agitation-propaganda work in the army is weak, in the navy a very little better. Your explanation that the quality of the members affected justifies the quantity is right in principle, nevertheless it would be desirable to have cells in all the units of the troops, particularly among those quartered in the large centres of the country, and also among factories working on munitions and at military store depots. We request that the most particular attention be paid to these latter. [. . .]

The Military Section of the British Communist Party, so far as we are aware, further suffers from a lack of specialists, the future directors of the British Red Army. It is time you thought of forming such a group, which, together with the leaders, might be, in the event of an outbreak of active strife, the brain of the military organisation of the party. [. . .]

Desiring you all success, both in organisation and in your struggle.

With Communist Greetings,

President of the Presidium of the ECCI [Executive Committee of the Communist International]

ZINOVIEV [. . .][9]

The letter bore many of the hallmarks of typical Bolshevik prose: verbosity, didacticism and condescension – with apologies for the pun, a certain 'bolshy-ness'. Its main aim seemed to be to give orders, and yet its author could not resist accompanying these commands with full-scale analyses of Britain's and the CPGB's problems, as if this would be news to the recipients. Much of the content was entirely routine. A comparison with the Comintern letter that British Intelligence brought to ministerial attention on 8 March 1923 shows how each focussed on British workers and the unemployed, while also looking at current British government policy towards Russia. Instructions to organise more, influence more, agitate more and generally prepare for all eventualities were the mantras that had echoed through all CPGB dealings with the Comintern from the moment of the party's creation.

And yet some aspects of the September 1924 letter were un-doubtedly more eye-catching than usual, and these were under-standably the passages that set alarm bells ringing in British Intelligence, the military and the civil service. The recent negotiations and resulting treaties were dwelt upon at length, and there was apparent confirmation that Moscow-inspired forces had indeed 'compelled the Government of MacDonald' to come to terms. Reference was also made to 'the group in the Labour Party' that sympathised with the Russians, and there was an implication in the phrase 'it is imperative that [they] should bring increased pressure to bear upon the Government' that these individuals, too, were somehow within Moscow's control.

In the first few days after the letter arrived, some members of British Intelligence described it as being nothing 'out of the ordinary run of things', according to Gill Bennett, the Foreign Office's official historian who has published a definitive account of the episode.[10] Yet far more common was the reaction of Desmond Morton, the senior SIS officer who was responsible for circulating the document across Whitehall. Morton was a Conservative supporter and anti-socialist who saw instantly the potential impact that the text could have in the election campaign. He, along with others, among them the senior MI5 officer Joseph Ball and the Foreign Office's Sir Eyre Crowe, became convinced of the need to publish the text as soon as possible, and definitely ahead of polling day (29 October). Sir Eyre, according to Bennett, 'attached great importance' to this, because, he said, it would provide a way of exposing the Russians as 'quite shameless liars'.[11]

By contemplating such an approach, however, the intelligence community and other government officials had put themselves in uncharted territory. Normally letters from the Comintern and similar pieces of evidence took much longer to emerge from the agencies that intercepted them, with careful checks being made as to their authenticity and analytical work being done to place information into context. Even then, documents were seldom, if ever, made public; rather, they were shared with the cabinet, which might take months to decide what to do about them, and often decided to do nothing. In this instance, however, government employees wanted to release the letter to the nation almost immediately and – in another significant departure from the norm – as a stand-alone document. British Intelligence's approach had previously been to avoid placing excessive importance on any single piece of evidence, but now many in the intelligence world felt they had found the single source that, above all others, would make their problems go away.

From the moment the Zinoviev Letter reached London, Morton and almost everyone else who read it assumed it to be a genuine Comintern document. 'The authenticity of the document is undoubted,' Morton wrote on 9 October – at a point before he could have had much if any basis for holding this view.[12] When Sir Eyre Crowe subsequently decided to forward the letter to Ramsay MacDonald, on 15 October, he too asserted that it was authentic, based on Morton's assurances. Crowe spelled out to the Prime Minister what he now thought should happen: the only way to be 'fair to our own people', he said, was to share with them 'our knowledge of these Russian machinations'.[13]

The letter was indeed evidence of 'Russian machinations', but not on the part of *Soviet* Russia. It would turn out to be a forgery, dreamt up by a group of White Russians who were working in the Baltic states and wanted to put pressure on Britain's Labour government. There had been other forgeries in the past, including some of similar provenance, but British

Intelligence had got progressively better at spotting them. On this occasion, however, it seems Britain's spies saw the letter's contents as too good to be anything other than true, which in turn allowed the Whitehall bureaucratic machine to push with atypical vigour for the document to see the light of day.

Among the people who had early sight of the Zinoviev Letter, MacDonald alone was absolutely sure that it was fraudulent. The Labour leader was suspicious both of the letter's contents and of the breakneck speed at which he was being asked to respond to it. On both fronts, he scented a right-wing conspiracy. From the depths of the campaign trail, he therefore wrote back to Crowe on 16 October demanding a copper-bottomed guarantee that the document was authentic, and also requesting that the Foreign Office draw up a protest note in case, after all, it should be necessary to confront the Soviet government.

Of course, it is possible that some members of British Intelligence actually knew the Zinoviev Letter was forged. As cited by Bennett, as early as July 1924 Desmond Morton and Joseph Ball had been considering the clandestine leaking of a well-timed piece of Comintern correspondence to bring Labour down. 'All these letters are addressed in the same way and signed, generally speaking, by the same people,' Morton had written to Ball at that time, before adding in cloak-and-dagger tones, 'I will not recapitulate what it is we are out to do, as I think my description on the telephone must have made it quite clear to you.'[14] By the autumn, the pair may have felt desperate and, thus, turned to counterfeiting. Yet there is no proof of this, nor of any other British spy actually being aware that the September letter was a fake.

Instead, the British state's descent into conspiracy began with its response to MacDonald's absolutely reasonable request for proof of the letter's authenticity. Morton misled Crowe into believing that an informant of his within the CPGB had confirmed that the letter was genuine, when in fact the informant had not mentioned the letter. This untrue statement was then taken at face value by Crowe, who saw no need to ask further questions on the Prime Minister's behalf. Later in the debacle, Morton's bosses lied further, saying that they were 'aware of the identity of every person who [had] handled the document on its journey from Zinoviev's files to our hands' – a complete fabrication – and even (after the letter had been published) suppressing a report from their own office in Berlin which raised the possibility that it had been forged.[15]

While MacDonald continued to ponder, British Intelligence personnel became ever more agitated at the delay in making the letter's existence known. They assumed that this was a deliberate stalling tactic by Labour and feared that it actually might work. Bennett has uncovered three separate instances of the intelligence agencies trying to increase the number of people who knew of the Zinoviev Letter before the Prime Minister decided how to respond to it (and there may well have been more). First, around mid-October, someone in the secret services tipped off an ex-MI5 officer, Donald Im Thurn, that the letter had arrived in England. As had presumably been intended, Im Thurn went straight to Guy Kindersley MP and to the Conservative Party treasurer, Lord Younger, to tell them the news. Secondly, on 21 October, Sir Vernon Kell told staff in MI5 to circulate the letter to every military command in the country, an act that he would doubtless have defended on the grounds of protecting the armed forces, but which he surely knew would increase the chances of a full-scale leak. Thirdly, and conclusively, Ball or Morton or some other high-ranking intelligence officer passed the letter in its entirety to journalists at the *Daily Mail*, the very best means, then as now, of maximising a controversy's value as scandal.

On 24 October, five days before polling day, MacDonald finally made up his mind – against his better judgement – to send a toughly worded protest note to Moscow complaining about the content of the Zinoviev Letter. Before he could do so, however, the *Daily Mail* informed the Foreign Office that it already had a copy of the Zinoviev Letter and would be publishing it the next morning alongside a story about what it called Labour's conspiracy to hide the document until after the general election.

Sure enough, the *Mail* ran the story on 25 October, explaining MacDonald's now hastily despatched note as just further proof of the conspiracy that its journalists had smashed. The headlines were damning:

CIVIL WAR PLOT BY SOCIALISTS' MASTERS
MOSCOW ORDER TO OUR REDS
GREAT PLOT DISCLOSED YESTERDAY
PARALYSE THE ARMY AND NAVY
AND MR MACDONALD WOULD LEND RUSSIA OUR MONEY
DOCUMENT ISSUED BY FOREIGN OFFICE
AFTER "DAILY MAIL" HAD SPREAD THE NEWS

The detailed coverage, and the use that right-wing politicians made of it, were more ruinous still.[16] Churchill, speaking to a crowd that day, described how MacDonald had been 'driven on by his extremists' and had ended up demonstrating 'comradeship and unity with these foul, filthy butchers of Moscow', who now wanted to establish 'germ cells [. . .] in our regiments and on our ships [and] to disturb and defile our streets'. Backing him to the hilt, Sir Laming Worthington-Evans, a Tory MP, said 'the issue' was now 'whether we were to be governed by Britons or "Bolshies"'.[17] And an editorial in *The Times* concluded that it was 'hardly credible that the nation [would] again entrust the conduct of great Imperial affairs to a leader who has, on his own confession, allowed himself to be cajoled and outwitted by the worst enemies of our country'.[18] Taking once more to his diary, on 29 October, H. Rider Haggard wrote that 'everything that is evil in the land is at the back of these Socialists who love the Russian anarchists because they have reduced that great empire to a condition which they hope to see re-duplicated in Britain and her empire also'.[19]

On election day, Labour lost forty of its 191 seats, despite its total tally of votes rising by one million. The increase in its popular support shows how the crisis manufactured by British Intelligence had failed to resonate in the party's heartlands, where its real policies and agenda were well known. However, thanks to tactical voting, the Conservatives ended up with 412 MPs, more than two thirds of the 615 seats in the House of Commons. Even if Baldwin's victory had been all but assured, there can be no question that the scale of the triumph was boosted by the Zinoviev Letter. Traditional Liberal voters – now not daring to split the non-Labour vote – had deserted the party for the Tories, who ended up more than two million votes better off. A year of scaremongering had culminated in the deployment of the scariest tactic of all: the production of apparent proof that the first Labour government in history had been in cahoots with a hostile foreign power.

Later in the Cold War, commentators would often talk of 'deep states' existing within democracies and acting whenever necessary to prevent those democracies taking supposed wrong turns. 1924 is the moment when such a 'deep state' first made its presence felt in modern Britain, the moment when a concerted and thoroughly illegitimate attempt was made to subvert a national democratic process. Whatever the real extent of the ruse's impact, it is worth bearing in mind that the protagonists themselves believed it to have been highly effective. Meanwhile, although the Labour Party would rise to power again, it was to suffer long-term damage, with many thousands of Britons continuing to believe these lies for decades to come.

ON THE LOAN TRAIL.

[In a document just disclosed by the British Foreign Office (apparently after considerable delay), M. ZINOVIEFF, a member of the Bolshevist Dictatorship, urges the British Communist Party to use "the greatest possible energy" in securing the ratification of Mr. MACDONALD's Anglo-Russian Treaty, in order to facilitate a scheme for "an armed insurrection" of the British proletariat.]

Just one example of the anti-Labour propaganda that poured out of the British media after the Zinoviev Letter was revealed, this Punch cartoon – published on election day – depicts a supposedly archetypal Bolshevik (frighteningly dishevelled) campaigning for Ramsay MacDonald and hoping to get Labour back into power. 'In a document just disclosed by the British Foreign Office (apparently after considerable delay)', the caption reads, 'M. ZINOVIEFF, a member of the Bolshevist Dictatorship, urges the British Communist Party to use "the greatest possible energy" in securing the ratification of Mr. MACDONALD's Anglo-Russian Treaty, in order to facilitate a scheme for "an armed insurrection" of the British proletariat.'

PART 4

DRAGNET

What is the point of having an enormous parliamentary majority if you do not use it to achieve daring things? And what is the point of uncovering (or engineering) the worst British scandal involving the Bolsheviks since the Russian Revolution if you do not use it to terminate Anglo-Soviet relations? Such were the questions that buzzed in the heads of many Conservative MPs and most British Intelligence employees during the dying days of 1924 and into the years that followed, as Moscow's hostility towards London showed no let-up and yet Soviet citizens continued living and working in Britain.

Stanley Baldwin, as leader of the Conservative Party, had been the greatest single beneficiary of the increased anti-socialist fear that marred Labour's final months in power. Quite deliberately, he had made no attempt to curb the worst excesses of Tory election rhetoric during the campaign. He fought for the largest victory he could get, hoping to exorcise the defeat he had inflicted on his party in 1923. But once he returned to office, Baldwin reverted to the more conciliatory style that had been his hallmark during his previous six months as Prime Minister, backing away from direct confrontation with the Russians and trying to calm the now turbulent waters of domestic politics. Although Baldwin did not share Labour's view that the Zinoviev Letter had been forged, very soon after his re-election he found a way to bring the scandal to an end, making it clear that Labour's treaties with

Moscow would never be ratified while he was in Downing Street and instructing the Foreign Office to assume an 'attitude of strict correctness' towards Russia.[1] There was to be no more unnecessary friendliness in Britain's dealings with the country, but equally there would be no unnecessary breach.

In British Intelligence, it was an approach that caused perplexity and anger. The risks Baldwin was taking with the safety of the nation and the empire seemed indefensible, as did his demand for further patience after all the effort that had gone into exposing radical socialism during 1924. Instead of basking in the glory of their famous victory, the counterespionage community began 1925 with the very same Soviet threat looming over them as before, and, in all likelihood, they could look forward to an increase in homegrown left-wing extremism as well, following Labour's controversial defeat. They soon learned that they would have fewer resources with which to combat these dangers, too, since the fiscally orthodox government tightened departmental budgets yet again.

Nevertheless, British Intelligence found a way to rise to the challenge, casting its nets wider than ever, and displaying a heightened sense of urgency in all it did, as well as a greater determination to make every discovery count. In the wake of the Zinoviev Letter, all counterespionage organisations, and especially MI5 and Special Branch, seemed much more aware of the potential publicity value of the intelligence information they collected, and of how an eye-catching story or leak could help them achieve their aims.

Moscow, too, had changed its tactics. By the mid-1920s, the Bolsheviks were beginning to take their first tentative steps into the field of foreign military espionage, and predictably using Britain as a test bed; simultaneously they started signalling an intention to infiltrate the British civil service. Understandably, British Intelligence was extremely agitated about this, yet it was also to react equally strongly to other developments, which, on the face of it, should have worried it less. During 1924, for example, Moscow supported the creation of an organisation to promote mutual understanding between Britain and Russia, the Society for Cultural Relations, or SCR as it became known. British Intelligence fretted constantly about this club's role in British life and, in spite of its own reduced resources and the fact that most SCR meetings discussed nothing more dangerous than contemporary Soviet theatre or Communist arts and crafts, it devoted precious time and energy to prying into the SCR's motives and activities. Similar effort was expended on the small group of Britons who showed interest in the films of Sergei Eisenstein, as the authorities believed that these, too, might spark revolts or even a revolution if they were shown to mass British audiences.

Whereas the agencies had previously focussed on activists and agents, they now began to show greater interest in people who expressed mere curiosity about the Soviet state. The names of members of the Bloomsbury Group started appearing in the MI5 files for the first time in the years after 1924, along with those of a number of left-wing vicars and priests who had fallen for Moscow's soft propaganda but who – quite obviously in hindsight – posed little or no threat.

These shifts did not feel like a descent into paranoia at the time, even if that is what they look like now. Or at least they did not feel like paranoia to those who were orchestrating them. Rather, they seemed like the bare minimum that ought to be done. British Intelligence had a prime minister in Stanley Baldwin who was far from ideal, and even King George V was known to have urged restraint in post-Zinoviev Letter responses to British socialism. (In a memorandum of 4 November 1924, Lord Stamfordham, the King's private secretary, had written to Baldwin to say that His Majesty had 'dwelt upon the importance of combating the idea of anything like class war' in the aftermath of the election. 'The Opposition would come back to Westminster disappointed and embittered,' George had said, before expressing 'an earnest hope that the Prime Minister would restrain his followers from doing anything in the House of Commons to irritate their opponents.')[2] Beyond these two figureheads, a large proportion of the establishment, including most press barons and scores of Conservative MPs (belonging to what had become known as the party's Diehard wing), were determined to increase pressure on the left and, yes, to 'irritate' them, while also finding ways to punish Russia for her misdemeanours. These men spoke out constantly about the government's need to act, but they also understood that only another revelation like the Zinoviev Letter could force Baldwin's hand, and they knew instinctively that this was most likely to come from the shadowy world of espionage.

The strength and self-confidence of the right wing of the Conservative Party was much greater in the years after 1924 than it had been before. The Diehards felt energised by the unveiling of a major left-wing conspiracy that confirmed their worst fears and seemed to prove them right in the eyes of the general public, and they took hope from the increasing strength of popular reactionary and even proto-fascist and fascist groups. Initially, it looked as though Baldwin had structured his cabinet so as to immunise himself from such influence, especially in matters of foreign policy, but in time it would become spectacularly clear that this was not the case.

The most obvious trap that Baldwin had sought to avoid was appointing Winston Churchill (who had been re-elected thanks to his anti-left rants, and had rejoined the Conservative Party) to a position where he could once again do battle with socialists. Baldwin made him Chancellor of the Exchequer, even though Churchill would have preferred to go to the Home or Foreign Office. According to an entry in the diary of Kathleen Hilton Young (the widow of Scott of the Antarctic and Baldwin's close friend), the Prime Minister had explicitly 'given Winston

Exchequer' so that he was in a place 'where he wouldn't be able to talk about Labour, nothing but finance'.[3] Similarly, Curzon was denied the post of Foreign Secretary – though in his case this was largely due to frailty – and was replaced by a noted moderate, Austen Chamberlain, who was determined to get a deal on global arms limitation and who saw almost no mileage in anti-Bolshevism.

The Diehards, of course, needed to be given some prominent positions in the new government, if only to buy their loyalty (many actively despised the Prime Minister). Baldwin's biggest mistake – if keeping a lid on left-right tension was what he really wanted to do – was to appoint the relatively little-known Diehard William Joynson-Hicks as Home Secretary. Joynson-Hicks, or Jix as he was known to friend and foe alike, was a reactionary through and through, but he had spoken out much less than other reactionaries on the subject of the political left, preferring instead to focus on issues of Christian morality (teetotalism and anti-drugs crusades in particular) and on Britain's right to defend her empire in whatever way she saw fit (a favourite topic was General Dyer, the Butcher of Amritsar, and his justification for massacring Indians in the Jallianwala Bagh gardens in 1919). During 1924, however, Jix's personal concerns about socialism had suddenly come to the fore, and he was now much more interested in the Red threat. His allegation during the election campaign that MacDonald was 'heart and soul in favour of union with Bolshevism' was a typical example of this.[4]

Perhaps Baldwin was unaware of the shift when he decided to appoint Jix, or perhaps some other measure of political expediency was at work: the Prime Minister may have calculated that Jix's famous bluster would be enough to keep the grassroots happy on this issue, while his poor track record of actually getting things done would mean that little damage ensued. A hint of this dismissive attitude, and of the Home Secretary's reputation for hot air, may be read in Baldwin's remarks to

Lord Curzon at the end of the first official meeting of the new cabinet on 21 January 1925. The Prime Minister described Jix as 'carrying 200 lb of steam to the square inch till every rivet in him [was] strained to the uttermost'.[5]

But Baldwin was wrong to underestimate the man. Because once Jix achieved power, he was to use it relentlessly in wide-ranging attempts to shore up Britain's traditional values and hold back the tide of what others called progress. During his term of office, he cracked down on nightclubs; successfully fought off attempts to update the Church of England's Book of Common Prayer; and, most importantly, fought the Russian and British Communists as hard as he possibly could, constantly questioning his colleagues' do-nothing policies and eventually deciding to take the law into his own hands. If an incoming Ramsay MacDonald had been shocked by the first Special Branch intelligence summary he saw, Jix turned out to be equally surprised by his first encounters with the secret services. He discovered that he had completely misjudged the brazenness with which Moscow flouted the normal rules of diplomacy. The situation was so much worse than he had imagined; the frequency and breadth of Soviet wrongdoing appalled him; and so, too, did the *laissez-faire* responses of his own and previous governments.

Over the next few years, Jix, even more than the Prime Minister, exerted a kind of political magnetism over Britain. His anti-socialist ideology not only altered the tenor of Britain's relations with Russia but also warped the internal dynamics of British society. While he sought constantly to outmanoeuvre Moscow and its followers in the United Kingdom, he also increasingly accepted assistance from right-wing domestic extremists and deliberately stoked the fires of class conflict. And it was with his explicit blessing that British Intelligence now followed its worst instincts and searched ever more intrusively for the proof of Bolshevik contamination throughout British life.

13

THE OLD BUSINESS GOES ON

Other things being equal, problems only tend to get more complex as time goes on, and this certainly turned out to be the case for British Intelligence in the 1920s. The longer its investigations continued, the wider its web of suspects grew and the more intricacy it detected in Bolshevik plots. If this was sometimes a measure of the British authorities' oversensitivity to conspiracy, it also reflected the reality of Soviet espionage and subversion, which became more diffuse and elaborate over time. Initially, Moscow had despatched agents overseas with only a single operation to carry out, but when they were successful, these agents were typically given dozens more tasks. To start with, the creation, funding and direction of the CPGB had accounted for most of the Soviets' secret activity in Britain, but gradually other interests developed. And as ARCOS and the Russian Trade Delegation turned out to be surprisingly resilient to repeated public scandals, Moscow understandably began to use them as hubs from which to meddle in other, non-British, parts of the world.

The two major spy cases that loomed largest for MI5 and Special Branch during 1925 and 1926 exemplify these tendencies: each had its origins in the earlier part of the decade but was to prove harder and harder to understand and unravel as the years went by. The first was the case of Jacob Kirchenstein, or

Johnnie Walker, the Latvian spy who had successfully evaded the British state when he first arrived in the country and who would continue to bamboozle it for several more years.[1] It was only after 1924 that the facts about Kirchenstein's work began to be clear to the secret services and, thus, became a source of serious consternation. Simultaneously, British Intelligence uncovered a network of suspected secret agents who worked for or were connected with the *Daily Herald* newspaper, an institution that had long been a cause of concern. This network appeared to be led by the paper's foreign-news editor, W. N. Ewer, a journalist of considerable public reputation who nevertheless seemed to be taking orders from Moscow.

It was understood that each of these cases might well supply British Intelligence with the grounds for another attempt to get rid of the Bolsheviks. Yet they also both presented the agencies with formidable logistical and tactical challenges. Distracted by other aspects of their voluminous and ever-expanding agenda, and to an increasing degree outwitted by their targets' mastery of the dark arts of secrecy, intelligence officers wanted nothing more than to close the Kirchenstein and Ewer rings down. But they also had a growing sense that to do so would leave vital questions unanswered.

After a brief stay at the Savoy Hotel following their return from America in November 1922, Jacob and Vallie Kirchenstein went on to enjoy another fifteen months as Soviet agents without so much as a hint of British Intelligence interference. During this time, Jacob managed to relocate many of his original helpers from the north of England and Scotland to well-paid positions in London, while maintaining other members of his agent network *in situ* and testing the feasibility of a range of new ways of working. He and Vallie lived in considerable comfort and ostensible respectability in the middle-class London suburb of Richmond-upon-Thames, while Jacob worked cover jobs, first in the Hides, Leathers and Tanning Materials department of ARCOS, and then at the ARCOS Steamship Company. At the same time, he masterminded several secret projects, operating through agents on Soviet and British ships, communicating by telegram and mail with Comintern workers in a dozen or more countries, and also by mail with his and Vallie's left-wing friends in the United States.

Perhaps Jacob had become somewhat complacent after so many years of successfully, often effortlessly, evading the British authorities, because in May 1924 he made a slip that was to give Special Branch its first real glimpse of his secret double life. Some of Jacob's post had been under surveillance since February 1924, as part of an investigation into the activities of Charles Douglas, one of his original Scottish contacts. Kirchenstein and Douglas had corresponded regularly since 1920; the latter was an engineer who worked in the ship-repair business in Edinburgh, while also couriering messages and parcels for Jacob to and from Communist sailors at the port of Leith. For the first three months that the check was in place, Jacob's intercepted letters to Douglas revealed nothing of interest and the Latvian might soon have been excluded from inquiries. But in a letter postmarked 28 May Jacob revealed in less cryptic terms than ever before some key details of his London life – details that, though sketchy, gave the authorities a vital lead and a clear rationale to probe further. 'Your note received last night,' he had written. 'I am working now in the City in that big building in one of the Departments (it was my own wish) but the old business partly goes on so I am pretty busy but I don't mind a bit. It does a lot of good.'[2]

This was something of a breakthrough, with British Intelligence correctly identifying that 'the old business' meant secret work. Yet Britain's spies had been on the back foot with Jacob and Vallie for almost four years by this point and progress with the case was still to remain agonisingly slow. From the material Special Branch intercepted over the next eighteen months, officers detected that Jacob sometimes travelled outside Britain

on shady Soviet business, including to New York, and that he
was in regular contact with other parts of the world where the
Soviet state generally wanted to increase its influence. A number
of the Kirchensteins' closest associates were also identified,
including Peter Miller and Karl Bahn, both of whom had jobs at
ARCOS, and some of the couple's radical contacts in America,
among them Jon Bankin and Otto Purin. Significantly, Special
Branch discovered that Jacob's presence at ARCOS had never
been officially notified to the British authorities – his American
citizenship meant he did not need to apply for a working visa. It
also established that, outside a trusted inner circle, most ARCOS
and trade delegation employees had nothing to do with Jacob;
he kept himself very much to himself.

In August 1925, a second key revelation occurred. The wife of
Charles Jurgenson, one of the Kirchensteins' American friends,
wrote to Vallie telling her, 'Don't send me those packets! All
the envelopes were split open and on each one could be read
to whom they were to be given over. The postman hesitated
and asked me a lot of questions before he gave them to me'.[3] As
the authorities correctly speculated, the contents had been some
sort of illegal propaganda or sensitive Comintern instructions
(probably a combination of the two) and the Jurgensons had
suddenly become unwilling accomplices.

The truth about the Kirchensteins was slowly coming into
the light. However, as late as September 1925 Special Branch
still struggled to join the dots and see the full picture, answering
a routine enquiry from elsewhere in Whitehall by saying that
'our information about [the Kirchensteins] is of a very indefinite
nature'.[4] Only in the weeks after that admission did the police
finally think to compare Jacob's handwriting with samples they
held for unidentified agents. This exercise included a comparison
with the *SS Sterling* letter of December 1920, the one Jacob had
signed 'Johnnie Walker'. And thus did the British state finally
realise that Jacob was someone whom it had been looking for

since the turn of the decade. The discovery was quickly followed
by an additional bombshell: Kirchenstein's fake Stormonth passport. Now the whole intelligence community was required
to comb through its files to try to explain how this apparently
mundane couple had got away with serial subterfuges for so
many years and how, in particular, the Passport Office's checks
had been so comprehensively rubbished.

Eventually, at the end of 1925, Special Branch produced a
dossier that listed everything it currently knew about Jacob and
Vallie. The report set out twelve central facts about 'KIRCHEN-
STEIN and his associates'; but, while impressive-looking at first
glance, it became clear on a more thorough perusal that many
of these supposed insights were very generic and left lots of
questions unanswered:

1. KIRCHENSTEIN's headquarters are in Moscow,
and he collects information regarding the activities of
the British Communist Party.
2. In May, 1924, KIRCHENSTEIN took up an official
position in the Arcos Steamship Company, while still
continuing his revolutionary activities.
3. KIRCHENSTEIN is a close follower of the
revolutionary movement both in the United Kingdom
and in America.
4. KIRCHENSTEIN's wife assists her husband in his
revolutionary activities.
5. As far as possible KIRCHENSTEIN carries on
his activities independently of the [Russian Trade]
Delegation, who in their official capacity are afraid of
disclosing any connection with the Third International.
6. KIRCHENSTEIN was anxious that the British
Authorities should not know of his connection with
Arcos.
7. KIRCHENSTEIN's work is of such a secret nature

that not even those in the movement and in Arcos are informed of his activities [. . .]

8. KIRCHENSTEIN is anxious regarding his personal safety and the possible censorship of his correspondence.

9. KIRCHENSTEIN [. . .] maintains touch with Peter MILLER [. . .] [Miller had already featured in British Intelligence lists of suspected secret agents.]

10. [In] 1925, KIRCHENSTEIN intended to visit this country by illegal means should he have been refused a visa in New York. [The authorities suspected, incorrectly, that Jacob still had access to a fake passport.]

11. KIRCHENSTEIN still receives reports from the British Colonies and from Moscow.

12. KIRCHENSTEIN appears to contemplate a visit to Palestine, possibly in connection with the recent growth of Communist activity [there].

The most significant passage was arguably the grave admission that Jacob's 'communications are sent either through seamen [. . .] or through the diplomatic bag' but 'beyond the fact that they are of a particularly secret nature and clearly deal with revolutionary matters, nothing is known of the contents'.[5]

A few years earlier, the unmasking of such a significant agent would have led to immediate calls within the intelligence community for arrest and deportation (as happened with Mikhail Borodin). But now the authorities paused. They were keen to discover what else Jacob had been up to and who else he might be connected with. Certain hints in his letters meant that they were especially eager to understand if Jacob was involved in military and industrial espionage.

This brand of espionage against the West had been a step too far for the Soviet state in the initial aftermath of the Russian Civil War. The country had made concerted attempts to keep tabs on White Russian groups abroad, particularly those that harboured ambitions to send agents to Soviet lands, but infiltrating the upper echelons of other nations' armed forces or stealing designs for military hardware were beyond it, either because such acts were genuinely too difficult or because they were not seen as a high enough priority. During late 1923 and 1924, British Intelligence worried briefly that Bolshevik effort might be about to shift in this direction and, as a result, some resources were put into the surveillance of ARCOS employees who had business links to companies that fulfilled British military contracts. An ARCOS worker called Leonid Vladimirov, for instance, was followed for a time because he had meetings with the Vickers and Handley Page companies. Despite some bold assertions, however, ('I tell you those Russians know all that Vickers and other large firms have in hand,' an informant was quoted as saying; 'So as to get an order or two the firms are willing to worship even a Bolshevik') no proof of wrongdoing was established and the matter was dropped.[6]

Kirchenstein's forays into military espionage seem to have begun in 1925, and this time they were in earnest. He had reconnected with one of his oldest acquaintances in Britain, James Messer, a Scottish Communist, who arranged for Jacob to be put in touch with other Communists employed in factories doing military work. Earlier, Messer had been among Kirchenstein's most trusted assistants: he was one of the only people the Latvian consulted before procuring the Stormonth passport. Now Messer's contacts gave Jacob access to employees at Armstrong Whitworth, an automobile, locomotive, aircraft and military armaments company, and at A. V. Roe (often known as Avro), a producer of military aircraft.

British Intelligence first confirmed the connection between Kirchenstein and Messer in March 1926, and then, that July, tracked the pair to 'a meeting [. . .] held at [Charles] DOUGLAS's house' in Edinburgh.[7] Douglas himself and Jacob's helper Karl Bahn were also said to have been present. Special

Branch speculated – though on what basis the archives do not reveal – that the subject of their discussion was the 'very secret organisation of Comrades who, working through the Shop Stewards in certain factories, were [. . .] obtain[ing] information on military and economic questions'.[8] By September, Special Branch had further established that Messer's men (Charles Henry, Tom Smith and F. E. Walker) – in factories as far apart as Barrow-in-Furness, Hendon and Manchester – had already leaked plans to the Bolsheviks, including detailed designs for British Army ordnance and a new RAF aircraft. Guy Liddell, one of Special Branch's senior officers, was convinced that before long, if he had not already done so, Jacob would secure contacts within the British military itself. Yet neither Liddell nor his colleagues knew the best way to address this, since any disruption might drive the traitors further underground.

During his confession to the American FBI about his life in Britain in the 1920s, Jacob admitted to almost everything that other sources indicated he had done. He also supplied many details that would not otherwise have come to light. However, on the subject of military espionage he remained tight-lipped, despite much prompting from his interrogators (who had been briefed by British Intelligence about the right questions to ask).[9] While Kirchenstein's account sometimes diverges from that of British Intelligence in ways that suggest mistakes on the latter's part, on this occasion there can be little doubt that Jacob was lying for fear of the consequences of having been a military spy.[10] On the subject of Messer, Jacob would only say that 'in the summer of 1926' another ARCOS colleague had come 'to me and asked me to recommend a person for light work who was capable [. . .] in journalistic circles. I recommended James Messer [and] this was the last time I saw or heard about [him]'.[11] As an intelligence official in London would note in 1951, 'For a man whose recollections of thirty-year-old events are meticulously detailed [. . .] he suffers curious lapses of memory [. . .] I think KIRCHENSTEIN has more to tell us.'[12]

The case against W. N. Ewer at first appeared to be more manageable than that against the Kirchensteins. Indeed, the circumstances in which Ewer became a suspect lulled officers into a false sense of security, leaving them with an initial impression that he and his contacts were rank amateurs. Soon enough, however, the full extent of Ewer's endeavours began to emerge and British Intelligence realised that this matter, too, was out of control.

William Norman Ewer has a good claim to being the first Cambridge spy, a precursor to Philby, Burgess and Maclean. Born in 1885 and educated at Trinity College, Cambridge, Ewer — who was known as Trilby by most of his friends — had been a conscientious objector in the Great War and then spent the postwar years as a campaigning left-wing journalist. He first attracted the attention of the secret services because of his wartime pacifism (he was made to work on a farm for refusing to enlist), but his file was kept open after the Armistice because of the interest he showed in the radical left. At the start of the 1920s, Ewer became an early member of the CPGB and also a senior *Daily Herald* journalist, serving as the paper's foreign editor and dedicating many articles to subjects like abuses of colonial power, oppressed peoples' quests for national self-determination, and the fortunes of worldwide socialism.

Until 1924, Ewer had been very much an also-ran in British Intelligence's long list of people of interest. Special Branch periodically noted his attendance at meetings of groups that it was following, but his own postal and telephone communications were untouched and he was generally believed to play little if any role in underground work. Even when the *Herald* came under enhanced scrutiny for accepting Bolshevik funding,

Ewer's name did not feature in the inquiries because he was not involved in the paper's business side.

All that changed, however, on 21 November 1924. That day, as every day, MI5 staff members' first task was to comb through the press in search of relevant information. The *Herald* was always read with especial care because of its political slant and its past reputation for supporting Moscow. Among its pages, on that particular morning, one of the clerks spotted the following classified advert:

> SECRET SERVICE – Labour group carrying out investigations would be glad to receive information and details from anyone who has ever had any association with, or been brought into touch with, any Secret Service department or operation. Write in the first instance Box 573, Daily Herald.[13]

The request was laughably overt. It seemed clearly connected to the continuing fallout from the Zinoviev Letter (which had been published the previous month), an attempt on the part of some left-wingers to get to the bottom of rumours that the state had conspired to deny Labour victory. Yet, naive as it was, it could not be ignored. MI5 always wanted to know if someone was prying into its existence and what, if anything, they already knew.

The organisation launched a classic sting operation. It imposed a warrant on Box 573, to intercept all the post that was sent there before it could reach the *Herald* (though, in the event, nothing whatever was sent). At the same time, it drafted its own response to the advert, signing it D. A. Reinmann, the alias of an MI5 employee who was already operating as a mole inside the CPGB:

29, Alderney Street
Pimlico, SW1
To Box 573, D.H.
Dear Sir,

In answer to your advertisement in D.H. of 21.11.24.

Having been associated with the British Intelligence service for four years my services may be of some use to you. You will appreciate, however, that I am not disposed to go into any detail here with one who is, as yet, a complete stranger to me, but, if you would care to arrange an interview at your convenience we could, no doubt, discuss matters to our mutual advantage.

At present I am engaged in teaching languages and am hoping shortly to obtain a post on the managerial staff of perhaps the biggest industrial concern in the country as confidential translator and interpreter. Under these circumstances I should be glad of an early interview as a change of my plans might become necessary.

Yours truly,

D. A. Reinmann.[14]

To MI5's puzzlement, the letter elicited no direct contact. The agency, therefore, despatched a follow-up, expressing 'not a little surprise' on the part of its fictional Mr Reinmann that he had not received 'at least an acknowledgement' for his previous efforts, but adding for good measure that 'perhaps I did not make it clear [. . .] in certain directions I am prepared to offer my services voluntarily'.[15] On this occasion the anonymous recipient took the bait, which led, during the course of January and February 1925, to a series of encounters between Reinmann and the suspect.

For the first of these, Reinmann received instructions to go to the Bodega Wine House on Bedford Street, off the Strand, and seat himself at a table near the entrance. 'Carry with you or be reading a copy of the "Daily Herald",' his correspondent said, in the best traditions of clandestine tradecraft.[16] It took MI5 no time at all to establish that the other man who turned up at the Bodega and at each subsequent venue was W. N. Ewer. Ewer presented himself as the advert's author, but in fact he was doing exactly the same as MI5: having happened upon the text in the paper, he had decided to abuse his position at the *Herald* to intercept any reply that came in. (Only in 1950 did Ewer reveal that, to the best of his knowledge, the advert had been placed by a Labour MP who wanted to write a book about British Intelligence, though the name of the MP has never come to light.)[17]

Reinmann attempted to build up trust with his new acquaintance by sharing 'secrets' he said he had picked up from serving intelligence employees, and also by suggesting that his new job as a 'confidential translator and interpreter' could bring him fresh contacts with the War Office and possibly SIS. Reinmann advised Ewer that 'advertising in a paper' was 'a rather peculiar way of finding agents' and suggested that he would be 'much safer' recruiting 'civil servants holding labour views'.[18] He also touched on what he correctly assumed would be a raw nerve for any left-winger at the time, stating that many intelligence employees were in close touch with the Conservative Party, the Anglo-Russian Club (a White Russian group) and anti-socialist organisations like 'the British Empire Union' (the BEU) and 'the Fascisti'. In fact, he added, he was confident that *all* officers 'were on good terms' with such groups while 'most [. . .] were members of the BEU, [the] Freemasons [and] the Primrose League. They were all friendly with each other and exchanged information; [in just the] same way they were connected with the conservative press.'[19]

MI5 hoped to trick Ewer into accepting Reinmann as his confidant so that the journalist's secret work could be mapped. But in these opening exchanges it was actually Reinmann and

MI5 that ended up being tricked by Ewer. The authorities quickly realised that the journalist was accompanied at each rendezvous by assistants who watched him and Reinmann from afar and then tried to follow the MI5 man home. Reinmann believed he was being successful at shaking off these shadows, but Ewer's men worked out soon enough that their quarry was actually a British secret service employee. Reinmann then found himself cut off not just from contact with Ewer but also from the CPGB he had worked so hard to infiltrate. (According to information that MI5 received only several years later, comrades in the Communist Party were particularly incensed to discover that the fake Reinmann had conducted a romantic affair with a genuine and unsuspecting party member called Minnie Birch – an echo of the infiltration tactics that would be used, and would also draw sharp criticism, in later eras.)

MI5 now found itself in a terrible mess. It had telegraphed its suspicions directly to Ewer himself, meaning that he would proceed with extra caution in future. It had also burned one of its best-placed agents. And its principal discovery in return for this significant outlay was that Ewer's network was more sophisticated and more extensive than had initially been thought. Intelligence chiefs now went back to the drawing board and commenced a spell of painstaking information-gathering to try to claw back some of the initiative.

Trilby Ewer had first been approached to consider secret work for the Bolsheviks during a 1922 trip to Moscow.[20] This visit had been an opportunity for him and other influential British left-wingers to get a taste of the new Soviet state, but Trilby must have been taken aside at some point and offered the chance to make an enhanced contribution to the cause. The reasons for his recruitment were no doubt complex, but among them was a desire on the part of the Bolsheviks to increase the number of British secret agents they had outside ARCOS and the Russian Trade Delegation.

Ewer's first efforts for his new masters appear to have been quite limited. But after Nikolai Klyshko's removal from the United Kingdom in response to the Curzon Ultimatum in 1923, the Soviet authorities elected to put the journalist in charge of more sensitive operations. Ewer was instructed to run these various projects under the umbrella of a genuine news agency, the Federated Press of America (FPA), which was based in Chicago, but which had its London offices at 50 Outer Temple. These offices began to function as a front. Ewer supplied news–agency-style copy back to the FPA in America – so as to maintain the ruse – but the material was all lifted directly from the columns of the *Daily Herald*. For the next six years, he and his team spent almost all their FPA time on a host of other shady activities, including stealing foreign secrets, following British government spies, and distributing illegal propaganda at British military bases.

In February 1925, a short time after the Reinmann encounters, MI5 placed the FPA offices at Outer Temple under postal and telephone checks, as well as intermittent physical surveillance. Unsurprisingly, the telephone conversations held at the agency were mostly 'very guarded'.[21] Yet British spies did manage to get some idea of the various people involved in Ewer's network. They included Walter Dale and Albert Allen (who seemed to be the men who stalked Reinmann), and at least one other *Herald* journalist, George Slocombe, the paper's Paris correspondent. There were also three women, none of whom had previously featured prominently on British Intelligence's books: Rose Edwardes, the London FPA secretary; Rose Cohen; and Eva Reckitt. MI5 managed to intercept material that had been sent to the FPA by Slocombe in Paris. At a glance this seemed to comprise French intelligence reports about political affairs in Bulgaria, Italy, Morocco and Yugoslavia. British Intelligence instantly worried that, so far from being a naive and amateur outfit, Ewer's group might already have its own informants hidden deep within the British state, too.

Surveillance now embraced everyone and anyone who came into contact with 50 Outer Temple. The predictable result, in the short-term at least, was that the investigation slowed to a snail's pace. There was a proliferation of shallow suspicions and little deep analysis to help make sense of them. Ewer and Slocombe, it was discovered, were corresponding frequently with one another, using aliases and some kind of simple but nonetheless impenetrable code ('Spaghetti 5000 a month; Goulash 5000; Native grown cereals 5000; Hospitality, foot-men etc. 5000' and so on).[22] Special Branch's views on the pair were sought. But the police had nothing whatsoever to say about Slocombe, while their opinion on Ewer amounted to what was already obvious: that he was 'not an agitator in the street corner sense' but someone who 'as the Foreign Editor of the *Daily Herald*, as well as in his private capacity, [was committed to] advancing the revolutionary causes which he has at heart'.[23]

Meanwhile, Ewer's sidekicks, Dale, Allen and Edwardes, were all placed under physical surveillance, which was an extremely foolish move given that MI5 had already caught Dale and Allen following its own officers. As a case history later put it, 'MI5 watchers attempting observation on these people found themselves watched in turn'.[24] Dale and Allen, it would transpire, were actually former policemen who had been sacked from the Metropolitan Police in 1919 for their participation in an illegal strike.[25] Rose Cohen and Eva Reckitt were regularly in Ewer's company and thus also warranted being watched. The women were both CPGB members, and Reckitt, who was heiress to a considerable fortune, was one of the party's most generous financial backers (referred to disparagingly by a fellow comrade as the CPGB's 'milch cow').[26] The correspondence between Ewer and the women proved to be extensive. It seems that at least two of them (he and Rose) were having a romantic affair, yet amongst the pleasantries and declarations of affection there were enough passages that might be espionage-related to keep MI5 engrossed.

In March 1926, Rose wrote to Ewer from Paris:

> *Moi dorogoi* [Russian for 'my dear']
>
> I too dislike being here. I'm terribly lonely. I haven't enough to do and I want to come home oh so badly, my love!!!
>
> I shall at least touch London one way if not both on my journey to Sussex. So I shall most certainly see you. At the moment I am not quite sure when I am leaving here, but I think it will be Thursday. If it is at all possible, I shall persuade him that I ought to see people in London and so snatch a day, if not two, in London. I'll write to you again when I know more definitely.
>
> How alone one can be in a strange big city. I've discovered the thing I like least is feeling alone. I wonder if I shall be reduced to picking up someone! Don't be alarmed. I find French men most unattractive.
>
> IMM's little holiday was spent in Paris. Bob is here, but I haven't seen him yet. Unfortunately I am cut off from the A. I'm very glad to hear that Yerbukova has gone – I hope you will take your time at the cash box.
>
> I'm so sorry about the Bink. I hope it's quite mild. Poor old Bink does seem to catch what's going [. . .]
>
> I must go and dine. I wish you were coming too.
>
> See you very soon,
>
> *Tvoya Roza* [Russian for 'Your Roza']27

Rose's references to 'IMM', 'Bob', 'Yerbukova', 'the A' and 'the Bink' were tantalising mysteries.28 They added to the bad feeling that MI5 had about Ewer's whole outfit, but despite drowning in clues about him, the agency still could not say clearly what was going on.

And it continued to be entirely unaware of many of the most damaging facts. In particular, it persistently failed to understand the extent to which Dale was spying on British Intelligence's own employees, and had been since long before the *Daily Herald* advert. Dale, and under his instruction Allen and occasionally another ex-policeman called Marsden, had been intermittently tracking MI5, SIS and Special Branch workers since 1922, often following them between their work and home addresses, and sometimes watching them as they met White Russians and other contacts. The trio continued to do this, mostly without being noticed, after the Reinmann-Ewer debacle, while Dale also helped Ewer to recruit two serving Special Branch officers to pass secret documents and other 'live' intelligence to the FPA. These officers, Inspector Ginhoven and Sergeant Jane, were relatively low-ranking and, therefore, had limited access to the most sensitive information. Nevertheless, their existence on Ewer's payroll represented a huge coup for the Bolsheviks and at least some of what they passed over was extremely useful.

Perhaps the most damaging leak occurred in October 1925. During that month, Joynson-Hicks, the new firebrand Home Secretary, ordered a raid on the CPGB headquarters in Covent Garden. Ever since taking up office, Jix had been under strict instructions to avoid rocking the boat of Anglo-Soviet relations (Austen Chamberlain, the Foreign Secretary, had written to him in May 1925, reprimanding him for making anti-Bolshevik comments in public: 'I do *not* want an open breach if we can avoid it [. . .] no pinpricks on our part', Chamberlain had said).[29] Yet the Diehard minister was determined to find some way to get at the Russians. In the autumn of 1925, he hit upon the notion of authorising a police incursion into the CPGB's head office. The resulting raid led to sack-loads of material being carted away and the arrest and trial of twelve high-ranking Communists.

Ostensibly, the episode was an enormous success for the

authorities – the biggest since the Zinoviev Letter – with twelve convictions for incitement to mutiny secured on the basis of the evidence. But behind the scenes, spy chiefs were extremely surprised at the mildness and limited nature of what they seized: plenty of leaflets, pamphlets and draft newspaper articles, all of which sought to rouse the working class, often in intemperate language; lots of planning documents and minutes of committee meetings and speaker events; but very little that was truly shocking. There was no evidence, for instance, of direct orders from Moscow, or of military and industrial espionage, or of direct contact with ARCOS and the Russian Trade Delegation. The missing material seems to have vanished thanks to Ginhoven and Jane – a fact that British Intelligence would only discover four years later. The moles became aware of the raid while it was at the planning stage and tipped Dale and Ewer off. Long before officers set foot in King Street, therefore, the most incriminating evidence had already gone, probably hidden in comrades' houses or, possibly, at the ARCOS offices on Moorgate. Following the tip-off, Ginhoven himself participated in the raid, and later even gave evidence against the CPGB defendants at Bow Street Police Court. (According to *The Times*, he reported finding 'publications headed "Bolshevising the Communist International" and "What the Young Communist League Stands For"'.)[30] But, in reality, the bent copper had done more than anyone else to limit the damage that the action could cause.

Ginhoven and Jane were among the CPGB's very best British friends in the 1920s ('primarily Communists and not merely mercenaries' was the compliment that Ewer would later pay them).[31] Ewer himself, of course, though not 'an agitator in the street corner sense', was also one of the Soviet state's most valuable British assets during the era – a man heavily suspected by British Intelligence but one who, nonetheless, managed to keep pulling the wool over its eyes.

Copy of letter addressed to Mrs. J.
KIRCHENSTEIN, 43, Lancaster Park, Richmond.

(Translation from Lettish T.785B.)

2486 Valentine Av.
Bronx N.Y.
America.   July 26 - 1925

Greetings, My dears,

Thank you for the letter and for the photos
of the boy.   It is worth while having such a son.
He will no doubt one day be a help to his Mother.
I met your boy's Godmother at the Jahnis' and she
sent you her greetings.   I asked her if she had
had any letters from you and she said that you were
no longer in correspondence.   She said "I don't
know what has happened to them," and that there had
been no time to write because of her mother having
to be massaged in Bellevue Hospital, which also
costs a lot.   Dear Mihxe, don't send me those
packets.   All the envelopes were split open and on
each one could be read to whom they were to be
given over.   The postman hesitated and asked me a
lot of questions before he gave them to me.   Let
the Jews get themselves what belongs to them.

                    Chas. Emily.

1.
   ? BANKIN's wife

2.
   John or Jahnis
   BANKIN (Vide
   Appendix B)

3.
   Vallie
   KIRCHENSTEIN (Vide
   Appendix C.)

4.
   (Vide letter No.
   39)

5.
   Probably refers
   to the leaders of
   the American Commu-
   (nist Party who are
   held in contempt by
   the local Lettish
   Group)

6.
   Charles & Emilia
   JURGENSON (Vide
   Appendix F)

*A marked-up British Intelligence translation of Emily Jurgenson's letter to
Jacob and Vallie Kirchenstein, dated 26 July 1925. The casual antisemitism
that appears in the letter's last line is a common feature of many documents
in the MI5 archives of this era, some of them produced by people on the
Soviet side, but others written by MI5 employees.*

```
The Daily Herald.

21.11.24.
```

```
            NOTICE
SECRET   SERVICE.—Labour   Group
    carrying out investigation would be
glad to receive information and details
from anyone who has ever had any asso-
ciation with, or been brought into
touch with, any Secret Service Depart-
ment or operation.—Write in first in-
stance Box 573, DAILY HERALD.
```

A photograph of the original classified advertisement that led MI5 to pay close attention to W. N. (Trilby) Ewer, the respected Daily Herald *journalist who also performed numerous clandestine services for the Soviets during the 1920s. British authorities initially thought that Ewer was a naive amateur, but they came to realise that it was they who had been duped by his extensive undercover enterprise, which included moles within their own ranks.*

14

BOLSHEVISM IS CATCHING

'We are far more conscious of our condition than we were, and far less disposed to submit to it. Revolution [. . .] is now a possibility so imminent that hardly by trying to suppress it in other countries by arms and defamation, and calling the process anti-Bolshevism, can our Government stave it off at home.'

George Bernard Shaw, June 1919 Preface to *Heartbreak House*

As the months turned to years, investigations into the likes of Kirchenstein and Ewer often seemed set to drag on indefinitely, with British Intelligence trying and failing to catch the conspirators out or take other decisive action. Partly this was because the intelligence community could never devote itself fully to such top-level threats, but instead was increasingly distracted by Bolshevik assaults on what might be described as the soft underbelly of British culture and society. These lesser threats seemed to take on ever greater prominence, and the authorities accordingly felt obliged to expend more and more energy tackling them.

Alongside Soviet rhetoric that emphasised the regime's implacable enmity towards Britain's rulers and its deep solidarity with British workers, there was another strand to Anglo-Soviet discourse which purported to ignore such distinctions and insisted instead that everybody in the Russian state just wanted to be friends with everybody in Britain. This happy fiction was allowed to float in the ether between the United Kingdom and Russia from the dawn of the trade negotiations in 1920 until midway through 1924, at which point it was explicitly and deliberately harnessed by an organisation called the Society for Cultural Relations Between the Peoples of the British Commonwealth and the Union of Socialist Soviet Republics. Known as the Society for Cultural Relations, or the SCR for short, this body welcomed interest from, and offered membership to, anyone in Britain who had a benign attitude towards Soviet life, irrespective of whether they belonged to the CPGB or believed in revolutionary Marxism.[1]

The SCR presented itself as an enthusiastic interpreter of the realities of the new Soviet state. It was always meant to have an equal commitment to interpreting *British* culture back to the people of the USSR as well, but this aspect of its endeavours remained underdeveloped. Instead it focussed on extolling Bolshevism's achievements in the arts, literature and the sciences, and on proving that Britain and the rest of the world had nothing to fear, and much to gain, from contact with Soviet society.

At the SCR's inaugural meeting, in London's Caxton Hall in July 1924, the presiding chairman Margaret Llewelyn Davies (a veteran of Britain's cooperative movement) 'expressed the hope that in reopening the channels of communication interrupted by the ten years of war and revolution, the Society would make a contribution to the international intercourse through which alone civilisation can reach its highest expression'.[2] Following this, the SCR sought to advance its goals via a series of eclectic events and publications that considered subjects as diverse as new Russian poster art, village folk theatre, penal reform, Soviet music, and a major celebration in September 1925 to mark the bicentennial of the Russian Academy of Sciences.

The SCR's core target audience was a group of Britons who have become known as 'fellow travellers', an English translation of the Russian word *poputchik*, which initially referred to Russian citizens who sympathised with, but did not actively participate in, the Bolshevik revolution. British and other foreign fellow travellers tended to be men and women working in cultural and academic professions who supported the Bolsheviks' right to rule and felt that Moscow had things to teach a moribund world of privilege, tradition and compromise. SCR events, which were almost always in London, were attended by some of the most Bohemian people of the age, who were eager to believe that somewhere there existed a state which was sympathetic to their ideals. From 1925 onwards, the SCR also sponsored trips to the magical place itself, leading to an expansion in the number of British people who got to see aspects of Soviet life first-hand.

The SCR always maintained that it was above politics, or rather that the everyday dirt and confusion of international politics and diplomacy were beneath it. In a letter to the *Manchester Guardian* timed to coincide with the society's creation, the executive emphasised that 'the work of the Society [would] be strictly cultural'.[3] That said, right from the outset, British Intelligence saw in the SCR a new ideological threat that needed to be marked and monitored no less keenly than other ideological dangers.

There were a number of reasons for this. First, the loud protestations about being apolitical were in themselves thought to be suspect. Llewelyn Davies and her co-founders genuinely believed they were building an organisation from the grassroots up, responding to demand from the social circles in which they moved. Yet they always enjoyed significant support from the Comintern and the CPGB, and many of their members were Soviet citizens who, at the very least, had been encouraged to sign up to the SCR by their bosses in ARCOS and the Russian Trade Delegation. Secondly, British Intelligence worried about the role played in the organisation by the known secret agent Andrew Rothstein. He was closely involved with the vast majority of the SCR's work, sitting on its committees and helping to arrange the trips to Russia; he also put the considerable resources of the Russian Telegraph Agency (ROSTA) at its disposal. Why would he do so, British spies wondered, if he did not see the SCR as a way of furthering Moscow's clandestine agenda?

The final alarm bell for British Intelligence was the staggering level of interest that the SCR managed to drum up among key members of the intelligentsia. In hindsight, the subject matter of its events might appear a bit safe, even humdrum, but the organisation's creation coincided with a moment in British culture when interest in all things Russian (pre-revolutionary as much as post-revolutionary) was soaring.[4] This meant that what might have been just a dilettantish sideshow for people already committed to Communist politics quickly turned into one of the most vibrant links between Britain and the Bolshevik regime. Already by the time of the first meeting, the organising committee comprised – in addition to Llewelyn Davies and Rothstein – Leonard Woolf, Ruth Fry and Leonard Hobhouse, all leading figures in Britain's liberal elite. They were rapidly joined by other notable individuals, including several members of the celebrated Bloomsbury Group. John Maynard Keynes, E. M. Forster and Virginia Woolf all agreed to be 'vice-presidents' and have their names printed on the SCR letterhead. Bertrand Russell, Ben and Winifred Nicholson, Vita Sackville-West and H. G. Wells were members, too, as were many whose names may no longer resonate but who were, in their day and in their fields, no less eminent: Julian Huxley, the evolutionary biologist; H. N. Brailsford and Henry Nevinson, both famous journalists; C. R. Buxton, a noted philanthropist and Labour MP; Evelyn Sharp, the suffragette; R. H. Tawney, the historian; and Havelock Ellis, the sexologist.[5]

For British Intelligence, these people were participating in yet another ruse that Moscow had engineered to boost its influence in the United Kingdom and bypass the elected government. It had not escaped British spy chiefs' attention that the CPGB's membership had remained quite small in the years since its foundation (though this was not something from which they ever derived much comfort). Fewer than five thousand of the United Kingdom's forty-five million citizens (or about one in nine thousand people) had signed up to the CPGB by the mid-1920s.[6] But now the Bolsheviks had deliberately set out to target a group of influential people who did not feel like becoming card-carrying comrades. On hearing of the SCR's creation, some in the British state wondered if the organisation constituted a direct breach of the no-propaganda clauses that Moscow had signed up to in the 1921 treaty and re-committed itself to following the Curzon Ultimatum in 1923. But the SCR, it was quickly accepted, was unlikely to furnish the grounds for a much-sought-after Anglo-Soviet split, given that successive prime ministers had failed to act on much more serious provocations. Nevertheless, officers agreed that the club had to be watched.

Surveillance of the SCR and its supporters in one form or another was constant from its inception and probably lasted until the collapse of the Soviet Union. (The SCR's successor body, the Society for Cooperation in Russian and Soviet Studies, still exists today, though in a much less well-funded and glamorous form than its forebear.) During the 1920s, British Intelligence initially kept tabs on the SCR through Special Branch's and MI5's monitoring of Rothstein and ROSTA, but it also watched the group directly at times. What the British were looking for was harder to articulate than in many other cases, and what they found was patchy at best.

A typical document records an approach to Rothstein by a left-leaning vicar, the Reverend William Dick of Trinity Congregational Church in Poplar, east London, in June 1925. The Reverend Dick had written to ask a number of questions that had been puzzling both him and his worshippers:

1. Are all members of the Soviet Government

Communists? If not, what proportion are not Communists?

2. Would it be possible for a 'Christian' to attain a place in the Soviet Government at present?

3. Have Priests been executed who have not taken part in political programmes?

4. Was the Revolution accompanied by bloodshed and killing? If so, to what extent? And who were the authors – the leaders, or the mob with excited passions?

5. Have the peasants accepted Soviet Rule? Are they much influenced by it? Is it true to say that on the whole Soviet Rule ceases to be effective 5 miles on each side of the Railway track? Is it true that in some cases the peasants have cast out their Communist teachers?

6. What is the death-rate for infants and adults in town and in country?

7. Are musicians, poets, literary people, journalists, teachers, doctors, lawyers, ministers of religion (in a word brain workers only) regarded as 'workers' and do they have a vote? Is it only the 'manual worker' who has a vote?

8. What became of the 'employers' after the Revolution? Were their factories confiscated?

9. Would the present form of Soviet Rule be advisable for Britain?

10. Could not the great benefits accruing to Soviet Russia be achieved at once in this country through ordinary parliamentary methods – in view of the fact that the workers in this country constitute the vast majority of the electorate?[7]

The Reverend Dick's letter was intercepted by Special Branch and then transcribed and shared with MI5. It must have grabbed the imagination of some intelligence officer or clerk who saw the potential for connecting this cleric's left-wing enthusiasms with the more general problem of worker radicalisation in London's East End. But the questions are interesting for their naivety rather than any revolutionary intent.

In the next month, July 1925, MI5 got its hands on a complete membership list of the SCR, after the society's assistant secretary wrote to Rothstein enclosing the information and asking for a photostat. All the famous names were present, alongside those of other members of the public and CPGB and Soviet representatives. MI5 thought the document important in part because it demonstrated what officers described as the SCR's 'Russian parentage'. Of the 353 names, MI5 calculated that 'approximately 25 per cent' belonged to one or other of the Soviet organisations in London.[8]

But what did this juxtaposition of eminent Britons and Soviet citizens actually signify? By no means all SCR members were enthusiastic pro-Bolsheviks. John Maynard Keynes, for instance, was famously scathing about Bolshevism in his essay *A Short View of Russia*, which was written after a visit to the country in 1925 ('how can I adopt a creed which, preferring the mud to the fish, exalts the boorish proletariat above the bourgeois and the intelligentsia who, with whatever faults, are the quality in life and surely carry the seed of all human advancement?').[9] Keynes joined the SCR merely because he found Russia interesting. Many other members *were* fellow travellers who had more time for the Bolsheviks and, in hindsight, their enthusiasm for the Bolshevik state raises questions. Modernists who dreamt of living in a more dynamic and daring version of Britain, they sincerely wished the Soviet Union to be a template for the rest of the world, and, thus, many of them ended up being duped by Moscow.

But British Intelligence's concentration on them was only partly based on an understanding that soft support for Bolshevism could be valuable to the Russian regime. It was also fuelled by a belief that such soft support masked more dangerous and illegal types of assistance. Without doubt, a certain amount of scouting for talent and recruiting of secret agents did go on at SCR events, but this was something that British Intelligence's approach to surveillance was never likely to spot.[10] Instead, the authorities' focus seemed to be on maintaining an ever-longer list of people who were potentially – though not verifiably – a cause for concern.

The watching of Clare Sheridan from the middle of 1920 was an early example of British authorities directing surveillance at an artist and public figure who was not actually a spy. At least in Sheridan's case, the connections to Churchill and Kamenev justified the initial interest. But the decision to start focussing on the SCR led MI5 and Special Branch to wade further into these waters, and arguably they got out of their depth. A tendency developed to place prominent British cultural workers under surveillance without anyone being clear what the surveillance was for. Over time, the British secret state would open files on scores of notable individuals, including George Orwell, Christopher Isherwood, Ewan MacColl, Joan Littlewood, Cecil Day Lewis and Sam Wanamaker, none of whom presented an imminent threat to British national security.[11] For cash-strapped and perennially overwhelmed organisations to show so much interest in these people, while details of known spy rings remained murky, was questionable prioritisation.

Perhaps even more dubious was British Intelligence's involvement in the monitoring of output from the burgeoning 1920s Soviet film industry.

On certain afternoons in the mid-1920s, hard-pressed British Intelligence officers, who might otherwise have been trying to uncover the truth about various military and political conspiracies, would stop what they were doing and head to Wardour Street, in Soho, where they would watch films that hardly anyone else in the country could see. The Bolsheviks intended their 'Soviet Hollywood' to produce a new kind of cinema which had proletarian values, the overarching aim being to have a significant revolutionary impact around the globe. The intelligence agencies in Britain got drawn into watching Soviet films almost as soon as they hit the international market, partly out of their own interest and partly at the request of the Home Office, the War Office, the Admiralty and the British Board of Film Censorship (the forerunner of today's British Board of Film Classification, which is still known as the BBFC). Across the British state, officials wanted the censors to reach quick and effective censorship decisions in order to try to protect the nation's impressionable viewers.

Early Soviet cinema is probably the most celebrated product of the first decade of Bolshevik power, with students of film studies still guaranteed to encounter Sergei Eisenstein at some point in their course and also having a good chance of coming across other 1920s Soviet directors, like Vsevolod Pudovkin. Students learn about Eisenstein's theory of the 'montage of attractions', his commitment to the sensory and visceral impact of films on their watchers, and the many ways in which his works, including *Battleship Potemkin* and *October*, were cinematic departures from everything that had gone before. Less attention, however, is generally paid to the reactions Soviet cinema elicited at the time, particularly in the international arena – even though this was a key measure of success for both the directors themselves and the Bolshevik state that supported them financially and politically.

In the declassified archives of the British government, a large file records the many exchanges that took place between government ministers, officials and censors about early Soviet filmmaking and the risk that some United Kingdom cinemas might try to show Bolshevik films. The films had caused a stir among the world's critics, who were excited by what was widely believed to be a major leap forward for cinematographic art. The authorities worried that film reels might be smuggled into Britain and that cinema clubs or left-wing local councils might show them either privately or in public. With 'talkies' still a couple of years away, silent movies were transnational – they could easily be adapted for display in any country just by the addition of a few language-specific intertitles. Soviet cinema, therefore, seemed to be yet another way in which the Bolsheviks might speak directly to the British people without official permission and in a context that appeared apolitical but was actually not.

Soviet films would have been a cause for official concern regardless of when they were first produced and irrespective of their content. But the threatened release of *Battleship Potemkin* during the first half of 1926 was particularly undesirable, given the recent Soviet attempts to influence British affairs, the hostility that many in the Baldwin government already felt towards the Bolsheviks, and, most acutely, the immediate backdrop of Britain's first general strike (described in greater detail in the next chapter). The subject matter of the film seemed to have been deliberately chosen to fan the flames of class conflict, depicting as it did the moment in 1905 when mutinous sailors took control of a ship – the battleship of the title – during the first Russian revolution. While critics and cinema aficionados argued that Eisenstein's work should be shown because of its great originality and artistry, the authorities agonised about the damage it might do to British class relations, and in particular to the loyalty of the armed forces. They determined that *Potemkin* must not be seen in any form by anyone outside their own circle.

Film censors in Britain had always operated with a degree of blurriness in relation to the state. During the 1920s, cinemas across the country were technically free to show any film they chose so long as the local council approved it, but in reality it had become almost unheard of for a council to go against the recommendations of the national censor, the BBFC.[12]

The BBFC itself was theoretically independent of central government, being funded through industry levies, yet it shied away from controversial decisions without first consulting senior government officials and politicians. As no decision could be more controversial than whether or not to show a Soviet film, civil servants were confident, without even bothering to check with the BBFC, that it would ask for their views about *Potemkin* and any other 'Red' releases. As one Home Office official wrote to another in June 1926, 'the Censors would never pass a film of this character [. . .] not without consulting us'.[13]

Whitehall's official involvement with Eisenstein began on 21 June 1926 when the Permanent Secretary of the Admiralty, Sir Oswyn Murray, contacted the Home Office to share the concerns of his boss (the First Sea Lord) about *Battleship Potemkin*. He had read in the press that the film had already been shown outside Soviet borders, in Berlin. The film, he said, 'appears to be a fantastic representation of a mutiny on board a Russian Battleship, worked up so as to constitute very objectionable propaganda against the discipline of the Fighting Forces'. 'We presume that there would be no likelihood of such a film being allowed to be exhibited here,' Sir Oswyn continued, 'but should there be any question of it, the First Lord hopes that the [Home Secretary] will do everything possible to prevent it.'[14]

In the weeks and months that followed, this was exactly what the Home Secretary did. The reels of film were successfully tracked as they entered the country and made their way to the Film Booking Offices of a Mr F. A. Enders at 22 Soho Square. There were then rumours, first picked up by the navy, that this 'amazingly well produced' feature had already 'been shown privately at the Capitol [Cinema on Haymarket] to a considerable number of members of the film business'.[15] These rumours turned out to be baseless, but they, like Sir Oswyn's letter, indicate how jumpy officials had become.

To start with, Mr Enders made clear to the BBFC that he

had no intention of showing the film in Britain, saying instead that he had only wanted to see it for himself because he 'looked upon [Eisenstein] as the leading exponent of his art throughout the world'. He added that he had now decided to consider hiring the Russian director to make more films, which would be 'purely of entertainment value', and therefore might stand a better chance of being approved for display in Britain.[16]

Officials dared to hope that this might mark the end of the episode. But instead Mr Enders, somewhat mischievously, let his contacts in the press know that the BBFC had effectively told him there would be no point trying to get a version of *Potemkin* passed, because any version would be banned, no matter how many cuts he made. Matters became increasingly sensitive after screenings of Eisenstein's masterpiece were allowed to occur in other European countries, leading Britain's liberal and left-wing commentators to castigate the British government for patronising British audiences. An article in the *Observer*, on 11 July 1926, wrote of 'the forbidden film' that was now being shown to new audiences in Berlin and Vienna even as it 'has been banned by the British Censor' (a statement that was not in fact yet true). *Potemkin*, the journalist concluded, would 'go down in the annals [. . .] as the finest example of expressionist art: men under military orders acting as machines, a ship under individual hands taking on human personality' – but British cinema-goers would not be there to see it.[17] In even more fervent terms, the CPGB-run *Workers' Weekly* wrote of a film 'banned in Britain while all Europe is stirred'. 'Described by capitalist critics as the greatest ever produced,' the article continued, 'the Soviet film "Armoured Cruiser Potemkin" has been banned in Britain while it is being shown to enthusiastic audiences in nearly every other country in Europe.' The paper noted the contrast between the suppression of Eisenstein's supreme cinematic achievement and a series of decisions by the BBFC to pass low-quality, low-morality films that included the likes of the 'Mack Sennett Bathing Girls', 'Shooting Niggers', and what was described as 'American undress cabaret'.[18]

Mr Enders eventually decided that he would try to get *Potemkin* shown, perhaps in an attempt to make good on his investment (that was certainly what Mr Brooke Wilkinson, the secretary of the BBFC, felt) but no doubt also from a genuine desire for British film lovers to see the masterpiece. At the start of September, Enders signalled to the censor his intention to offer an edited version of the work for certification. As soon as it received Enders's proposed cut, the BBFC then hastily arranged a meeting at 'the Censorship's Office' in Wardour Street for mandarins from across government to come together 'to view the film and to help the Board with advice'.[19] That meeting took place on Wednesday 8 September; the invitees were surprisingly numerous: two from the Home Office; one from the Admiralty; a Mr Neale from Special Branch; and no fewer than three officers from MI5 – Oswald Harker and Captains Boddington and Tomlins. They all watched the film and then shared their judgements and fears. A detailed note of what transpired was circulated to those involved, and to William Joynson-Hicks, the next day.

The note consists of an extended description of the film, as seen through the eyes of a posse of British security officials and secret policemen, and a series of recommendations to inform the BBFC's official reaction. The viewers were especially struck by the work's visual force, in particular the images of 'a brutal Quartermaster lash[ing] one of the [*Potemkin*'s] crew'; of meat 'rotten and alive with worms'; of the body of a dead mutineer 'laid out on the quay side [at Odessa], a placard having been pinned on his chest with the words "All for a spoonful of soup"'; and of 'soldiers firing on [a] crowd' which included 'women, children and cripples'.[20] Everyone present at the Wardour Street screening agreed that the film seemed to have an exemplary, didactic quality (as Eisenstein had intended), by which they meant that they saw clear risks that ordinary viewers would generalise from what they saw and take it as instructional. At the conclusion of the screening, Mr Wilkinson said he felt absolutely sure that his boss, the chief censor T. P. O'Connor, would deny *Battleship Potemkin* a certificate. He stated this was because the film showed 'mutiny against properly constituted authority' and scenes of the 'armed forces firing upon the civilian population', both of which were banned under the BBFC's code. But he added that he was eager to know 'if the Board would have the backing of the Government' in taking this step. 'All present at the conference were in agreement,' the memo noted, about 'the undesirability of any public exhibition of the film in this country.'[21]

The discussion then turned to the matter of how the BBFC and the state should respond if any local council decided to authorise the film against the recommendation of the national censorship body. Government officials, including those from the intelligence agencies, were deeply worried about this prospect, believing that a small number of councils, those with what they described as 'an extremist majority', would likely allow *Potemkin* to be shown. Mr Wilkinson was asked if he knew of 'any means of overcoming this danger'.[22]

He replied with surprising bullishness. 'The danger was more apparent than real,' he said, because 'Mr Enders [is] the sole agent for the film in this country [and has] his living to earn in this industry.' Preemptively, the BBFC 'would give him clearly to understand that, if he approached any licensing authority [i.e. any local council] behind the Board's back, to obtain permission to exhibit this film, the Board would have nothing more to do with him and would not censor any future films that he may desire to exhibit. This would jeopardise his living and Mr Wilkinson said he was confident that Mr Enders would not run this risk.'[23] In the event that a different kind of organisation that was not part of the film industry (for instance the CPGB) should plan to show the film, officials agreed that anti-mutiny legislation would need to be used to seize the reels and prevent the film being displayed.

Needless to say, such conversations and such plans were highly contentious. Theoretically, the BBFC was totally independent of government, and yet here it was pre-clearing its decisions with both the civil service and government spies. It is no surprise, then, that the Home Office folder containing this note is covered with warnings. 'Memo of an unofficial conference held at the offices of the British Board of Film Censors' it says, and on the front cover someone has added for good measure that 'the Conference was entirely unofficial and it was definitely understood by all who took part in it that the Board of Censors, in conveying their decision to refuse a certificate for the film, would do so on their own responsibility and would not, without permission, mention that they had consulted any Government department'.[24] Jix's reaction, scribbled inside the folder on 14 September 1926, was one of approval. He wrote that he was 'much pleased with the action taken by the H.Office and other govt. departments' and that he would 'support to the utmost both in P[arliamen]t and out the decision to prohibit this film'.[25]

Through this unprecedented series of actions, *Battleship Potemkin* was successfully suppressed – at least for a time. However, any sense that this was a unique event was quickly dispelled by the threatened arrival of other revolutionary films, and by the secret services' perception that they now needed to keep track of all matters connected with Britain's radical cinema. In November 1926, fears surfaced about the possible screening of another Eisenstein feature, *Strike*, a film that the director had made before *Potemkin*, which would become known at the Home Office as *Black Sunday*. It covered similar ground to the tale of naval mutiny, being a restaging of events that had taken place during a pre-revolutionary strike in Russia, culminating in a massacre of innocent workers. For added effect, the great director had interspersed images of human cruelty with footage of dead cats and of cows being slaughtered. Special Branch's Captain Miller said the film was 'suspected of being subversive in character' and he therefore arranged a warrant to detain it should anyone try to import it into Britain.[26] In 1927, Special Branch's concern switched to the arrival of Vsevolod Pudovkin's *Mother*, a film which Miller described in a letter to the Home Office as 'a sermon on class hatred [. . .] intended to show the brutality of the police forces'.[27] (A second secret government screening at the BBFC's Wardour Street offices took place to view *Mother*, the ensuing note commented on the 'very high order' of acting throughout the picture but again expressed worry that the director's intent had been to indicate that 'the lessons of the film [were] of general application'.)[28]

Around this time, British Intelligence began to take an interest in those British individuals who were in contact with the Bolsheviks about cinema. This included Eva Reckitt and Rose Cohen, and also a young man called Ivor Montagu, the son of the banker and political activist Lord Swaythling. In 1925, when he was still in his early twenties, Montagu created the Film Society, an elite membership organisation that was committed to showing the best of world cinema to small groups of cineastes at exclusive events in London movie theatres on Sunday afternoons. Being a members-only club, the Film Society did not have to submit to the BBFC's censorship regulations, so long as it could find venues that were willing to host it. This was obviously a matter of grave concern to the authorities, not least because Montagu was a known member of the CPGB ('a convinced Bolshevik', as Special Branch's Miller put it in one letter).[29] The noble's son wrote widely to Russian bodies, begging them to send him anything that had been produced by Soviet film directors, especially films like *Battleship Potemkin* and *Mother*.

Warrants were placed on the addresses where Montagu

lived and worked, and gradually these began to shed light on his plans. In one intercepted in September 1927, he wrote to cultural officials at the Soviet trade delegation in Berlin to set out his Film Society's *modus operandi*. It was not, he said, 'a commercial renting firm' but rather 'a group of intellectuals and technicians engaged in or interested in the Film industry'. 'We give only one performance of each film,' he went on, 'a private one attended only by our members and the press, and for this reason our showings are exempt from the censorship.'[30] Many of the members of Montagu's exclusive club were also in the SCR, including H. G. Wells, Keynes and Julian Huxley. From the perspective of the authorities, of course, this all confirmed the notion that such people and such organisations were suspect. But was there any real risk?

Contemporary opinion on the matter, and views about the power of cinema more widely, were finely balanced. Soviet thinkers tended to concur with British spies, censors and the chiefs of the armed forces that revolutionary subject matter, if persuasively depicted on the silver screen, could push viewers towards a revolutionary state of mind – the theory of imitative behaviour. This was certainly an element in Eisenstein's own understanding of his art form; for him the manipulation, in all senses, of the watcher was crucial to cinematic success. Leon Trotsky, similarly, explicitly referred to *Potemkin* as a way to make British workers more radical, writing in May 1926 that he 'would very much advise [. . .] British workers and sailors' to 'see the Soviet film' because it showed 'graphically the mechanism of the revolution inside an armed mass of people'.[31]

In general, there was also widespread agreement about the unique potency of the moving image and the unusual vulnerability of the masses when sat in front of it. The BBFC seldom banned entire films in the 1920s – with the exception of *Potemkin, Strike* and *Mother* – but it was constantly clipping and snipping at movies in order to try to protect audiences from things they might not be able to handle. Often these were things that people were permitted to read about in books or look at in paintings (where state censorship was considerably rarer), but cinema was treated differently because it was deemed to provide a heightened experience of reality. In its annual report for 1926, the BBFC listed no fewer than seventy-three reasons why a film might be banned or cut. Alongside 'inflammatory sub-titles and Bolshevist propaganda', these included 'painful insistence of realism in death bed scenes'; 'lampoons of the institution of monarchy'; 'white men in [a] state of degradation amidst native surroundings'; 'officers in British regiments shown in a disgraceful light'; 'female vamps'; 'methods of crime open to imitation'; and 'the drugging and ruining of young girls'.[32]

Yet not everyone felt it would be dangerous for ordinary Britons to see Soviet cinema. According to the Home Office archives, even the right-wing *Daily Express* thought it might be unwise to ban *Battleship Potemkin*. In July 1926, at the time of the *Observer* and *Workers' Weekly* pieces, the paper ran an article 'expressing surprise that it was felt necessary to stop the film [since] the public might be trusted to judge [it] properly'.[33] Going still further, Lord Beaverbrook, the *Express*'s proprietor, requested his own private viewing via the Home Office, though we do not know whether his request was allowed.

Officials and ministers seem to have taken it for granted that, if *Battleship Potemkin* or similar films were licensed, the cinema-going public would flock to see them in large numbers. They seem to have assumed that the Bolsheviks were cunningly exploiting a pre-existing appetite among the British masses for proletarian drama. But the evidence for this was mixed at best. In Germany, it was said that over a million people had rushed to see Eisenstein's masterpiece during the spring and summer of 1926, a number that frightened the British authorities. But in Russia itself, as the historian Denise Youngblood has persuasively shown, it was films from the United States that consistently came out as the people's favourites. In the same year that *Battleship Potemkin* hit Soviet screens, for instance, Youngblood demonstrates that Douglas Fairbanks's appearance in *The Thief of Baghdad* was a much bigger draw for cinema audiences, while several other Hollywood movies also featured among the most popular films.[34] Fairbanks and Hollywood generally were immensely popular with British audiences too – a fact that had caused the government of Stanley Baldwin to mandate a quota of British films to be shown alongside American ones in cinemas.

Battleship Potemkin would remain banned in Britain until the 1950s, at which point the BBFC permitted it to be displayed with an X rating. Thus, the authorities were never able to test whether the majority of the British public in the interwar years would really have been interested in, or susceptible to, the Bolsheviks' cinematic messages. During the 1920s, there was just one British showing of Eisenstein's film, orchestrated by none other than Ivor Montagu and the Film Society (because it was private, this screening was, as Montagu had said, exempt from state censorship). It took place at the New Gallery Cinema on Regent Street on Sunday 18 November 1929 and – sensationally – the great director, Eisenstein himself, was present, having arrived in the country a short time before on a Soviet fact-finding mission.[35]

The event turned into a gala for London's great and good, with plenty of fellow travellers in attendance but also many effete and glamorous figures from London's Bohemian scene. Film critics for every major newspaper came and there was a spate of colourful write-ups in the press during the week. Among the funniest was a vignette that Herbert Thompson penned for *Film Weekly*, in which he contrasted the harshness of Eisenstein's subject matter with the delicacy of fashionable London dressed in its Sunday best:

> Bearded young men, famous authors, famous actors, effeminate young men, film directors and technicians,

are all jumbled up together in the auditorium. Among the audience [. . .] I noticed H. G. Wells, the famous novelist, Anna May Wong [the American film star], Jameson Thomas [the British film star] [and] Adrian Brunel, the film director [. . .] Some of the Film Society crowd is typified by the following charming little interlude: – In a tube train on my way to the show, I noticed two effeminate young men, very animatedly discussing the Film Society's programme which one of them held in his hand. Suddenly the train, with many screeches and groans, came to a jarring stop. One of the young men, apparently fearing an accident, turned to his companion, and said, in a piercing whisper, 'Darling, I shall scream! I'm terrified.' I wonder now what their feelings were when they witnessed some of the excessively barbaric incidents of *Potemkin*.[36]

S. C.R.

The Society for Cultural Relations between the Peoples of the British Commonwealth and the Union of Socialist Soviet Republics

President : Prof. L. T. Hobhouse
Vice-Chairman : Miss A. Ruth Fry
Hon. Secretary : Mrs. Catherine Rabinovitch

Chairman : Miss Llewelyn Davies
Hon. Treasurer : Henry J. May

Telephone :
Museum 5254

23, Tavistock Square,
London, W.C.1

Vice-Presidents :

15. July. 1925.

Prof. Lascelles Abercrombie

E. M. Forster

David Garnett

Julian Huxley

Prof. A. A. Ioanne

J. M. Keynes

Prof. A. N. Kriloff

Dr. V. P. Lebedeff

Dr. Albert Mansbridge

N. M. Minsky

Prof. M. N. Pokrovsky

Prof. W. A. Stekloff

H. G. Wells

Mrs. Virginia Woolf

Prof. O. J. Schmidt

Dear Mr Rothstein,

Herewith the list of our members and first subscriptions which you kindly said you could get duplicated for us. There are a few blanks instead of subscriptions, but these are people who gave some service to the S.C.R instead of a subscription.

I think 30 or 40 copies should be quite sufficient.

We are very grateful to you for this help.

Yours sincerely,
C. B. Hutchinson
Assistant Secretary.

One of several early items related to the Society for Cultural Relations that British Intelligence intercepted, this letter, which came with a complete membership list, shows how overwhelmingly un-revolutionary the society's leaders were. Moscow would surely have waited a long time for such a group to start an insurrection.

FILM THE CENSOR
DARED NOT PASS

Banned in Britain While All Europe is Stirred

"ARMOURED CRUISER POTEMKIN"

"Shooting Niggers" Spectacle Preferred to Anti-War Film

Workers' Weekly
16.7.26

Headlines in the Workers' Weekly, *a Communist newspaper, correctly predicted the BBFC's later decision to ban* Battleship Potemkin. *The film would not be exhibited publicly in Britain until the 1950s, and then only with an X rating. British Intelligence was closely involved in the decision to censor it.*

15

SPIES, FASCISTS AND THE GENERAL STRIKE

'Something goes wrong with my synthetic brain
When I defend the Strikers and explain
My reasons for not blackguarding the Miners.
"What do you know?" exclaim my fellow-diners
(Peeling their plover eggs or lifting glasses
Of mellowed Chateau Rentier from the table),
"What do you know about the working classes?"'

Siegfried Sassoon, 'The Case for the Miners', 1926

Whether or not any British workers could have been incited to rebellion by watching the films of Eisenstein, the fact remains that both Soviet propagandists and the British state believed it to be a possibility. It was a belief originating partly in wishful thinking and paranoia, but also from the very real class tensions that were circulating in the air in Britain, especially in 1926. Worker dissatisfaction had been growing for decades and it now reached crisis point. A British revolution was still a remote prospect, of course, but a general strike suddenly seemed much more likely. A few in British society had been predicting such a mass organised withdrawal of labour since the first half of the nineteenth century, when industrialisation and the machine-based economy had first taken root. By the start of the 1900s, there had been plenty of false dawns, so that the idea of a general strike had even taken on something of a mythical quality for those who saw it as the ultimate way to demonstrate where true power lay in the capitalist system. For their opponents, meanwhile, it remained a bogeyman, fundamentally anti-constitutional and anti-democratic.

After the Bolshevik victory in the Russian Revolution, the perceived significance of general strikes increased worldwide. This was partly because they had been an important expression of social unrest in late-Tsarist Russia, and partly because the Comintern had started to advocate for them strongly as a revolutionary weapon. There was also an increase in the number of them across the globe. Between 1917 and 1920 – a time when social tensions were exceptionally high in many countries – general strikes or events that were depicted as such occurred in Australia, Germany and Hungary, and in major industrial cities including Seattle, Winnipeg, Vancouver and Glasgow.[1]

Unsurprisingly, it was the events in Glasgow that had the biggest impact on British government thinking. During January 1919, a campaign for a shorter working week had mobilised some sixty thousand workers from a variety of Glaswegian factories and industries, convincing them to put down their tools and take to the streets. Rioting erupted when protesters did not get their way, and some of the movement's leaders used Bolshevik slogans in speeches and pamphlets, predicting a Russian-style future for their city, including workers' soviets (the grassroots councils that had been the original hallmark of the Russian Revolution) and a dictatorship of the proletariat. The government responded in dramatic fashion, with the Secretary of State for Scotland labelling the incident an attempted 'Bolshevist uprising' and deploying ten thousand soldiers with machine guns, tanks and a howitzer.[2]

In fact, the problem of what became known as 'Red Clydeside' abated relatively quickly, but the authorities' fears lingered much longer, being rekindled in 1921, when a national general strike suddenly seemed a serious possibility. The major coal-mining, railway and transport unions had banded together in 1914 to form a Triple Alliance, whereby they agreed to interpret a threat against any of their memberships as a threat against all of them. Wartime restraint had prevented these unions from taking radical action. But in 1921 post-war austerity and deregulation left coal miners facing large wage reductions, and transport workers and railwaymen indicated that they would walk out in solidarity, a move that would achieve the same impact as a general strike by bringing the country to a standstill.

Ultimately, the walkout did not come off and the episode was remembered as a bitter failure for the labour movement, with miners deserted at the last moment by their supposed comrades. The coal union struck alone but, shorn of wider support, was unable to protect its members' terms and conditions. This was the point at which the Comintern decided to smuggle Mikhail Borodin into Britain, in order to help the fledgling CPGB exploit these cowardly unions' woeful performance. In government circles, however, the debacle was seen as a frightening harbinger in spite of its failure, demonstrating the need for better preparations and a greater willingness to use active countermeasures.

Four years later, in April 1925, the coal industry faced another crisis. There had long been oversupply of coal on the world market, but the consequences of this for Britain's industry were suddenly exacerbated when Winston Churchill made the controversial decision to return sterling to the gold standard, further driving up the comparatively high cost of British production.[3] In response, mine owners signalled their intention to reduce miners' wages and extend their working hours in order to increase efficiency. Unions immediately opposed the measures and argued instead for a major restructuring, preferably one that included nationalisation. (This was not as fanciful or radical as it may now sound: a post-war government commission, reporting to the Liberal-Conservative coalition in 1919, had recommended nationalisation but its suggestions were ignored.)

Matters first threatened to come to a head in July 1925,

the month when owners planned to terminate earlier accords about minimum rates of pay and maximum working hours. A newly expanded alliance of trade unions agreed to resist these impositions by ordering their members, on the railways and in factories, power stations and other walks of life, not to handle any coal – an act of resistance tantamount to a general strike. At the eleventh hour, however, on 31 July 1925 (a day some nicknamed Red Friday), Stanley Baldwin's government suddenly intervened and agreed to pay a subsidy of several million pounds to mining companies so that miners could retain their current wages for a period of nine months, while fresh inquiries were made about alternative solutions to the crisis.

Miners and other workers celebrated wildly in the days that followed. As the *Manchester Guardian* put it in an editorial on 1 August 1925, this seemed to be 'the first occasion on which a British Government had been terrorised by the threat of a general strike into doing what it was exceedingly reluctant to do and really believed to be wrong'.[4] The newspaper, which then had a liberal tilt, deplored this state of affairs, though it agreed with Baldwin's decision to pay the subsidy. It worried that future trade unionists would 'take [this] as an encouragement to go ahead with [their] new-found weapon and threaten a general paralysis of industry' whenever things looked like not going their way.[5]

Wisely, however, the paper's editor also allowed room for an alternative interpretation of what was going on. Some people, he wrote, felt that 'there must [. . .] be a catch [. . .] somewhere' in what the government had done.[6] And, indeed, this was the case. The Baldwin administration abhorred the idea of a general strike and believed that it warranted massive resistance from the state – even greater than the response Lloyd George's government had made in Glasgow in 1919. Irrespective of how ministers felt about other issues connected with the political left, they all concurred that workers must not be allowed to force an elected government to change its policies by threatening to shut the country down. Baldwin did not view his concession of a subsidy in July 1925 as a capitulation, but rather as recognition that a general strike, while probably inevitable, was not something the government could deal with yet. He had bought himself and his ministers some time in which to make what the cabinet minutes called 'unostentatious preparation [. . .] for maintaining the public services', so as to be ready when the fateful day eventually came.[7]

The nine months between 31 July 1925 and 30 April 1926 were filled with planning, practising and drilling for the presumed future strike. Jix, as Home Secretary, took the lead. His decision to raid the CPGB headquarters in the autumn of 1925, and to arrest the bulk of the party's leadership, was one of the more conspicuous actions taken. But there was a surge in other activity as well. Ministers calculated the best ways to stockpile resources and ration goods and services in their respective areas of expertise. They made estimates of the number of workers in different sectors of the economy who were likely to join industrial action, and assessed the adequacy and elasticity of existing legal frameworks for dealing with civil disturbance. As the hiatus progressed, the public began to get glimpses of the mammoth planning exercise that was under way. Predictably, it was Jix who most often let things slip (whether accidentally or deliberately). At a meeting in Greenwich on 12 October 1925, he said, 'Red agitators were deliberately out to destroy any chance of confidence between master and man', adding cryptically that 'the best work of the Home Secretary [is] work that [is] never seen', at least not 'until the right moment'.[8]

But what kind of work did Jix mean? Behind the scenes, British Intelligence was employing all the tools at its disposal. Agent networks and moles were feeding back information about the plans of trade unions and other left-wing groups. Simultaneously, the whereabouts and pronouncements, public and private, of a large and expanding number of British and Russian figures were being tracked closely, with Special Branch, MI5, SIS and GC&CS all on the lookout for references to strikes. After several years of bemoaning the harsh financial settlements that the Treasury had imposed on them, intelligence chiefs got a temporary reprieve when the April 1926 deadline started to loom. Briefly they would be allowed to increase their manpower, for the most part doing so by reactivating old officers who had worked for them during the war and who now gave their time for little or no money.[9] Additionally, Special Branch and MI5 received tacit clearance to increase informal collaborations with private patriotic groups, many of which had substantial and eager memberships dotted throughout the country.

Right-wing patriotism in its modern form was an important feature of British cultural life from the first decade of the twentieth century onwards. Tapping into fears about threats to the empire and homeland, a range of jingoistic groups had sprung up around the time of the Second Boer War and in response to the radical reforms of the Liberal government of 1906. These groups, along with others that came into being in the 1910s, found a clear focus for their efforts during the Great War but inevitably had to seek new ways to justify their existence thereafter. The ones that survived the transition tended to switch their attention to concerns about socialism, which in the interwar years became the best glue for holding right-wing patriots together. The main organisations that populated the chauvinistic scene during the 1920s were the Anti-Socialist and Anti-Communist Union (founded in 1908); the British Empire Union (founded in 1915); the National Citizens Union (founded in 1919); and the British Fascisti (founded in 1923).

When Ramsay MacDonald had asked Sir Wyndham Childs what he was doing to track right-wing extremists in Britain at the start of 1924, the Labour Prime Minister had doubtless had some or all of these bodies in mind. They were known to be involved in a variety of misinformation campaigns and dirty tricks against the mainstream British left, which they liked to depict as indistinguishable from other forms of socialism, including Bolshevism. Childs had been unable to give a convincing answer, because in truth the British secret services were not monitoring these extremist patriots. On the contrary, as the mole D. A. Reinmann mischievously, but truthfully, hinted, many intelligence officers sympathised with, and may even have belonged to, these organisations. Certainly, their members included numerous aristocrats, high-ranking officers and other establishment figures, as a half-page advertisement for the British Empire Union in *The Times* in 1924 proudly declared. 'Some prominent supporters of the BEU,' the advert announced:

His Grace the Duke of Northumberland
The Right Hon the Earl of Plymouth
The Right Hon the Earl of Leven and Melville
Viscount Astor
Lord Leith of Fyvie
Lord Dunleath
Lord Ampthill
Duke of Bedford
Duchess of Atholl
Earl of Derby
Sir John Hewett
Brigadier General RBD Blakeney
Brigadier General Sir Henry Page Croft
Admiral Sir Edmund Fremantle.[10]

The exact moment when British Intelligence began thinking of private patriots as part of the solution to their problems with left-wing activism is unclear. The links had been forged in the immediate post-war period, or, in many cases, even earlier, through lifelong personal connections. But they were undoubtedly strengthened during the year of Labour government and again after the threat of general strike resurfaced in the spring of 1925. Patriotic groups liked to flirt with running their own in-house intelligence and espionage departments – a reflection, among other things, of the pedigree and inclinations of their most active members. Over time, and perhaps with direct British Intelligence support, these unofficial spy units became more ambitious and successful, and the country's official spy chiefs came to look to them to provide spare capacity.

The historian Gill Bennett has unearthed deep connections between the intelligence agencies and the founder and head of the British Empire Union, Sir George Makgill. 'Approached by a group of like-minded industrialists [in the early 1920s]', she writes, 'Makgill set up a private industrial intelligence service (the Industrial Intelligence Bureau), financed by the Federation of British Industries and the Coal Owners' and Shipowners' Associations, to acquire intelligence on industrial unrest arising from the activities of Communists, Anarchists, various secret societies in the UK and overseas, the Irish Republican Army and other "subversive" organisations.' Makgill was extremely close friends with Desmond Morton of SIS and also 'from an early stage [. . .] had personal links with some members of MI5, and in particular with its head, Sir Vernon Kell'.[11] Bennett speculates that Kell probably offered Makgill some of his old MI5 informants and agents at the point when the head of the British Empire Union was commencing his own work and MI5 was downsizing. Similarly, it is known that during 1924 and 1925 Kell struck up a beneficial working relationship with the head of the British Fascisti's in-house intelligence cell, a man named Maxwell Knight. Knight subsequently went on to be a long-serving MI5 officer, and while working for the service continued to belong to the Fascisti as well as being married to its director of women's units, Gwladys Poole.[12] The British Fascisti drew inspiration from Mussolini's new Italy and, while not embracing all tenets of classic fascism wholeheartedly, the group was both institutionally anti-Labour and eager to use paramilitary methods to break up strikes.[13]

As the date of the possible general strike came closer, the lines between the state's secret services and these cloak-and-dagger jingoistic organisations grew progressively more blurred. So-called intelligence reports from the British Empire Union, the Fascisti and others were shared with British Intelligence officers, who, as far as we know, treated them as welcome additions to their supply of information. Manpower was offered too, both generally and for specific operations. For instance, a British Empire Union secret agent, James McGuirk Hughes, is known to have accepted funding from Special Branch to spy on, and possibly run dirty-tricks campaigns against, dockers in Liverpool in early 1926.[14] Maxwell Knight attempted to get working-class thugs into the CPGB, knowing that the eventual fruits of this effort would be available equally to the Fascisti and MI5.[15] And another man, known as Jim Finney (alias: Furniture Dealer), was said to be feeding intelligence back from within the CPGB to both the British Empire Union and SIS.[16]

Jix, meanwhile, went out of his way to reference the far right in a letter he wrote to the Prime Minister detailing progress with anti-strike preparations on 1 September 1925. 'There exist the Fascists,' he stated, 'they are well known and, I think to be depended upon [. . .] I have seen their leaders several times.'[17] He went on to outline the parameters of a new group, called the Organisation for the Maintenance of Supplies (the OMS), which was still in an embryonic state. This had been set up by close supporters of the government, but officially at arm's length from it, and was intended to provide a pool of sympathetic men under a single command who would do the state's bidding in the event of a strike. At the government's insistence, the OMS's organisers were refusing to permit other patriotic groups, like the British Fascisti, to affiliate on a corporate basis, but this was mere window-dressing since rank and file Fascisti and British Empire Union members were free, and indeed encouraged, to enrol as individuals.

At the start of October 1925, in a public letter printed in *The Times*, Jix offered his warm support to the group. 'I told the promoters of the OMS that there was no objection on the part of the Government to their desire to inaugurate [a] body [. . .] that, if and when an emergency arose [. . .] would be a very great assistance to us.' 'Classified lists of men in different parts of the country who would be willing to place their services at the disposal of the Government', would, he added, be most useful, and citizens 'who would desire the maintenance of peace, order, and good government in times of difficulty would be performing a patriotic act by allying yourselves with this or any other similar body'.[18] Around one hundred thousand men are said to have signed up by the eve of the strike, only a minority of whom were fascists in any sense of the word – but in this and other ways the state was clearly signalling that some varieties of political extremism were more acceptable than others.

On 4 May 1926, just four days after the coal subsidy expired, the General Strike began. Predictably, no solution had been found that could bridge the gap between the miners and their bosses, and the government refused to intervene further to prevent what it saw as the natural laws of economics taking their course and business owners exercising their natural rights. The final straw for Baldwin and other relative moderates came when a Trades Union Congress ultimatum threatened a walkout and – like petrol on the flames – the unionised print-workers of the *Daily Mail* refused to set the paper's anti-miner editorial for printing on the night of 3 May.

The ensuing strike lasted ten days and saw between two and three million workers abandoning their jobs. On the left, there was initial rejoicing because so much of the country's unionised workforce had obeyed the call to strike – around half of all union members and far more in the industries belonging to the Triple Alliance. Labour and the TUC also took pride in the fact that, as they saw it, the strike was conducted responsibly, with minimal violence and a prior commitment to maintain essential services being upheld. But there was anger, too, at what was perceived as the government's deliberate misrepresentation of the workers' aims and behaviour.

On the right, the strike was treated as an outrageous provocation and an existential threat. OMS volunteers and many others tried to fill in for strikers in a variety of roles. Among them was the young writer Evelyn Waugh, who was later to say that he had participated somewhat thoughtlessly, and in order 'to escape boredom'.[19] In his semi-autobiographical novel, *Brideshead Revisited*, Waugh's character Charles Ryder drives a convoy of milk vans around the East End of London for a week, but only occasionally makes contact with 'the enemy' (that is to say, the striking workers), otherwise having a dull and uneventful time.[20] Waugh would write, in a letter to the *New Statesman* in March 1938, that 'only once was there anything like a fascist movement in England [and] that was in 1926 when the middle class took over the public services' – an indication that, deep down, the author had understood the momentousness of what was at stake.[21]

In government, the most anti-socialist voices – Jix, Churchill and Lord Birkenhead – now came to the fore. Churchill, whom a canny Baldwin had tried to keep away from anything labour-related for the preceding eighteen months, exploited the crisis to the full. He appointed himself editor of the *British Gazette*, an official government propaganda sheet printed on the presses of the right-wing *Morning Post* with the aid of OMS manpower, and peddling an exaggerated state version of events.[22]

In reality, there was little doubt about who the eventual

winners in the conflict would be. The TUC did not want a revolutionary situation to develop in Britain and, almost from the moment the strike began, the majority of its general council was desperate to find an honourable way of calling the whole thing off. Union leaders were universally angry about the treatment of the miners, but this did not mean that they wanted to bring down the existing structure of British society. On 12 May 1926, the TUC visited Downing Street and said it would be willing to end the strike if minimal guarantees were given about the future treatment of strikers and about further talks on the coal dispute. When Baldwin refused to issue guarantees of any kind, the TUC shamefacedly terminated the strike anyway.

For anti-socialists, the days and weeks that followed were a paradoxical time. It was abundantly clear that the state, with the support of its external helpers, had easily vanquished Britain's unionised workers. But leading right-wingers also felt that it was vital to continue reminding the public that the strikers had (somehow) posed a credible and considerable threat. With the coal miners once again continuing their industrial action alone (in some parts of the country their strike would persist into the autumn), the hardship, hunger and destitution that they and their families faced became undeniable. Yet the authorities continued to stress that the General Strike was the product of a dangerous, organised anti-democratic machine – not, as the facts might have suggested, the last-ditch action of a desperate movement with no other options left. Sir Vernon Kell walked this tightrope in his internal letter of thanks to MI5 colleagues shortly after the TUC's capitulation. Kell was clearly gleeful about how the whole episode had unfolded and there is something undeniably jaunty in his choice of words, yet he also drew parallels between what had happened and the war: 'I desire to thank all Officers and their Staffs, and the Ladies of the Office, for their splendid work and cooperation during the General Strike. The manner in which all hands have put their shoulders to the wheel shows that the ancient war-traditions of MI5 remain unimpaired.'[23]

An obvious way to answer the riddle of how a strike could simultaneously be very menacing and relatively easily batted away was to allege, and then prove, that it had been directed from abroad by the Bolsheviks. This was what many ministers, all patriotic groups and most right-wing newspapers believed. As Birkenhead wrote to the new Viceroy of India, Lord Irwin (the future Lord Halifax), on 30 May 1926, 'the people tolerate up to a point Russian infiltration, trade unionist tyranny [and] Red Flag demonstrations [. . .] but the spirit of old England is stronger than the spirit of new Moscow'.[24] Churchill had similarly warned just before the walkout that it would 'inevitably lead to some Soviet of Trade Unions with real control of the country'.[25]

Ever since 'Red Friday' in July 1925, British Intelligence had been attempting to demonstrate precisely how Russian infiltration lay behind the General Strike. Reviewing the cases they already had on the books, they initially felt it would be quite straightforward to identify the ties that linked ARCOS and the Russian Trade Delegation with the British people who were agitating for a general strike. But finding concrete facts to pin the strike on Moscow turned out to be a much trickier feat.

During this period, state surveillance of Russian nationals and other trade delegation employees was in overdrive. The close attention paid to Edith Lunn's miscarriage in August 1925 was probably one sign of how the impending strike had altered British spies' behaviour. What were Lunn and Rothstein doing in Devon? Why was there so much urgency about the latter's visit there? Why so much secrecy? Just a few months earlier, such matters would not have warranted the rapid scrutiny they received, especially given the fact that the intelligence services were typically quite London-centric. But now anything potentially connected with local agitation was of paramount importance. The Chief Constable of Devon Constabulary, in his response to MI5's request for all possible information on the couple, even gave orders for Lunn's doctor be interviewed. Obviously there was nothing significant that he could tell the authorities (except about Miss Lunn's gynaecological condition), but the officer still sent word back to London that Dr Twining had seen 'on the table' in Edith's room 'four or five books and leaflets on Communism, which he believes [were] of Russian origin, because on the top of each was an emblem like an Eagle'. Similarly, the local man who drove Andrew Rothstein to Edith's bedside at the Kingsbridge Cottage Hospital was interrogated, but all he could say was that he had not understood 'anything of [his passengers'] conversation as it was in a foreign language'.[26] There was no obvious connection to the strike.

Similarly, with Kirchenstein and Ewer the secret services drew complete blanks, as they did with their raid on the CPGB (a fact that had at least something to do with Ewer's two moles inside Special Branch). Other monitoring of ARCOS and the Russian Trade Delegation was equally disappointing – routine misbehaviour remained detectable, but there was nothing to indicate a causal link to the strike. At the time, this was interpreted as evidence of how sensitively the Bolsheviks were handling their involvement, yet in reality these were all signs that Moscow was keeping its distance from events rather than risk destroying Anglo-Soviet relations for good.

In a sense this reticence could be read as a victory for Britain's Diehards and others who had taken a strong line against Soviet misdemeanours in the past. As the historian Daniel Calhoun has written, 'the Soviet government deemed it impolitic to rhapsodise over England's agony' too openly because 'a diplomatic break with Britain would be inconvenient, and the Russian leaders did not want to give the hotheads in Baldwin's cabinet any excuse to insist on such a rupture'.[27] High-ranking Soviet politicians and officials in the Comintern actually offered little more than warm words to Britain's strikers, and even these were often combined with equally warm insults about the uselessness of the country's trade union leaders, the very people responsible for coordinating the action. At ARCOS and the Russian Trade Delegation, the new chargé d'affaires, Arkady Rosengolz, actually placed a ban on Soviet staff becoming involved in any strike-related activity.

Throughout the ten days of industrial action, the newly expanded British intelligence agencies tracked their top suspects day and night, including Andrew Rothstein. They discovered that the British ROSTA chief and Soviet spy was travelling around London's picket lines and other strike hotspots in a hired car, collecting news stories to send back to Russia. But they unearthed little else, and other avenues of inquiry terminated in similar dead ends.

What was much more telling was the letter the British intercepted on 9 June 1926, which had been sent by Rosengolz at the Soviet embassy to Rothstein at ROSTA. In it the diplomat reacts very negatively to some lines in a story Rothstein had just wired to Moscow. 'Urgent need [for] continued intensified assistance illustrated via fact [that] 400 babies born weekly [in] mining areas,' the secret agent was quoted as having written, and, 'already 2,000 babies born [to] miners families since commencement [of] lockout.' Rosengolz exclaimed that he found 'such expressions of opinion' from Rothstein 'most undesirable'. It was 'the duty of [ROSTA] to report actual facts,' he went on. 'Every Soviet institution, official or otherwise, has, as you are aware, the strictest instructions not to interfere in the internal affairs of Great Britain. In view of this, such a statement as quoted above is very imprudent.'[28] MI5 would note the outburst, and indeed filed it for posterity, but it was apparently not accorded much weight in the organisation's thinking.

The simple but inconvenient truth was that the General Strike was entirely homegrown, with the largely foreign-funded CPGB playing only a very minor role and, according to the historian James Hinton, not coordinating at all with the actions of the mainstream trade unions.[29] There was, however, just enough material indicating Soviet support for the strike to enable the government's most vehement anti-socialists to make the case that the whole saga had been 'engineered from Moscow', the phrase that Jix memorably deployed at a public meeting in Hounslow on 28 June 1926.[30] For starters, the authorities would focus on the loose ties of affiliation that existed between Britain's TUC and the equivalent body in Russia, the All-Russian Council of Trade Unions. These ties had come into being in 1924 and were known as the United Front, but there was little to them beyond friendly exchange trips and other exhortations of comradely goodwill.

Secondly, ministers collated all the positive references to the strike they could find in Soviet sources, including secret intercepts, and spun these as proof of Bolshevik orchestration. Many different bodies assisted in the effort. Keith Jeffery, in his official history of MI6, shows how on the first day following the strike the head of SIS (nominally the overseas arm of British Intelligence) sent a memorandum to Sir Wyndham Childs at Special Branch, saying he had demonstrated 'beyond doubt' that the idea of the General Strike had been 'conceived many months ago in Moscow' and that the Soviet 'directors of the movement' had used British trade unions as their 'facile accomplices'.[31] Unfortunately, we do not have access to the memorandum itself, but Jeffery reports that it links 'Soviet statements about labour activism [and] British trade union attendance at international workers' conferences and organisations such as the Anglo-Russian Trade Union Unity Committee'.[32] If this describes the document accurately, it could hardly be seen as a smoking gun, except by those who were already convinced that such a gun existed.

Thirdly, and most persuasively, the authorities seized on

the fact that Russian trade unionists had offered large sums of money to British strikers to alleviate their hardship and help prolong the industrial action. The head of Russia's equivalent of the TUC had instructed Soviet trade unionists to donate a quarter of a day's pay to support their British counterparts. More than £26,000 (over £1 million in today's money) was raised, with larger sums flowing in during the weeks and months that followed. The offer of aid was presented to TUC leaders in London, via an intercepted telegram, but it was a gift that they immediately rejected. Later, however, the long-suffering Miners' Federation of Great Britain, which was willing to take assistance from any quarter, accepted the cash – thereby giving the government its most solid proof of Soviet state interference in British affairs.

Sending aid to striking miners – the total would eventually rise to a staggering £1.2 million (equivalent to £60 million now) – was not the same as organising the strike, but this was easily brushed over by ministers and right-wing journalists. In reality, mutual assistance from workers in one country to workers in others was a venerable tradition that had nothing to do with Bolshevism: during the 1926 strike, the Russian contributions may have been the largest, but donations came in from many other overseas sources as well. Anti-strike commentators legitimately suggested that the sums given by Russian workers were surprisingly generous in light of the nation's impoverished status and there was speculation that the money had actually come from Soviet government coffers or, failing that, had been extracted from labourers' pay packets without consent. The connection between 'Red gold' and what many thought of as the most convincing attempt yet to stage a British revolution was sealed, and thus Diehards had the perfect way to demonstrate that Britain's brush with disaster had a Bolshevik cause.

Publicly, the right was in uproar throughout June and July 1926, as spokespeople for various patriotic groups joined with politicians and journalists to demand that punitive measures be taken against Britain's errant and supposedly uncontrollable labour unions. The charge of being in cahoots with Moscow was repeated endlessly. This also became the basis for the strongest calls to sever Anglo-Russian relations. On 16 June, Jix, Churchill and Lord Birkenhead approached Baldwin and recommended that he take instant, strong action against the Bolsheviks in order to protest at their involvement in the previous month's crisis. Baldwin agreed to act but, as ever, applied a large degree of caution to his plans. He would publish an official record of Soviet interference in the General Strike, he said, and write to the Soviet government rebuking it for what it had done, but he refused to go further.

Three days after seeing Baldwin, on 19 June, Winston Churchill publicly broke ranks with his boss in what may be seen as the first open skirmish in an increasingly rancorous cabinet conflict. To an audience at Alexandra Palace in London, the Chancellor of the Exchequer set out his own analysis of the General Strike and the appropriate response to it. He said that the episode had been part of the 'incessant campaign levelled upon us by the Russian Bolshevists', adding, in an echo of SIS's description of 'facile accomplices', that the Soviets 'had their dupes' within Britain's trade union movement, 'their feather-headed hirelings and allies in this country'.[33]

Wading still deeper into the waters of controversy, Churchill went on to note that 'he had heard the question asked several times, and it was a perfectly fair question: Why do you let them stay here?' He gave his own answer (which was quite different from Baldwin's): 'I am sure it would give a great deal of satisfaction if they were thrown out. Personally, I hope I shall live to see the day when either there will be a civilised Government in Russia or [. . .] we shall have ended the pretence of friendly relations with men who are seeking our overthrow.'[34]

Churchill, Jix, Kell, Childs and many others in Westminster

felt great consternation that Britain and Russia were even on speaking terms. But Baldwin's moderation, shared by Austen Chamberlain, seemed unshakeable. There was, therefore, much bafflement about what it would take to bring the 'pretence of friendly relations' to a close. In hindsight, however, successfully depicting the General Strike as a problem of Moscow's making really did mark the beginning of the end for the post-war Anglo-Russian settlement.

The BRITISH LION

FOR KING AND COUNTRY

THE OFFICIAL ORGAN OF THE BRITISH FASCISTS

(WITH WHICH IS INCORPORATED THE YORKSHIRE FASCIST WEEKLY.)

Editorial Office - - - - - - - - - 297, Fulham Road, London, S.W. 10

Phone KENS. 9486.

No. 14.   JANUARY 7, 1927.   Price TWOPENCE.

THE BRITISH FASCIST OPINION.

*'For King and Country', but certainly not for the right to a general strike,
Britain's fascists stood shoulder to shoulder with the government in its
opposition to the 1926 walkout. In advance of the dispute, a leading fascist
activist, Maxwell Knight, had developed a connection with MI5. Fascists
and Diehards were in total agreement that getting rid of the Russians was a
prerequisite for making Britain safe.*

PART 5

THE ARCOS RAID

For six years, the issue of how to deal with Soviet Russia had created significant rifts within the British state. The tensions ran not just along party lines, between left and right, but between serving British governments and the civil service and intelligence agencies that were supposed to support them. Time after time, prime ministers managed to get their own way on Russia policy, in spite of stiff opposition from their advisers and followers. Lloyd George's 1921 trade treaty had come off only after he prevented Churchill and Curzon from scuppering it. MacDonald kept his promise to renew negotiations with Moscow and, without any assistance from the Foreign Office's diplomats, he and Arthur Ponsonby had thrashed out two further treaties (although they were never ratified). Baldwin himself had three times gone against the wishes of committed anti-socialists in his party: over the Curzon Ultimatum; after the Zinoviev Letter; and now following the General Strike, when he issued only a rebuke to Russia despite what others perceived as massive, state-sponsored interference. After the middle of 1926, however, a decisive shift took place, in which Baldwin was left increasingly powerless against the Diehards in his midst.

This shift was the result of numerous factors, not least the sheer persistence of personalities like Jix and Churchill, but also – and this was perhaps the crucial change – the conversion of a critical mass of ordinary people (by no means a majority, but a highly vocal and influential minority) to the cause of getting the Russians out. Within the rank and file of the Conservative Party, support for the Diehards on the matter of Russia swelled greatly after the strike. At the party's conference, in the Yorkshire seaside resort of Scarborough, in the autumn of 1926, delegates rarely spoke of the year's dramatic labour unrest without condemning the supposedly pivotal role that Moscow had played in it, and this was underlined by an unusually harsh resolution, carried unanimously, which bore the following message:

> This conference views with alarm the continuance of subversive propaganda in this country on the part of the agents of the Union of Socialist Soviets of Russia [*sic*] and is of the opinion that, in view of the flagrant breaches by such agents of the agreement made between [the] Russian Soviet Government and Great Britain, it is in the paramount interests of our own people [that] such an agreement should be terminated forthwith and immediate arrangements made for the closing down of all official Russian Soviet Agencies in Great Britain and for the return to their own countries of all foreign personnel engaged therein.[1]

In wider society, newspaper readers were now more likely than ever to encounter articles and editorials that called for the Russians to be expelled, or that enthusiastically supported and publicised the new grassroots movements that had been founded as a result of anti-strike activism. The 'Clear Out the Reds' and 'Hands Off Britain' campaigns were the brainchildren of Commander Oliver Locker-Lampson, a Conservative MP who had served in Russia during the Great War and had seen the chaos of the revolution at first hand (he was also rumoured to have been asked to participate in the 1916 assassination of Rasputin).[2] Locker-Lampson's organisations held several mass rallies during the second half of 1926 and the first half of 1927, regularly filling the five thousand seats of the Royal Albert Hall in London. Members of the British Fascisti volunteered as stewards at these events.[3] Potently, Locker-Lampson argued that 'Bolshevism was the symbol of all that was ugly and ignoble in public life' and he asked for help in a 'crusade to strangle this hydra-headed monster'. 'The Bolshevist peril was the concern of every English citizen,' he contended, 'the crusade against it must go into every corner of the land [. . .] The "Reds" are running [. . .] Keep them running until we have driven them into the sea.'[4]

This was all music to Jix's ears. But it was a source of worry to others like Baldwin and Chamberlain, who wanted to take the heat out of Anglo-Russian relations. Chamberlain remained in charge of Britain's foreign affairs but he felt undermined. He began to despair of his ability to maintain the line of restraint that he had held for so long, writing to his sisters in early 1927: 'for the time being we have not broken with Russia [but] I fear that it will come nevertheless, before long [. . .] the toes of my colleagues are itching to kick them even tho' it be but a useless gesture'.[5]

However, most Diehards also understood that in order to get their way, and give Moscow the kicking it deserved, more than public exhortation was needed. So much previous evidence of Bolshevik misconduct had come and gone, with what seemed like untenable outrages being overlooked or swept aside by Baldwin and Chamberlain. Following the General Strike, there was, therefore, more focus – in intelligence circles in particular – on finding the one undeniable scandal that would force the Prime Minister's and Foreign Secretary's hands.

The spider's web of Soviet connections, cash and influence in Britain had long been mapped by British Intelligence, even though important knowledge gaps remained. Anti-Soviet civil servants and politicians were now determined to move on and somehow tear the web down. If previously this *modus operandi* had been clandestine and imperceptible, the authorities now took a different approach: a direct and open attack that would see the intelligence agencies emerge from the shadows into broad daylight. Finally able to bypass the leader of their country, they would go straight for the symbolic heart of Russia's presence in Britain: the headquarters of ARCOS and the Russian Trade Delegation.

16

THE LANDLORD OF THE DOLPHIN

'Week after week, we gave startling proof that the Russian revolutionaries' main objective was the destruction of the British Empire and a bloody revolution in this fair England of ours. We have been laughed at, jeered at, sneered at, but we steadily kept our course, probing into the revolutionaries' secrets.'

Advertising pamphlet for the *Morning Post* newspaper, mid-1920s[1]

For years the intelligence agencies had searched for a lucky break. In 1927, it finally looked like they got one. It came not from any existing cases or leads, but from an entirely new source: a whistle-blower who had until recently been employed by the Soviets and who had decided that he did not like what he saw.

Whistle-blowers and other kinds of tipster had been on the increase in Britain ever since the controversy of the Zinoviev Letter. The expanded media coverage of Bolshevik and Communist wrongdoing, and the importance that many politicians ascribed to it, motivated a growing number of people to come forward with their own tales of suspicious activity and dubious individuals. Typically submitted via local police, these allegations were then sent on to the relevant intelligence bodies in London, although, after investigation, they usually proved to be of little or no value – beyond providing yet more evidence of the putative omnipresence of left-wing extremism. (Early in 1927, one of the most unusual sources to land on Special Branch's desk was to arrive via the British Consul in Chicago. Harry Curran Wilbur, an American citizen who had no apparent connection with the United Kingdom or Russia, went on to correspond with British Intelligence over several months, always through the Chicago consul, sharing his conspiracy theories and antisemitic rants, which may well have been the product of a deluded mind. For a long time both Special Branch and the Indian secret service showed themselves reluctant to shut down this prodigious new source, however unhinged he might be, but eventually officials began to wonder whether he ever said 'anything of value' and if it was 'time to stop this outflow'.)[2]

The only whistle-blower who really mattered in 1927 was a man with considerably better credentials: an ex-employee of ARCOS who bore the organisation a grudge *and* had concrete evidence to back up his claims. Edward Langston – this is the first time in almost a century that his name has been associated with the ARCOS raid because declassified British Intelligence documents and historians have always referred to him as 'Y' – was a low-ranking ARCOS employee who worked in the company's photostat department from some point in the mid-1920s until February 1927, when his employment was abruptly terminated.[3]

After Lenin's death, London's Soviet organisations had become more and more fractured, mirroring the divisions in the USSR itself. Tests of loyalty were frequent, so that over time the number of non-Communist workers, which had once been quite large, diminished. Langston, whose work never seems to have been criticised, fell victim to such a test. Just before his dismissal, however, he saw which way the wind was blowing and collected sensitive information that he could use to punish his former employers after he departed.

Langston, it seems, had dreamed for some time of running his own pub. After being sacked, he moved to Uxbridge, on the outskirts of London, and set about turning this dream into reality. He took over ownership of The Dolphin, a watering hole that was picturesquely located by a bridge over the Grand

Union Canal, and began doing it up while simultaneously applying for a landlord's licence. He was still smarting from his dismissal and he, therefore, also decided to press ahead with a revenge plan; some sense of public duty undoubtedly played a part, too. Langston's tip-offs were to be unlike the others British Intelligence received, which its clerks or officers mostly glanced at, minuted and then forgot. Instead, they would go on to change the course of world events.

On 24 January 1927, when it was already clear that he was likely to lose his job, Edward Langston was hard at work in the company's basement photostat room at 49 Moorgate; a senior staff member, Joseph Dudkin, had come in and handed him a classified British army training manual, instructing him to copy it. Langston had duly made the copy, but on seeing what the document was and believing it to have no business in Soviet hands, he had secretly made an additional copy for himself. It was this document that he took to the British authorities after his dismissal from ARCOS. He did so not via the traditional route of going to a police station and having a frustrating conversation with a weary, sceptical sergeant at a front desk, but through an unusual sequence of events that brought him almost instantly into contact with British Intelligence. Langston, it turned out, had a friend in ARCOS (also British) who was the neighbour of an SIS officer called Bertie Maw. (How this friend, who is referred to in the archives only as 'X', came to know Maw is a mystery, as is the matter of whether or not 'X' was formally in SIS's pay, though we can probably assume he was.) In any case, Langston confided in 'X' about the document and 'X' recommended that he meet his secretive neighbour. The would-be publican duly agreed and went on to tell his story to the SIS officer face-to-face. Maw, highly interested, told him he should expect further contact with the secret services in the very near future.

Later that same day, Sir Hugh Sinclair, the head of SIS, nobly resisted the temptation to claim the case as his own (it was not uncommon in the interwar period for the intelligence agencies to usurp each other's powers) and instead passed it to MI5, whose rightful duty it was to investigate all threats to the British armed forces arising within the United Kingdom's borders. There then ensued six weeks of interviews with 'X' and Langston. These took place both at The Dolphin and in central London. For one of them, Sidney Russell Cooke – Clare Sheridan's friend and Oswald Harker's brother-in-law – offered Harker the use of his flat, a secluded residence located on King's Bench Walk within the walls of the Temple (a kind of impromptu safe house and perhaps, therefore, an indication that in the 1920s MI5 could not afford permanent safe houses of its own).

Meanwhile, Sir Vernon Kell and Harker also checked out various aspects of Langston's story. They established that the manual he had photostatted was intended to show army officers how to use a piece of basic signalling equipment, and managed to trace the original stolen copy back to the British Army's biggest barracks, in Aldershot, where the commanding officer confirmed that one (at least one, he said!) of his assigned copies was missing. Kell and Harker ascertained that there was nothing obvious in Langston's past which meant he could not be trusted. It was, of course, theoretically possible that he was a stooge put up by the Soviet authorities to deceive and embarrass the British, but the man appeared to have no connections to the CPGB and his anger at his old employers seemed both genuine and deep.

The files make clear that MI5 treated this case with the utmost urgency. And yet the wheels ground agonisingly slowly, with officers constantly distracted by other projects and generally struggling to keep on top of their workload. This meant that the initial inquiries lasted through March and April. Kell had known from the beginning that Langston's document had the makings of a major public scandal. But it was not until MI5's investigations were nearing an end in early May that he finally decided to brief ministers about what had come to seem a shocking and sensational theft. If this indicated an admirable degree of restraint on Kell's part, it also meant a very long gap had opened up since the moment when Joseph Dudkin was last known to have had the manual at ARCOS headquarters – around one hundred days. Ordinarily this time lag might have been considered a significant limitation on the options the authorities had open to them.

On 11 May, Kell went to see the War Secretary (his official boss, Sir Laming Worthington-Evans) and, on Evans's advice, headed immediately to brief the Home Secretary, William Joynson-Hicks, accompanied by the head of Special Branch. At this second meeting, Kell described in detail what Langston had done and how it meant British Intelligence could now prove that classified military documents had been inside ARCOS. Jix was outraged at what he heard and, after pausing momentarily, shouted at the top of his voice: 'Raid ARCOS!', adding, 'Do you want it in writing?'[4]

The Home Secretary made no demand for further inquiries, no request for a night to sleep on the information before reaching a decision. There was no desire on his part to test the strength of Kell's evidence, nor any demand for alternative scenarios to be considered, nor even a perceived obligation to consult with his cabinet colleagues in advance. After two and a half years of frustration, this opportunity was exactly what he had been waiting for and he grabbed it.

During the preceding months, Jix had done his best to keep up pressure on Baldwin to take action against the Russians. He had, of course, continued to see plenty that justified such action (though nothing as clear cut as Langston's signals manual). At the annual dinner of the Primrose League on 7 March 1927, Jix had initially stuck to the government line in a speech before switching and, like Churchill before him, making it clear that he felt official policy on Russia was too soft. He started out by saying that it was better 'the cup should be filled to the brim rather than that his Majesty's Government by one false or one hasty step should have acted too soon'. There were 'limits', he went on, 'beyond which it [was] dangerous to drive [. . .] temperate self-respecting people'; the Bolsheviks had already pushed the British Empire 'almost to the extent' that it would 'allow them to go'. However, just before he finished, he added that he was 'not quite sure that we have not reached the limit of toleration in our own midst of a body of men who are out to destroy what we hold dear'.[5]

Jix now set the police and secret services the task of retrieving the stolen signals manual from ARCOS's headquarters at 49 Moorgate. This raises the possibility – impossible to verify – that Kell did not draw the Home Secretary's attention to the significant amount of time that had passed since the document had last been seen inside the building. Similarly, Kell may not have emphasised to Jix the ordinary nature of the manual – though in this instance it seems likely that neither man would have drawn much distinction between one sort of classified military document and another. Crucially, from their point of view, the front cover of the pamphlet carried the following unambiguous warning:

FOR OFFICIAL USE ONLY
THIS DOCUMENT IS THE PROPERTY OF H[IS] B[RITANNIC]
M[AJESTY'S] GOVERNMENT
NOTE
The information given in this document is not to be communicated,
either directly or indirectly, to the Press or to any person not holding
an official position in His Majesty's Service.[6]

In any event, Jix, Kell and Childs, along with others in the security community, felt certain that the manual provided sufficient grounds for raiding ARCOS and that it could easily be presented to the media and to their supporters in the House of Commons and the wider establishment as evidence of an escalation in Soviet aggression. These men were also convinced – as they had been for years – that once they got into the Moorgate offices they would find far more than just a single stolen document.

After the meeting had concluded, the Home Secretary found Stanley Baldwin and Austen Chamberlain and retrospectively sought ratification for what he was about to do. He did not mention the weaknesses he may have been aware of in the Langston case: neither the delay nor the document's moderate-to-low sensitivity. Afterwards, both Baldwin and Chamberlain would feel that they had been informed in great haste of a *fait accompli*, and also that the grounds for Jix's proposed action, as presented to them, had been somewhat exaggerated. But at the time they had to admit the seriousness of a proven act of military espionage and, weary of restraining their reactionary colleagues over so many years, conceded that the long-feared Anglo-Soviet altercation must now occur.

The following afternoon, on 12 May, two hundred police officers gathered near the ARCOS offices in the heart of the City of London. It was a Thursday and, in order not to give the Russians advance notice of what they were planning, the authorities left Moorgate itself open. Dozens of pedestrians and people on buses and in cars were, therefore, present at the moment when the lead officers first banged on the front door of ARCOS and then started piling into the entrance hall. A posse of British spies and senior civil servants appeared on the scene as well, but they were more inconspicuous. Working together, this small army went on to turn ARCOS's six floors and more than one hundred individual offices upside down, searching every employee – more than five hundred in all – and leaving not a single floorboard or piece of wooden panelling unexamined.

'Raid ARCOS!' the Home Secretary had said. And finally an endgame of sorts had begun.

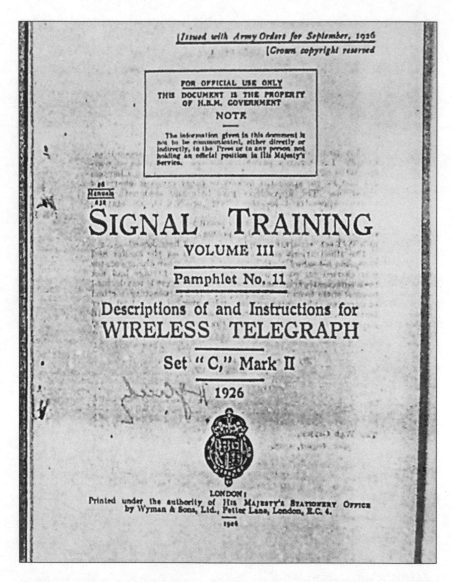

Signal Training, *Volume 3, Pamphlet no. 11, was never likely to be the lynchpin of a Soviet military invasion of Britain, but as its front cover shows – and as the ARCOS employee Edward Langston instantly spotted – the Official Secrets Act made it an offence for a Soviet employee to have this document in his possession. This, therefore, was the basis for the ARCOS raid that started on 12 May 1927.*

17

ONE IN THE EYE FOR LENIN

The raid was long, very long, by the standards of police raids in any era. A typical search for stolen goods lasts just a few hours and almost all are completed within a day. But the ARCOS raid was to stretch over five days, from Thursday 12 May 1927 until Monday 16 May. Apart from the large number of policemen and officials engaged at the scene, it also involved scores of people at the Home Office, the Foreign Office, MI5 and Special Branch, including top civil servants, every available intelligence officer, and as many trustworthy Russian-English translators as could be found.

In response to a request from Oswald Harker, the City of London magistrate, Sir Charles Batho, had issued a warrant allowing the search for the missing signals manual to go ahead. But this was never intended to be just a quest for a single document. The police were under orders to requisition everything that might be helpful in assembling a watertight case against Moscow and accordingly the effort was massive. They were told not to allow any ARCOS employees to leave the site without being searched, and not to leave behind any material of possible interest, however small. A gargantuan haul of evidence was seized, a haul so big that it had to be taken from 49 Moorgate in lorries, so as to be studied in greater detail at a range of government locations.

There was obvious disappointment when the searchers finally confirmed that no signals manual was among the spoils. But supporters of the raid, including Jix, did not get overly worried. It would have been satisfyingly clear and simple to discover the document inside the building, since so much was known about how it had got there. But, failing that, there was believed to be no cause for panic. On the contrary, all the early indications were that a mass of other suggestive and incriminatory evidence would come to light.

Acting on Langston's descriptions, a detachment of police had immediately made its way to the ARCOS basement, bursting into the photostat department and proceeding to search its occupants before going over the entire space in minute detail. Though they did not find the signals manual, the raiders saw much else that concerned them. They took special note of the inordinate number of different alarm mechanisms that the Russians had in place, alongside prominently displayed warnings that this part of the building was out of bounds to all but authorised personnel. There were also metal bars on the walls, which the police decided must be weapons to defend the space from attack (none of these so-called 'life preservers' was pressed into service on the day of the raid). On searching Langston's replacement, a man called Robert Koling, officers found envelopes in his pockets bearing the addresses of known Communists in Britain and America. And, upon later analysis, the contents of these envelopes turned out to include 'information and directions' from the Comintern to British and American left-wing organisations. As an internal Home Office report put it, this showed that 'ARCOS and the Trade Delegation [had] been habitually used as a clearing house for subversive correspondence'.[1]

Elsewhere, just minutes after entering the building, a second group of officers had come across a locked door. After seeing through its frosted glass panelling that some sort of frantic activity was taking place inside, they had forced the door open.

According to Inspector Clancy, everything about the room and its occupants gave cause for grave concern. 'On entering the room I observed that a quantity of paper was burning in the fire place,' Clancy wrote:

> I asked a man, whom I now know as Anton Miller, what he was burning and he replied in broken English 'decoded telegrams'. Noticing a steel deed box in front of Miller I asked him if the papers which had been burned were taken from this box. He did not reply to my question but after a few moments' hesitation addressed a remark in the Russian language to a man whom I now know as Khoudiakoff, as a result of which both rushed to obtain possession of the deed box. I restrained the man Miller who became extremely violent. The other man became so violent that it required the assistance of five officers to prevent him injuring personal property. During the struggle a bundle of papers fell from the breast jacket pocket of the man Miller. I picked these papers [up] and, noticing that they included a number of addresses, I put them out of reach of Miller.
>
> I might mention that P.C. Dore of the Special Branch, who is a fluent Russian scholar, informed me that he asked Khoudiakoff in Russian why he was burning these papers and he replied, 'we did not want the Police to get them'.[2]

When experts went through the papers, they concluded that these were lists of 'legal' and 'illegal' addresses of Comintern secret agents overseas – that is to say, the addresses to which, respectively, overt and covert information was sent. As Sir Wyndham Childs set out in a note, 'the documents are in fact the key to the underground movement of the Third International throughout the British Empire and foreign countries'.[3] The countries named included Australia, Canada, New Zealand, South Africa, Argentina, Brazil, Chile, Columbia, Guatemala, Mexico and Uruguay. Meanwhile, Miller's closely guarded metal deed box turned out to contain secret cyphers that were clearly for use by ARCOS staff when sending sensitive letters and telegrams.

Some time later, as they explored a room that housed the records of ARCOS's internal branch of the Soviet Communist Party, police came across an empty box-folder labelled 'Anti-British Propaganda'.[4] Elsewhere, they found a small number of rifles (estimates in the archives and other reports vary from one to five) and, underneath the carpet in several parts of the building and behind wooden panels on the walls, secret compartments. When officers asked ARCOS staff to open the safes that were inside some of these compartments and otherwise dotted throughout the premises, they met with absolute refusal. In some instances, keys were confiscated from their owners without permission. But when it proved impossible to gain access to the very large walk-in safes in the ARCOS basements – situated next to the photostat room – the authorities decided to use pneumatic road drills and oxyacetylene torches to blast and burn their way through the reinforced-concrete walls instead.

Certainly, the early findings of the raid offered anti-Soviet organisers much hope. And, while all this ought to have remained secret from the public until such time as the government decided to make it officially known, during the five-day raid Britain's major newspapers were in a position to carry many hints, and often much fuller leaks, of what the police were up to and what they were discovering. These leaks came from various sources: police themselves (an unusually large proportion of whom were in the pay of journalists during this era); angry employees of ARCOS and the Russian Trade Delegation; MPs and activists who claimed some sort of access to privileged information; and probably (though it cannot be confirmed) British Intelligence operatives.

'Raided at last' was the headline in the *Daily Mail* on the morning after the dramatic incursion. 'The public will learn with the utmost satisfaction that the police yesterday made a thorough search of the premises of ARCOS, the Soviet establishment in the City of London [. . .] The country will welcome the Government's vigorous action the more if it means that Ministers are going at last to do what the public and *The Daily Mail* have so long been urging upon them – to turn the Moscow plotters out bag and baggage.' Articles on other pages mentioned the meticulous search that had been made of the 'photographic department' and the discovery of the 'rifles and life preservers'.[5] Subsequently, another article described these objects as being 'far worse than any specimen in the "Black Museum" at Scotland Yard', so 'only a slight blow [. . .] would be sufficient to kill a person'.[6]

On Saturday 14 May, newspapers then revelled in the arrival in Moorgate of the pneumatic drills. According to *The Times*:

> [The] safes are really strong rooms, built of concrete and guarded by thick, heavy steel doors with enormously strong locks and bolts, and the only way of opening them in the absence of the keys was by drilling round the locks and then forcing the doors. During the afternoon arrangements were made with a firm to do the necessary work, and about 8 o'clock last night a powerful pneumatic drilling apparatus was taken to Moorgate [. . .] A gang of skilled workmen conveyed the tools into the building, went down to the vaults, and at once began operations on one of the two strong rooms. The noise of the pneumatic drills as they pierced steel and concrete was like the staccato sounds of the drills used in breaking up concrete roads, and could be

distinctly heard by the interested crowd assembled in Moorgate.[7]

The Times later said these strongrooms, along with much else in the building, demonstrated that ARCOS was a 'sinister establishment', 'the most powerful engine' in the Soviet state's 'hostile battery'.[8]

After two more days of shocked and sensational coverage, the raid came to an end on the evening of Monday 16 May. A Soviet official closed and padlocked the iron gates of 49 Moorgate behind the last police officer to depart. The headline on the *Daily Mail*'s main editorial the next morning had an air of finality about it: 'The People Know Their Own Minds'. The paper argued that the British public now demanded that 'the Cabinet, having taken the first step, shall at last muster up courage to rid us of the Red menace in our midst'.[9] There was hope, expressed here and in anti-Bolshevik circles more widely, that the resolution would be swift. How could Anglo-Soviet relations survive such revelations? What more needed to be discovered before the state would take decisive action?

And yet, during the week after the raid the familiar pattern of vacillation and delay seemed to re-emerge. Official silence reigned and a number of planned ministerial statements were postponed without explanation. In the country, some radical anti-socialists began to express dismay. The case against the Russians was as clear-cut as any they could imagine. The severity of the actions that the police had taken and the nature of what they had reportedly retrieved surely meant that anything short of a complete break in Anglo-Soviet relations was unthinkable. Could Baldwin and Chamberlain somehow evade doing their duty once again?

It is debatable whether Jix, Churchill and Lord Birkenhead shared the anxiety felt by their supporters. They understood that as soon as the authorities had entered the ARCOS building, a fundamental line had been crossed. Almost irrespective of what the police found – and these men all believed the stash of evidence to be compelling – the raid itself meant that the Prime Minister had little or no room for manoeuvre. A raid on this scale which did not culminate in a diplomatic breach would be widely interpreted as a failure. The left would accuse the government of having succumbed to dangerous paranoia and sabre-rattling, while supporters of campaigns like 'Clear Out the Reds' might well take to the streets in anger. The state could not seize possession of the trading arm of a foreign country one weekend and then continue normal relations with that country the next.

So it was that, eventually, on Tuesday 24 May 1927 Stanley Baldwin stood before a packed House of Commons to announce that Britain's diplomatic relationship with the USSR was at an end. He spoke at length and in his usual measured tones. Some thought his words tinged with reluctance and regret, but his conclusion was nonetheless emphatic. In a formulation that Lord Curzon had first used back in 1923, he started by asserting that 'His Majesty's Government' had shown 'patience and forbearance' towards Russia that was 'probably without a parallel in international relations', and then went on to say that this could no longer continue. 'Diplomatic relations when thus deliberately and systematically abused are themselves a danger to peace and His Majesty's Government have therefore decided that [. . .] they will terminate the Trade Agreement, require the withdrawal of the Trade Delegation and Soviet Mission from London and recall the British Mission from Moscow.'[10]

Elation surged through the right wing of Baldwin's party and among its backers in the press and in patriotic groups. Many Diehard MPs who were present in the chamber wanted to rise to their feet and congratulate the Prime Minister there and then, but he encouraged all members to reserve both remarks and questions for a separate day-long debate later in the week. It was on Thursday 26 May, therefore, when the House gathered for that debate, that the fate of Britain's Soviet diplomats was finally sealed, with the government's large majority backing the proposed expulsion 346 votes to 98.[11]

When Jix spoke in the debate, his own sense of triumph was clear. There was, he said, no country on earth which had 'degraded itself in the manner in which [. . .] Russia has'. He went on to state proudly that 'we [i.e. the government] are responsible for our actions, and we stand by those actions'. 'We make no apology for the course we have adopted and we intend to see that course carried out to its conclusion.'[12] For the firebrand Home Secretary, it was a fairly measured and mature performance – until, that is, he turned to the opposition benches to direct a broadside at the Labour Party. 'I have just one sentence to say in reply to the Opposition,' he began. 'On our side of the House, and I believe outside the House, there is a real patriotic endeavour to support Great Britain in these very difficult and troublesome circumstances. I say to the party opposite that until they realise that Great Britain is not always wrong, and that her enemies are not always right, they never will be able to represent this country.'[13]

The founder of 'Clear Out the Reds', Oliver Locker-Lampson, also spoke, making use of highly coloured and expressive language as he addressed his colleagues. Pointedly, he congratulated Jix rather than Baldwin or the cabinet as a whole. He praised the Home Secretary for 'his courageous and forceful visitation of the pirates' premises last week', by which means Jix 'has in effect stamped out the red rot which promised to spread everywhere and to ruin us'. Locker-Lampson continued:

> Indeed, there is only one element about the raid on ARCOS which can be considered as in any degree mistaken, and that is that [it] did not come sooner [. . .] The mystery house of ARCOS [was] a nest of

pestilential propaganda and [. . .] septic intrigue [. . .]
The discovery of this warren in the heart of peaceful
London explodes forever the fetish of Soviet affection
for England [. . .] What has been the answer of His
Majesty's Government to [. . .] assaults in the past? In
the name of peace [. . .] we have pleaded moderation
and have fed the Bolshevist bear – when he growled
– with buns. We had far better given him the knout
or the boot. He would have understood them a great
deal better.[14]

Locker-Lampson was just one among many Diehard Tories
who viewed the impending diplomatic breach as something
akin to an act of national renewal, hoping that there might now
be a post-war renaissance in Britain's self-respect and global
standing, and that Bolshevism's end might be nigh. 'This debate
[. . .] is historic,' he intoned. '[The government] recognise that
no longer can a proud people tolerate the shame of bondage to
a state of slaves. They have cut us free. Long may we remain
masters of our liberty.' He then expressed the conviction that,
shorn of British recognition, 'Bolshevism as a world force [was]
doomed'. 'The Communist state in Russia,' he said, 'enthroned
and strong though it be there now, could not continue and will
not continue if we do our duty tonight and throw out Russian
recognition.'[15] This was still an era – though only just – when
British politicians could claim such power and supremacy on behalf
of their country and not sound preposterous. In a private letter
to his friend Lord Irwin, the Viceroy of India, also dated 26 May,
Lord Birkenhead said he was 'personally [. . .] delighted' and
that he was able to 'breathe quite differently now that we have
purged our capital of these unclean and treacherous elements'.[16]

The Russians began leaving the United Kingdom the day
after the debate, Friday 27 May, and took some three weeks in
total to depart. Special Branch and MI5 both drew up blacklists

in order to track the most dangerous Bolsheviks as they left. In the event, however, Moscow's orders were for Soviet citizens to leave the country *en masse* and there do not appear to have been any attempts by secret agents who were Soviet nationals to remain. Many departed through the East Anglian port of Harwich, while others took trains from London's Victoria Station to Dover. In both instances, steamers delivered them to the continent from where they continued their journeys east. But to speed the Bolsheviks on their way, Britain's right-wing media and politicians treated them to a barrage of negative commentary. Articles in the press continued to push for even harsher responses from the government. Why were the Russians being allowed to take so long to collect their belongings and leave? Why had none of the evil-doers been arrested and put on trial instead of facing expulsion? Perhaps most shockingly of all, the *Morning Post* published the names and London addresses of a number of top Soviet officials.[17] The only apparent reason to do so was to encourage readers to send hate mail to these individuals or, worse, incite more direct kinds of vigilante action.

Come the end of June, most traces of ARCOS had vanished. The building at 49 Moorgate was more or less deserted. The keys to many other Soviet businesses and to the embassy at Chesham House had been surrendered. A skeleton staff stayed behind to maintain any contracts that Moscow decided to honour, and there remained just one or two contested cases of expulsion for British Intelligence and the Foreign Office to work through, but most of these were very slight. (A good example is the case of Fanny Karlinsky, a Russian-born woman who had worked at ARCOS but who had been living in the United Kingdom since 1909. The complicating factor here was that, in 1923, Fanny had accepted Soviet citizenship and a Soviet passport. She had never, however, set foot in the Soviet state and, sensibly, now wanted to remain in Britain. To resolve the matter, authorities contacted her old Oxford college, Somerville, for a testimonial.

Based on this they allowed her to stay: to turn 'this woman out', one official wrote, would be 'straining at a gnat'.)[18]

More broadly, the mood of right-wing jubilation continued for many months. During mid-July, the 'Hands Off Britain' campaign held a 'Victory Rally' at the Royal Albert Hall 'to celebrate routing the Reds'. Commander Locker-Lampson was there (of course) and spoke about the 'crimson ramblers' of Moscow becoming 'scarlet runners', while 'England stood free once again'. Also invited were a number of right-wing activists from France, who congratulated their British friends on the ARCOS raid and said that 'they hoped that the French Government, following the example of Britain and Italy' (Mussolini's Italy), would soon take measures to punish the Bolsheviks too. 'The fight was between the Soviet and civilisation,' they said. 'Great Britain had given to the world a great example [. . .] in that great fight'.[19]

When police raided the ARCOS headquarters, they signalled the end of the Soviet presence in Britain. A member of the ARCOS staff had already turned their calendar to the next day's date before officers took control of the building on Thursday 12 May 1927. It is thought, however, that it was a British police officer who mischievously, and many would say disrespectfully, squirted ink in Lenin's face.

18

ONE IN THE FOOT FOR BRITAIN?

'I expect you would sooner hear about ARCOS than about the garden. The warrant was to search ARCOS for a stolen Govt. document – a military manual, I think – which the police had good reason to know was or had been in their hands. When I last heard, they had not found it, but at that time they had not opened the safes, some of which were concealed behind panelling and some bedded in deep concrete in the basement. I can only trust that they will find something worth all the fuss. They and we will look foolish if they don't, but to tell you the truth I have no great faith in Sir Wyndham Childs or in some of his people.'

Austen Chamberlain, letter to his sisters, 15 May 1927,
The Austen Chamberlain Diary Letters

Upon retaking control of the ARCOS building on Monday 16 May 1927, the Russians were greatly shocked. The extent of the devastation that had been wreaked within was so enormous that it was clear the British government's actions had been motivated at least partly by spite and a desire to humiliate. Although the Bolsheviks themselves knew how to play tough, they were genuinely taken aback by what confronted them. They found devastated basements and corridors, torn carpets and splintered walls. It was like a bomb site. Shelves had been stripped of their books and folders, which had either been seized by the raiders, or strewn across the floor. Chairs had been knocked over and desks pushed aside in the police's hunt for trapdoors and secret compartments. On a Soviet wall calendar, Lenin's face had been deliberately splattered with ink.

In the days following the raid, protest statements from the Soviet government and its sympathisers drew attention to these perceived injuries and made more serious allegations as well. Ordinarily, Stanley Baldwin and Austen Chamberlain would have dismissed such Russian criticism as hyperbole or downright mendacity, but they now had their own concerns about Jix's and the police's actions. When Chamberlain wrote to his sisters on Sunday 15 May he still hoped that Jix would succeed in finding enough material to justify the raid. Very quickly, however, the Foreign Secretary was thrown into a damage-limitation exercise – one that, despite its scale, was unable to remove the impression that Britain's government had acted without due process and in a dangerously inflammatory way at 49 Moorgate.

Some in Britain, including many who were not Communists, had objected publicly to the raid from the start. Members of the Labour Party, for instance, had suspected a conspiracy because the raid coincided with a series of parliamentary debates on the new Trade Disputes and Trade Unions Bill, the government's controversial response to the General Strike (this was actually just a coincidence). The *Manchester Guardian* and other centrist and centre-left publications had worried, with more reason, about Jix's propensity to exaggeration and overreaction. 'Presumably Sir William Joynson-Hicks was not completely light-headed when he ordered the raid on ARCOS offices yesterday in London,' the *Manchester Guardian* mused on Friday 13 May, before voicing its own scepticism in coruscating terms:

> No one could reasonably describe him as a man of balanced judgment where Communists are concerned, but he is, after all, a Secretary of State and fully conscious of the responsibilities of that position. He cannot have sanctioned so serious a step without what

he at least believed to be strong *prima facie* evidence
that criminal proceedings were afoot. [. . .] A similar
raid was carried out eighteen months ago on the
headquarters of the British Communists with singularly
inconspicuous results. The memory of it may rankle
in the mind of the Home Secretary, but that should
be rather a warning than an encouragement to repeat
the experiment [. . .] If the Home Secretary should
be found to have discovered another mare's nest
[i.e. a much-trumpeted revelation that subsequently
turns out to be unimportant] it will be really time that
he should be removed to a sphere in which he can
indulge this peculiar hobby with less danger to serious
business and international relations.[1]

This sentiment was doubtless shared by Austen Chamberlain
as he began to engage with official Soviet reactions to the
raid. It was instantly clear that the Bolshevik regime was not
just objecting to the manner of the incursion, but believed the
search to be illegal in principle. This, the Russians said, was
because 49 Moorgate was the main office for both ARCOS and
the Russian Trade Delegation. While the former was a public
limited company registered in the United Kingdom and subject
to normal British law, the latter was an international entity
enjoying special privileges agreed by treaty and through long-
standing diplomatic conventions. Russia contended that there
was not 'the least doubt that the violent irruption of the police
into the premises of the Trade Delegation and the acts they
committed there [were] a flagrant violation of the Agreement
of 1921', while the British had also been guilty of ignoring 'the
requirements of international law' and subjecting individuals
who had 'the right of diplomatic immunity' to 'offensive
handling' by the British police.[2]

To Jix and his supporters in government, all this ran like water off a duck's back, but Chamberlain and – once he had been briefed – Stanley Baldwin instantly saw that it was of vital importance.[3] The substance of the Soviets' allegations was easy to confirm: 49 Moorgate, whose official name was Soviet House, was indeed the headquarters of both organisations, and the Russian Trade Delegation did enjoy privileges that made it corporately entitled to diplomatic immunity. In addition, several senior members of the delegation were also entitled to personal immunity, a right usually considered to extend to such individuals' offices, desks and paperwork as well as their physical person. The delegation was explicitly allowed to use codes and ciphers, and its premises were, in legal terms, defined as extraterritorial, meaning that the relevant sections of 49 Moorgate were effectively Soviet, rather than British, land. Worse still, no British official had ever thought it necessary to agree with the Russians precisely which parts of 49 Moorgate these were. It was arguable, therefore, that the whole building was a Soviet enclave with internationally protected status.

The Foreign Office frantically set about trying to pin down what had gone wrong with the planning of the raid. Having violated Russian diplomatic privileges, Britain's reputation for decency and fair play was on the line, as was the inviolability of *British* diplomatic property elsewhere in the world. If a state like Britain could march into other countries' diplomatic premises and ransack them, what was to stop other nations doing the same to British embassies and consulates?

Chamberlain demanded to know from the Home Office and British Intelligence whether they had intended to raid the Russian Trade Delegation and, if so, on what grounds. As the archives show, the answers he received deeply worried him. No one, it appeared, had even considered the Trade Delegation's special status before raiding it. The text of the search warrant Harker had drafted – which had been reviewed by the Director of Public Prosecutions – mentioned both ARCOS and the Trade

Delegation but made no allowance for the latter's special rights: it was 'a SEARCH WARRANT [. . .] to enter certain premises [. . .] occupied by and known as ARCOS Limited and the Russian Trade Delegation and therein to search the said premises so occupied and as aforesaid and every person found'.[4] Jix and the secret services had behaved as if they could go wherever they pleased, which indeed they believed. But, as a note of a meeting between the Home and Foreign Secretaries recorded, 'Sir Austen [felt] it might be difficult to defend the issue of such a warrant against the premises of the Trade Delegation'.[5]

In later discussions, some government officials attempted to argue that the Trade Delegation's immunity extended no further than the person of its head, the official agent, a man who had happened to be out of the country when the raid occurred. The Foreign Office, however, believed that his immunity 'must be held to cover more than the mere person of the agent. In order to give any value to such immunity it must cover the papers and archives of the agent.' The Foreign Office clearly had the matter of precedents in mind and this led its representatives to side with Moscow (albeit privately) by contending that 'any search of the papers of the Trade Delegation would be a violation of the [Anglo-Soviet] Agreement'.[6] Chamberlain and the diplomats who worked for him could then only fall back on the forlorn hope that what the police had found in the raid would be so staggering as to excuse the infringement. In strictly legal terms, however, the police raid on ARCOS looked like nothing short of a small-scale British invasion of Russia.

The other main cause of Soviet anger was the brutishness and excessive aggression of the raiding party. Here the boundaries between truth and lies were harder to pin down. While some evidence was undeniable (the pneumatic drills in the basement, the struggles between Inspector Clancy, Anton Miller and others) much relied on accounts which inevitably came from biased sources. The Bolsheviks' most eye-catching claim related to a series of allegations that female members of staff had been mistreated. In one letter of protest, which was reprinted widely in the British press, Mr Rosengolz, the chargé d'affaires, said:

> I must point out that during the raid the most ele-
> mentary guarantees and demands of common decency
> were violated. [. . .] All the employees of ARCOS and
> of the Trade Delegation, both men and women, were
> detained and subjected to a personal search. Among
> those detained were women possessing diplomatic
> passports [. . .] The personal search of the women was
> carried out by male police officers.[7]

These assertions were elaborated on in a number of sworn statements from 49 Moorgate's Soviet staff, statements that were sent to the Foreign Office and then hastily published by a group of CPGB members as an English-language booklet: *The Raid on ARCOS Ltd. and the Trade Delegation of the USSR: Facts and Documents*.[8]

According to the official British version of events, the police had indeed been under instructions to search all employees before allowing them to leave the building, but the authorities categorically denied that any woman had been frisked by male officers, or – worse still – that women had only been allowed to go to the toilet if accompanied by policemen. Only the women's handbags had been examined, ministers later said. Yet the claims of manhandling received considerable coverage and probably played well among those Britons who distrusted the police anyway. More generally, they supported an impression that the raid had been frenzied and ill-disciplined.

Each new claim by the Russians made the question of the quality of the material the police had seized more and more important. For anyone who was worried about the raid's legality, the failure to find the missing signals manual was damning. It meant that whatever else came to light would be the spoils of a fishing expedition, and would have to be sufficiently extreme to justify Jix's dramatic action. On this front, Chamberlain and Baldwin soon found themselves with another huge problem: just when they needed to be at the top of their game, Special Branch and the Home Office co-authored a first account of the raid's discoveries that was singularly unpersuasive.

Jix had initially placed his draft account before the cabinet on the morning of Thursday 19 May, three days after the raid and just a few hours before he intended to deliver an update to the House of Commons. Chamberlain was immediately concerned by the document's flimsiness and demanded that the Home Secretary postpone his public statement. Not only did the report confirm that the stolen manual was still missing, but it also made clear that no other British government paperwork had been found in the Soviet premises. The authors of the document, without stopping to address these glaring holes in their case, proceeded to focus on the things that had been found: the aforementioned ciphers; the list of public and secret Comintern addresses; and the suspect behaviour of staff members like Anton Miller. But Chamberlain saw inadequacies in all this evidence. Ciphers, as everyone would soon know, were explicitly permitted under the Anglo-Russian Treaty, and it would be very hard to demonstrate that any particular cipher had been used for illegitimate rather than legitimate purposes. Comintern secrecy was a well-known fact that had been established over and over through dozens of different sources; this was hardly likely to strike most ordinary people as a persuasive reason for deploying two hundred officers to make an assault on a pro-tected building. Finally, the behaviour of ARCOS staff, while clearly connected with attempts to conceal illegal activity, might now easily be explained as a reasonable defence of the Russian Trade Delegation's threatened diplomatic immunity. (By this point, even the much-vaunted matter of rifles had lost its potency; Soviet officials had produced evidence that these were just samples of British-made hunting guns that the Russian government had been considering purchasing in bulk.)

According to the Secretary of State for the Colonies, Leo Amery, who took part in that Thursday's cabinet discussion, Jix's report came across as 'colourless'.[9] A later inquiry went further, slamming it as 'an unconvincing production'.[10] Chamberlain now took over responsibility for trying to salvage the best story possible from the mound of irrelevant and trivial information that police had taken from 49 Moorgate. Indeed, having feared that such a situation might arise, the Foreign Secretary had already begun work on an alternative way to present the facts. In this task he would be assisted by SIS, the wing of British Intelligence that had originally encountered Langston but which subsequently had had least to do with the raid. Sir Hugh Sinclair, head of SIS, had only been told about the incursion two and a half hours before police entered Soviet House; he would now have the chance to vent his anger and wreak professional revenge on his careless colleague Sir Vernon Kell.

The Foreign Secretary and SIS quickly concluded that there was no possible configuration of existing evidence that would supply a sufficiently convincing explanation for the raid and hence a watertight justification for breaking off diplomatic relations. They therefore decided to fall back on the earlier part of Langston's story (which, bizarrely, Jix's report had dealt with only in passing) and on other pre-existing allegations of military espionage, including the Kirchenstein case. They chose to augment this narrative with translations from a selection of recently intercepted Soviet telegrams. Of course, all this evidence might have been assembled without ever entering ARCOS – a nuance that was not lost on the demoralised Foreign Secretary – but what mattered now was to save Britain's reputation and try to fix Jix's mess.

In his speech to parliament on 24 May, the Prime Minister

displayed the fruits of this hard work. Naturally, he devoted a significant amount of time to describing the raid. But in a departure from what listeners might have been expecting, he began and ended his address with unconnected examples of Russian wrongdoing. To start with, he gave a general account of British Intelligence's other investigations into Russian military espionage, implying a direct connection between these and the discovery of the missing manual – a connection that was not fully supported by the facts, but that served to make the raid sound more rational and less of a knee-jerk reaction. Moving on, he revealed the contents of some of the intercepted telegrams (details of others then followed in a government white paper).

Among the material there appeared a familiar name, that of Mikhail Borodin. He had recently been appointed the Soviet state's *de facto* representative in China, and had begun attacking Britain's considerable commercial and political interests there. In response to previous questioning from the British government, Moscow had been adamant that Borodin was just a private individual who happened to be living in China. But in a coded telegram from 12 November 1926, which GC&CS had intercepted, the Soviet government told its own employees that 'until a Soviet representative is appointed to Peking Comrade Borodin is to take his orders direct from Moscow'.[11]

The Prime Minister also described another communication, dated 13 April 1927, in which Rosengolz had been caught wiring the Commissariat of Foreign Affairs in Moscow to warn about 'the possibility of a raid on our [London] Embassy'. Though he 'very much doubt[ed]' that this raid would happen, he said it would be 'very useful', as a 'measure of precaution, to suspend for a time the forwarding by post of documents of "friends", "neighbours" and so forth from London to Moscow and *vice versa*.'[12] British government officials correctly interpreted the words 'friends' and 'neighbours' to be simple code for secret agents, and Baldwin told MPs that it was 'unnecessary' for him 'to speculate as to the character of the documents about which [Rosengolz had] showed such anxiety'.[13] This was probably the most compelling piece of evidence that the government presented, yet – possibly deliberately – it also contained an implicit rebuke for Jix. Had the Home Secretary acted less hastily on 11 and 12 May, the government might well have considered the possibility that Soviet buildings had already been cleansed of incriminating evidence because of the general deterioration in Anglo-Russian relations. Did Jix's vociferous anti-Bolshevism, in the months running up to May 1927, help explain the slim pickings that police came away with?

In the main internal government inquiry into the ARCOS raid, which occurred during June 1927, there was to be savage criticism of many aspects of the police's, MI5's and the Home Office's work. The inquiry was ordered personally by an angry Prime Minister and carried out by the Secret Service Committee, which reported its conclusions directly to him. One of the few bright spots in the final report – a report which only a handful of people ever read – was the assertion that, through their actions, Chamberlain and SIS had saved the day, pulling together 'a sufficiently formidable indictment', so that 'the public were convinced [. . .] that the authorities had no alternative but to authorise' the raid.[14] But even this limited success was more apparent than real, as many journalists and other commentators were able to piece together, and then set before the public, the chaos and discord that had reigned in the corridors of power in the aftermath of the raid. Significantly, on this occasion the criticism was not limited to publications that the Tories routinely ignored, like the *Daily Worker*, the *Daily Herald*, and the *Manchester Guardian*.

In the *Saturday Review*, a Conservative-leaning journal, the 'Notes of the week' section for 21 May 1927 recorded that 'the raiding of the offices of ARCOS and the Russian Trade

Delegation' was 'one of the most extraordinary incidents in the history of relations between Great Britain and Russia', before going on to say that:

> every embassy and every legation in London has in its files documents the publication of which might arouse the ire of the *Daily Mail*, and which have not always been obtained by very honest methods. The stolen document for which the police were searching may be in an altogether different category, but, since it was not found, the raid is very difficult to justify. A breach with Russia [. . .] would seriously affect British prestige throughout Europe, where our strength depends upon our impartiality. If Sir Austen really agreed to the raid, he was deliberately taking a step which will compel him to give way time after time to France, Italy, Poland, and the rest of them, in order to obtain their support against the Bolsheviks [. . .] If we do not ourselves strictly observe the terms of our Agreement with Russia, we hopelessly weaken our own case when we protest against her violations of it [. . .] Orders which were coming to England may now go elsewhere. It is not a question of sentiment, but of hard business facts. This country cannot afford to turn away trade, and the trade between it and Russia is not negligible.[15]

By the end of the following week, the Prime Minister had set out his case in the Commons and the breach had become official. Another *Saturday Review* story then stated, 'What seems [. . .] probable is that the raid was rashly undertaken, and that the Government have felt compelled to cover the first blunder by committing a second. By so doing they have saved the Home Secretary and pleased the *Daily Mail*, but it is hard to see what other benefits can result from their action. It may prove to be a heavy price to pay for making the world safe for Jix.'[16]

Similarly, in that week's *Spectator* – another right-wing periodical – the coverage of the crisis noted that there could not 'be any doubt that the Government are formally justified in what they have done [. . .] But though the Government are justified formally they may not have been wise'.[17] 'As a matter of fact,' the publication went on, 'the papers found at the offices of ARCOS and the Trade Delegation are less wicked than several documents that had already been published [. . .] We think that a little more patience, even though patience had already been practised for a long time, might have been the best policy.'[18] The journal wondered, 'What do we stand to gain?', and came up with the answer 'Nothing'. 'Our last vestige of bargaining power has been cast away [. . .] We shall undoubtedly lose some trade and, worse still, some gold. Propaganda will increase, and we shall have no right to protest, and no one to protest to.'[19]

At the first meeting of the behind-closed-doors inquiry, on 24 June 1927, the Secret Service Committee's four members (the permanent secretaries of the Treasury, the Foreign Office and the Home Office, and the Cabinet Secretary) attempted to analyse matters on their own before deciding that they would need 'to summon "C" [Sir Hugh Sinclair], Colonel Kell, and Sir Wyndham Childs [. . .] and get from each his own version of the story'.[20] In the meetings that then ensued, intelligence chiefs gave their accounts largely uninterrupted before being asked questions of clarification. The declassified minutes give no sense of witnesses being subjected to the third degree, yet inter-agency rivalries and rancour still surfaced and committee members found themselves staring many of British Intelligence's intrinsic weak spots in the face.

In hindsight, the determination of MI5 to go it alone until just before the raid was deemed utterly reckless. For Sinclair's SIS, learning of the proposed action only hours before it began had caused justifiable panic. 'On receipt of this news, "C" [Sinclair] immediately came over to the Foreign Office [. . .] with a view to the conveyance of a suitable warning to our people in Russia,' the minutes record, though it is unclear whether these 'people' were SIS secret agents or just the British chargé d'affaires and his staff.[21] The head of Special Branch had got slightly more warning (having been taken by Kell to his meeting with Jix on the Wednesday afternoon) but his organisation too had been caught off guard and harmed by the decision to raid.

Under senior officer Guy Liddell, Special Branch had spent much of the preceding year and a half investigating Jacob Kirchenstein's links to military espionage. As recently as December 1926, Liddell had taken the highly unusual step of writing to Sir Vernon Kell to notify him of the positive advances colleagues were making on this case. He warned that he did not want any action of MI5's to jeopardise this progress:

> Jacob KIRCHENSTEIN, who is at present working in the ARCOS Steamship Company, is one of the most important political agents of the Soviet Government in this country [. . .] It [. . .] seems clear that KIRCHENSTEIN, in addition to his political activities in this country, America and the Colonies, is also responsible in some degree to the Soviet Government for military or economic espionage. [. . .] It would, of course, have been possible to get rid of the Russian members of [Kirchenstein's] organisation on the grounds that they were *persona non grata*. This however did not seem desirable since they would have merely been replaced by others, the tracing of whose activities might have been yet more problematical.
>
> I have explained to you verbally how our prospects of getting to the bottom of Kirchenstein's activities have improved enormously within the last few weeks.

It is for this reason that I am particularly anxious that neither KIRCHENSTEIN and his associates nor MESSER's group should be disturbed in any way. Otherwise the work of months, and even years, may be rendered useless just at a time when there is, in my opinion, an opportunity of bringing the whole case to a successful conclusion.[22]

Of course, the ARCOS raid had triggered the dismantling of Kirchenstein's gang, which blew the chance of catching the culprits red-handed. As some journalists commented at the time, it was genuinely puzzling that the authorities had limited themselves to raiding only 49 Moorgate. The Soviets had several other business premises in London, while all ARCOS and Russian Trade Delegation employees had their own private homes. Kirchenstein, for instance, lived in Richmond and worked not in Moorgate but at the ARCOS Steamship Company offices in nearby St Mary Axe. No attempt was made to gain access to his home or office because no time was taken to weigh up the pros and cons of such action.

On this matter the secret inquiry report was withering. 'Had the combined interests of the three organisations been consulted,' it concluded, 'had there been a central authority to view the matter otherwise than piecemeal and from departmental points of view, had even the three Secret Service Heads met together to determine what action should be recommended, before irretrievable steps had been taken, action would probably not have been confined to a raid on 49 Moorgate'.[23]

And these were just the failings that affected the past, the 'work of months, and even years' that had now been 'rendered useless'. Still more concerning, and much more destructive, was the impact that the botched raid would have on the future. Secret intercepts had first been revealed by Lord Curzon in the 1923 ultimatum but, luckily, this did not seem to affect British

Intelligence's ability to read Soviet telegrams. After May 1927, however, the Soviet reaction would be quite different, as the Secret Service Committee inquiry already well knew: 'The publication of the telegrams automatically stops their source of supply for some years at least. [In this instance] it was authorised only as a measure of desperation to bolster up a case vital to Government'.[24] As Christopher Andrew has said in his official history of MI5, 'between 1927 and the end of the Second World War GC&CS was able to decrypt almost no high-grade Soviet communications [. . .] Alastair Denniston, the operational head of GC&CS, wrote bitterly that Baldwin's government had "found it necessary to compromise our work beyond question"'.[25]

What was originally planned as an attempt to convince doubters that the Soviet state's presence in London was actively threatening to British national security ended up as an exercise in preaching almost exclusively to the converted. Many MPs and other commentators – whatever their own views about Russia – were staggered that the government had managed to snatch defeat from the jaws of victory. The full cost, of course, would never be known by most of them: the bitter irony that in trying to retrieve a basic manual on signalling, British Intelligence had succeeded in losing access to all the USSR's most important signals traffic.

```
Dramatis Personae.

        For the purpose of this record

"C²"=   a certain officer on "C"'s
        staff.

"K" =   Colonel Sir Vernon Kell.

"K²"=   a certain officer on "K"'s
        staff.

"X" =   an accountant employed at Arcos
        and a neighbour of "C²".

"Y" =   an individual employed in the
        photostat department of Arcos.
```

*The Secret Service Committee presented codenames of some of the key
players in the ARCOS raid in appropriately dramatic fashion in its classified
report of June 1927. After talking to 'X' and 'Y' (whose real name can now
be revealed for the first time as Edward Langston) and passing the case to
Sir Vernon Kell, SIS heard nothing about it until police were about to enter
49 Moorgate. The ARCOS raid, which British Intelligence had done
so much to facilitate, would have disastrous consequences for British
counter-espionage for years to come.*

19

ESCAPES, LUCKY AND UNLUCKY

'The ARCOS raid might be regarded as a prodigious jest,' a contemporary commentator said, and indeed there are moments in the sequence of events that are hard to think of as anything other than comedy.[1] It is, in particular, easy to imagine the police who burst through the doors of 49 Moorgate, past the bewildered porter, as the Keystone Cops, Hollywood's legendary early-twentieth-century fictional policemen who delighted cinema audiences with harum-scarum chases and backfiring capers. But, of course, a central tenet of the Keystone Cops films was that no one really got hurt; the same cops – and often the same villains – survived unscathed and none the wiser to be able to participate in future entertainments. For the real-life politicians, police and intelligence officers who dismantled ARCOS, this was not the case. And they were not the only ones to be seriously and enduringly affected by the dramatic events of May 1927.

Among the first to suffer was a group that had very little connection with the raid, if available facts are to be believed. Inside the USSR, Britain's onslaught on ARCOS caused not just indignation but fear. The war scare that had followed Curzon's ultimatum in 1923 was repeated, and once again there were anti-British protests in both Moscow and Leningrad. William Peters, a diplomat in Britain's mission to Russia, wired back to London on 20 May to say that 'the Soviet Government has public opinion more behind it on this occasion than has been the case in incidents with foreign Governments in the past'.[2]

With Stalin now *primus inter pares* among the country's leaders, the raid and subsequent fallout also gave rise to a violent crackdown that was directed at Bolshevism's surviving domestic opponents. The crackdown began shortly after Stanley Baldwin announced the termination of Anglo-Soviet relations and was intensified in the wake of a rare bomb attack in Leningrad on 7 June, which injured twenty people. Both this attack and the assassination of Russia's ambassador to Poland – which took place the same day – were (probably correctly) pinned on White Russian terrorists. The Kremlin, predictably, said however that the terrorists had been British-sponsored, and, on 9 June, the head of the local secret police in Leningrad received permission from his bosses 'to exterminate the agents and spies of the British Government and all other enemies of the revolution'.[3] There were to be similar reprisals elsewhere. This could have been a genuine response to events, anchored in reasonable fears or sincerely felt Soviet paranoia, but it was probably something more calculating and staged. In any case, it led to numerous arrests and deaths.

The targets came mainly from aristocratic and Tsarist military backgrounds. About twenty people in all ended up being executed without trial. The largely implausible charges levelled against them included one man (Colonel Georg Elfvengren) conspiring with 'the British Intelligence Service' to assassinate the entire Soviet delegation at the 1922 Genoa Conference; one (K. N. Malevich-Malevsky) acting as a bodyguard for the British Intelligence Service in Persia and later becoming a British secret agent inside Russia; and one (A. E. Skalskii) supplying a British spy in Finland with 'information regarding [Soviet] aviation and war supplies'.[4] On the military island of Kronstadt, meanwhile, a naval commander in the Baltic Fleet was accused of spying for England and sentenced to death, while his wife was charged with complicity and imprisoned for three years.

The Foreign Office diplomat Thomas Hildebrand Preston wrote that he saw 'the whole country plunged into a state of nervous tension which finds expression in the subterranean organisations, be they Monarchist or opposition communist, peeping like rabbits from their holes and in isolated instances even venturing forth to hurl bombs at communists in session in their clubs. The answer to this wave of reaction has been, and will no doubt continue to be, the usual cruel reprisals and the exercise of red terror similar to that obtaining during the early days the revolution'.[5]

British and Soviet diplomats and other employees who had been residing in one another's countries were all, like Preston, permitted to leave without great obstacles being placed in their way. But their fates thereafter were very varied. British diplomats mostly returned to a hero's welcome, with respect and curiosity accorded to them by friends and strangers alike, and some sympathetic coverage in the press. The head of Britain's mission to Moscow, Sir Robert Hodgson, who had stuck at his posting for six long years ('trying conditions, physical and moral', Austen Chamberlain said), was already in London when the crisis hit, enjoying a period of leave.[6] Soon afterwards, *The Times* gave him a right of reply about some of the more fantastical claims that Moscow was levelling. On 13 June 1927, he wrote that among other spurious charges the 'allegations that Mr Vice-Consul Waite was involved in plots to blow up the Kremlin and the Grand Theatre [the Bolshoi], &c., are so grotesquely absurd that no good purpose would be served by attempting to disprove them. They are,' he went on:

> on a par with other charges made against the Brit-
> ish from time to time by the Soviet Press of having
> organised the Pilsudski *coup d'état* in Poland and the

overthrow of the Lithuanian Government, of attempting the destruction of the Leningrad Water Works, and
of planning to seize the islands of Dago and Oesel in
the Baltic, conspiring to murder Reza Shah, and so on
ad infinitum.[7]

Hodgson would lie low for a year but thereafter became
Britain's representative in Albania and later, in the 1930s, in
Franco's Spain.

For some of the Russians who returned home, reintegration
was also swift and pain-free. Arkady Rosengolz, for example,
departed from the world of diplomacy permanently but spent
three years as a member of the Soviet Communist Party's powerful Central Control Commission before becoming National
Commissar for External Trade, another high-ranking position.
Others, however, were to have a nastier time. Anton Miller, the
principal villain in Britain's case against Russia, and one of the
earliest operatives to go back, is thought to have been instantly
locked up in the Lubyanka, the old insurance office that served as
the headquarters of the Soviet secret police. He was subsequently
shot. And his brother Peter, another of Jacob Kirchenstein's
helpers, met the same fate after he was reputedly kidnapped by
Soviet agents in Germany in 1928 and forcibly returned home.
Karl Bahn, another Kirchenstein associate, was also lured back to
Moscow and disappeared.

What had these men – and perhaps several others – done to
deserve execution? This was a question that it was increasingly
illogical to ask in Stalin's state, where any act or thought, real
or imagined, could lead to retribution, but a combination of
knowing too much and being perceived to have failed probably
accounted for their demise. Moscow was well aware that the
ARCOS raid had been ordered by Jix and that its timing and
force had been unpredictable. Yet for all that, Anton Miller
was probably punished for losing the Soviet ciphers and the

lists of Comintern agents. The liquidation of the rest of the Kirchenstein group may just have signalled that they were now useless to the Bolsheviks, or it may have been a way for one faction in the Soviet elite to assert primacy over another.

Jacob and Vallie themselves would almost certainly have met the same end had they gone back to Russia as instructed. In his 1950s confession, Jacob told the FBI that he had been thinking constantly during his time in Britain about abandoning his work for the Soviets. This rings a little hollow when we consider the steady escalation of his activities and the significant role he clearly played in many of the Bolsheviks' most prized operations in the United Kingdom. Nevertheless, when disaster struck, Jacob proved less loyal than his comrades and put himself and his family ahead of whatever remained of his political ideals.

The couple and their young son departed Britain on 8 June 1927 and reached Hamburg two days later:

> We remained one night [. . .] and the following day took a train to Berlin. [. . .] The Russian Embassy in Berlin is much like a fortress or a city within a city. I went to the gate, told the gateman the cover name of the individual I was to see there. [. . .] I identified myself as RALPH, a cover name which had been assigned to me in England previously. In a few minutes I was admitted and guided through alleys and cellars to the office of the Third Secretary.[8]

At this point, Jacob still intended to follow orders. But the Third Secretary said 'there was bedlam in Moscow and [. . .] even he could not get any instructions' from Jacob's masters – an indication, perhaps, of the extent of the consternation that the ARCOS raid and other attacks had caused.[9] The diplomat asked Jacob to come back the next day and gave him a small amount of money to live off in the meantime. But the pattern was repeated on the second visit, with Jacob again being sent away.

Only on the third day did Jacob enter the Third Secretary's office and receive some enlightenment. Just as he went in, the man was decoding a message that he had received about the spy. According to Jacob, it said:

> In the event the American KIRCHENSTEIN appears there, take away his American passport and make up a Polish or Czechoslovak passport. Give him this new passport and immediately put him on an airplane for Moscow. Arrange the appropriate details. We repeat, under no conditions must he be permitted to travel on his American passport.[10]

Jacob's reaction was both intuitive and instant. 'When I saw this message, I knew that it was my death warrant, which I had been anticipating for a long time.'[11] Fortunately for him, the Third Secretary was not so quick and agreed with a now-dissembling Jacob that it would be better if he were to travel back to Moscow on his own passport, in case the British authorities were tracking him (this was not really a very convincing argument but somehow it worked). At Jacob's behest, the Third Secretary sent a telegram to Moscow requesting the spy's bosses to rethink. Jacob then returned to the Soviet embassy on two further occasions to see what the response was, though he had already made up his mind to defect. According to his confession, his final visit to the building was undertaken solely to deliver a 'farewell note' to his masters. In that note, he told the Bolsheviks that they were 'stupid to anticipate that I would accede to their instructions [since] as soon as I arrived in Moscow I would doubtless be arrested as a foreign spy travelling on a fraudulent passport, which would be the end of me'.[12] Thumbing one's nose at Stalin was a supremely high-risk gesture, and Vallie tried to dissuade Jacob from doing it, but he nonetheless managed to emerge alive.

On the very same day, Jacob took a taxi to the offices of the Hamburg American Steamship Line in Berlin – 'making sure I was not followed' – and booked a passage for himself and his family on the *SS New York*, which was sailing from Hamburg on Friday 24 June.[13] Eight days later, Jacob, Vallie and their son little John arrived in America, which they had forsaken for new adventures exactly ten years earlier. 'We arrived in New York,' Jacob said, 'and from that time on I have never been contacted nor have I been in touch with Soviet authorities, and since that date I have never engaged in any legal or illegal activities on behalf of the Comintern or the Communist Party.'[14]

Jacob went back to life in the Bronx and work on the railroads. But it was only natural that he should wonder what had happened to the rest of his team. He kept in touch just with his Scottish accomplices – and even that infrequently – and they knew nothing. He feared the worst but this was not finally confirmed until he saw an article in a Russian emigré newspaper in 1931. In a letter to his old Scottish comrade Charles Douglas, Kirchenstein shared that news, together with his own distinctive, embittered and antisemitic views:

Dear Charlie,
Your welcome letter received. Glad you are still in old haunts and keeping head above water. There is little to write about myself. I am working on my pre-war job, now six days a week [. . .]

Boy already 8 years old, 3rd year in school. Life comfortable enough and no worry about work.

First 2 years I almost got what one would call pettie [*sic*] bourgeois stupor – did not interest about anything and could not really believe that no one intrigued me in work; that free time was my own and no one was plotting intrigues on my account.

Then the last I heard of Carl and Peter Miller was in 1928. That was my last link which went with the past, but I have no regrets for I have always done the right thing.

This year in March I accidentally bought a White Russian paper published here and reading almost lost my senses. I did not know whether the paper refers to times of Turkish atrocities or Spanish inquisition, but here it was – year 1928 in workers' paradise – Russia. Miller's brother the cypher clerk shot on arrival in Russia in 1927 for swallowing in the ARCOS raid of old cypher instead of newest.

Peter Miller in the summer of 1928, while employed in Hamburg in Soviet shipping office in charge of bunkering ships, forcefully taken from Hamburg to Russia and shot for being a British spy!

Ye gods and little fishes! That International Jewish criminal thrash has some sense of imagination! But the real reason for shooting them both was that they knew too much of the dirty doings in upper Sovietist circles in London. As far as I could check up through Latvia they both have been shot and wifes [sic] exterminated. One had a little girl the age of my boy and no one knows what became of her. The rest of acquaintance of that time in London are so terrorised that they do not write, although some of them have parents living in neighbourhood of Miller's parents in Latvia.

I got in touch with one of Miller's brothers in Riga (he was 2nd mate on one of Arcos ships) and they did not know anything about this murder till I sent them the paper clippings.

Those news made me to make [sic] enquiries about

Carl by finding his mother in Latvia. She got from Carl one letter from Rotterdam in 1928 and postcard from Moscow in 1929, nothing since. Therefore I have not the slightest hope that he is alive. With his open talk he made so many Jewish enemies, that they wanted to get him in paradise when I was in London. Now since he was in their clutches no reason to have any delusions on that score – he is gone. Some of the filthy carierists [sic] made a big job and got a promotion by landing this 'counter revolutionary'. [. . .]

How he got to Moscow is a mystery to me. I warned him to steer clear. I told him that there is no justice there and not to get ensnared by fine speeches, that an ordinary criminal or crook has more honesty than the average Moscow communist.

He knew that, but he always insisted that things can and ought to be rectified – so they rectified him in Cheka cellars. I had very sickening experience to break this news to his mother, but it was better to tell her, than to let her live in hopeless illusions.

Miller's brother from Riga is trying to find out any particulars from Moscow, but he has a tough proposition. The secret executions are known only to a small clique. The other party members are so terrorised by intra-party espionage and keep silent, otherwise they would meet the same fate.

I still want to follow the trail and to find out more about this dastardly business.[15]

Whether he found out more we do not know. But Jacob Kirchenstein did eventually face his own retribution for the part he played in the ARCOS affair, albeit of a much less brutal kind than that experienced by his former partners in crime. At the dawn of the Cold War, the FBI brought Kirchenstein in for questioning. The Americans had been alerted to him initially by British Intelligence, probably at some point in the 1920s, but their interest in him had really only developed after the end of the Second World War. In the autumn of 1950, MI5 began to assemble accounts and recollections of the Kirchenstein case and forwarded these to America. 'KIRCHENSTEIN [is] shortly to be interrogated,' a note in one file states. 'We have been passing scraps of information on [him] to the FBI for some time, but in the last few months I have been pressed for a full account which I propose to compile from the interesting reports in SF.450/UK/3 [. . .] In view of the impending interrogation I think it is worthwhile trying to do this research as thoroughly as possible.'[16]

The research helped the interrogators to ask the right questions of the ageing spy, but Jacob himself was clearly minded to be candid too, not wishing to jeopardise his American citizenship and pleasant, ordinary life. His only significant omissions related to the military espionage that he had attempted to organise after 1925, but this was no longer thought sufficiently serious to warrant further action, and so he was left in peace.

By comparison with the demise of the Kirchenstein gang, the post-raid tribulations of Edward Langston, or 'Y', the landlord of The Dolphin, were negligible, and yet the surviving records leave us in no doubt that he felt them keenly. Langston could never have predicted the reaction that his disclosures would provoke but, when he was first told about the raid by Oswald Harker on the afternoon of 12 May (which is to say, a short time *after* it had begun), he seemed calm and even pleased:

> I visited Uxbridge yesterday afternoon, and, after considerable difficulty, succeeded in running to earth our informant 'Y', who was busily employed in putting in order the Public House into which he is moving on Monday next.

I explained to him that the information which he had given me was considered of such importance that it might result in immediate action being taken and that as a result of this action it was possible that the people at ARCOS might come to the conclusion that he had given information to the authorities.

'Y' said that he did not mind what action the authorities took so long as his name was not actually dragged into the matter. He said that as far as he could see it was possible that somebody besides himself might have given information to the police.

He further stated that if the authorities took any action on the information which he had given, he personally would be very glad as he thought it would be a very good thing if a lot of these people were turned out of the country.[17]

Langston's attitude changed rapidly, however, once he began to suspect that the Soviets in Britain actually had managed to work out his name. Langston's identity, and that of 'X', his one-time colleague, are among the most closely guarded secrets in the 1920s MI5 archives, an indication that Harker sincerely desired to protect the man's anonymity, and with it, of course, the full details of the basis for the raid. At the time, though, it would not have been hard for ARCOS managers to create a shortlist of people who might have tipped off the authorities about a stolen document, especially given that the raiding party had semaphored its interest in the ARCOS photostat room so obviously.

In the days after the raid, Langston was visited several times by a member of Harker's team, known in the files only as H.H. While H.H. believed 'Y' 'to be absolutely honest in his dealings with us' he was also of the opinion that the informant was 'inadvertently [. . .] drawing a certain amount of attention to himself'. H.H. went on to describe 'Y' as 'highly nervous'. But Langston felt he had good reason to be nervous after spotting in the newly opened Dolphin 'a shabby individual' whom he recognised as Marsden, the ex-police officer who conducted surveillance for Trilby Ewer's Federated Press of America group, and who had clearly been a frequent caller at 49 Moorgate. Langston told MI5 that Marsden had had some drinks in The Dolphin and, upon leaving, had said to the new landlord, 'Now don't forget – Gun-barrel for next Wednesday'. Langston had taken this as 'a subtle threat' so that 'visions of a violent end flashed through his mind'.[18]

'Utterly bewildered', Langston had rushed from the pub, leaving his wife in charge, and gone to the post office to send a telegram to Harker. He had been told to do this only in an emergency, which was what he now believed he faced. The message was despatched care of Sidney Russell Cooke at Cooke's personal flat – the safe house – in King's Bench Walk.[19] It read, 'Marsden is hanging around disguised as tramp. Please send revolver, if possible'.[20] Not satisfied with this, Langston furthermore 'called at the local police station and, the inspector being absent, saw the Sergeant in charge, telling him that Marsden was at his house and he did not know what to do'.[21]

H.H. had to impress on the publican the importance of staying calm at this point. He told him that 'it was extremely improbable that the Russian people would molest him in any way' and that 'if anyone connects him with the matter, it would come about solely through his own folly in not keeping his mouth shut and having more command over himself'.[22] Langston gradually grew more composed in the days that followed and no revolver was sent. By early June, Langston was no longer featuring in MI5 paperwork at all. Whether or not he ever learned of the short piece that was published about him in the left-wing *New Leader* for 3 June 1927 is unknown. But if he did, it must have made him shiver:

From Clerk to Publican
The dismissed member of the ARCOS staff who is suspected to have
supplied the 'information' to Scotland Yard which led to the recent
raid has, I hear, mysteriously become the owner of a public house. He
has not done it out of the wages which he received as a clerk.[23]

Were Marsden and Ewer behind this leak? Quite probably.
But, in fact, despite the slur, Langston had received no money
for his services to MI5. The only thing he ever asked for, and
received, was a guarantee from the authorities that his application
for a publican's licence would be granted without problem.
Paperwork in the MI5 archives shows that Harker made the
necessary approach to an Uxbridge magistrate, telling him about
the service that the future publican had rendered to the nation.[24]

Overall, the impact of the ARCOS raid was less impressive
than its orchestrators had wished. Not only was there no end to
the Soviet regime within Russia, but there was only a moderate
curtailment of Soviet wrongdoing in Britain and across the
empire. As it turned out, the structures of overt and covert
Communism in the United Kingdom were only partially and
temporarily disrupted by the spectacular expulsion that the
Diehards pulled off in May 1927, and many of the same old
suspects and the same lines of inquiry continued to be thorns in
British Intelligence's side in subsequent years.

Trilby Ewer's group is probably the best case in point. Even
as Jix and his supporters were crowing about their victory over
Bolshevism in the weeks and months after the raid, Ewer was
busy reconfiguring his men and women to cope with the loss
of ARCOS. Sending Marsden to The Dolphin was an early
indication that his team was not ready to abandon its work.
Instead they would continue, with some marked successes,
for another two years. There was, of course, an initial lull and
this was followed by important structural changes. It seems,
for instance, that the French dimension of Ewer's work dried

up altogether, the Soviets deciding instead to work directly through their Paris embassy. Meanwhile, in March 1928, the FPA surrendered its offices at 50 Outer Temple.

At this point, British Intelligence dared to hope that the whole enterprise had been abandoned. But in reality Ewer continued assisting the Russians under the guise of a new front organisation, the Featherstone Typewriting Bureau, which operated out of small premises in Featherstone Buildings, a secluded street off High Holborn. Ewer and Dale still jointly controlled Inspector Ginhoven and Sergeant Jane, their Special Branch moles, a fact about which the authorities remained in the dark. Dale and his other ex-coppers continued observing people around London and sometimes further afield. The Featherstone was their secure location, both for planning and debriefing meetings and for Rose Edwardes, who continued to be the group's secretary, to type up reports and copy the text of secret documents.

Midway through 1928, British Intelligence got its most sig-nificant lead on Ewer in years, when one of Dale's ex-coppers, Arthur Allen, left the outfit and offered to sell his story to an MI5 officer. Allen was similar to Langston in that his employment with the Russians was followed by an entry into the hospitality trade: he began running a tearoom in the south-coast seaside resort of Bournemouth. Over the course of several meetings in the vicinity of this tearoom, Allen told MI5 what he knew about Ewer's secret organisation. He bore no grudge against Ewer himself, he was at pains to point out to the authorities, but he did resent how the Russians had treated him. Open-mouthed with horror at what they learned, particularly about the Special Branch moles, the authorities started to plan an attack on the group. Eventually, in March 1929, MI5 spotted Dale at a meeting with Ginhoven and Jane in the Lyon's Cafe near Bank tube station. Armed with this corroboration, the police arrested all three men and, in a rare spot of good luck, managed to seize Dale's work diaries for the preceding eight years as well.

Ewer himself was not arrested and none of those detained ever found themselves charged with a crime. Finally, British Intelligence and its political masters seemed to be learning that discretion could be the better part of valour when it came to closing down espionage groups. Nevertheless, the softer approach did not mean that the authorities were indifferent to the conspiracy they had exposed. A careful perusal of Dale's notebooks revealed many periods during which he and his men had watched British Intelligence's own people. Among the most significant was an entry from late October 1924 – the height of the Zinoviev Letter affair – which recorded surveillance on none other than Sir Vernon Kell, MI5's head. He had been watched both at his home and at work and had had the details of his car registration number noted down: 'Obser. 34 Argyll Rd, High St Ken., res. of Lieu. Col. Sir Vernon Geo. W. Kell, Bart., KBE, CB, a Director of Mili. & Operative Intelligence WO [War Office] (office 35 Cromwell Rd, SW7) Car XT 1567.'[25] What was particularly worrying was that the authorities had known nothing about this until now, almost five years later. Many other intelligence addresses belonging to people in all branches of Britain's secret services had been compromised as well.

The people at Featherstone were busy right up to the moment when Dale, Ginhoven and Jane were arrested and the entire operation was shut down. Alongside the records of his own observation work, Dale seems to have used his diaries from 1927 onwards to keep shorthand accounts of the information Ginhoven and Jane leaked to him. When Special Branch carried out an investigation after the men's arrests, it discovered an almost perfect match between the files that Ginhoven and Jane had signed out of the confidential police registry each week and the corresponding entries in Dale's diary. It seems that Dale knew a great deal about the cases on which Special Branch had been working. Naturally, the authorities had to assume that all this intelligence had been forwarded to both the CPGB and

Moscow. Unlike with the signals manual, however, no public acknowledgement of the leaks was ever made.

In political terms, the ARCOS raid was equally unsatisfactory, as it failed to deal the fatal blow to British radical socialism that Jix and the Diehards had hoped for. Although ARCOS and the Russian Trade Delegation had disappeared, groups like the CPGB and its associated fronts and campaigns still endured. Men and women like Andrew Rothstein and Edith Lunn could not be expelled from the United Kingdom because they were British citizens, so there was a continuing requirement to track them closely. And interest continued to grow in people connected – sometimes only very tangentially – with groups like the Society for Cultural Relations and the Film Society.

The Diehards had also hoped that their attacks against the Soviets would permanently cripple the Labour Party, which had defended the Russian presence in Britain, and whose links to Bolshevism were held up as proof of its untrustworthiness and secret extremism. In the event, however, Labour quickly recovered its fortunes after the summer of 1927. During March 1928, a fresh parliamentary scandal even erupted over reports that the Zinoviev Letter had been deliberately leaked to Conservative newspapers in order to blacken the Labour Prime Minister's name. Naturally, government ministers and officials denied this – and also continued to insist that the letter was genuine – but this time coverage of the story was more balanced, helping to persuade some that MacDonald really had been attacked by hidden forces within the state. Around the same time, a string of local election results and by-elections showed consistent swings to Labour – the very opposite of the gratitude and caution that Conservatives like Jix had expected voters to display.

Anti-socialists responded to these developments in the only way they knew, by making speeches that continued to smear the left and urging people to ever greater vigilance and care.

A great deal was made, for instance, of a public espionage trial that took place during January 1928. In it, two men, Wilfred Macartney and Georg Hansen, were jailed for supplying British military documents to the Russians. Hansen was a German and Macartney was a convicted British jewel thief, who had sought to trade RAF secrets with the Soviet government in return for money. The Briton was imprisoned for ten years for his offences against the Official Secrets Act, but the court case against him had to be exceptionally carefully managed in order to avoid mention of the extent to which British Intelligence had entrapped him. MI5's own declassified records now reveal that the Soviets thought Macartney a thoroughly unreliable personality, which is what had led him to sell his secrets through a German intermediary in the first place.

Macartney's story is worthy of a book in its own right – indeed, after his release from prison, he wrote one.[26] Racing at breakneck speed across Europe, surviving run-ins with Romanian princes and wealthy heiresses, and always returning to the Café Royal for what one observer described as large quantities of 'hot grogs', he was completely different from the typical 1920s socialist secret agent.[27] The author Compton Mackenzie became an unexpected defender of Macartney, having served in the army alongside him during the Great War. Mackenzie was clear that the 1928 trial had been a staged event, with the government attempting 'to impress upon the people of Great Britain that between them and being blown sky-high by naughty Bolsheviks there was nothing except the vigilance and acumen of a Secret Service, the devotion and patriotism of a Conservative Cabinet, and the determination of the Law to support both'.[28]

In 1929, another general election took place and the British people faced the prospect of their fifth change of leadership in a decade. In February that year, Winston Churchill, who was still Chancellor of the Exchequer, spoke at the twenty-first anniversary celebrations of the Anti-Socialist and Anti-Communist Union, and reminded the two-thousand-strong audience that if Labour was returned to power it 'would be bound to bring back the Russian Bolshevists, who would immediately get busy in the mines and factories, as well as among the armed forces, planning another general strike'. Churchill added that 'he did not want to see the Conservative Party weaken in any way its attitude against subversive and revolutionary propaganda and conspiracy'. On the contrary, 'he wished to disperse the cursed apathy [. . .] with which the tremendous events of the next few months were being approached'.[29]

In traditional historical analyses, the Conservatives' most famous election slogan in 1929, 'Safety First', has been pilloried as among its blandest ever. Both the slogan and the set of mild, do-nothing policies that accompanied it have widely been described as overcautious. Yet for many who stood as Conservatives up and down the country, there was nothing bland about the kind of caution being urged. Led by Ramsay MacDonald, Labour campaigned on a manifesto that pledged bold state-led change: 'housing and slum clearance; land drainage and reclamation [and] electrification' as well as 'the reorganisation of railways and transport'. The party also promised to increase unemployment benefit and alleviate the 'tragic [. . .] distress in the coal field', paying for these and other activities by raising death duties and income tax on the rich. After once again spelling out that it was 'neither Bolshevik nor Communist' – as it still felt the need to do – Labour said that the Tories had made international relations worse during their time in office, and it explicitly committed itself to 're-establish diplomatic and commercial relations with Russia'.[30]

On 30 May 1929, Labour won the general election with its best result ever, netting 136 more seats than in 1924 and 2.8 million more votes. While just short of an outright majority, the party regained power and MacDonald re-entered

Downing Street. Only a few weeks later, he ordered the start of discussions, via the Soviet embassy in Paris, about bringing the Russians back to Britain. The negotiations, though tricky at first, ended in success and the permanent Soviet presence in the United Kingdom was restored. With it, of course, came all the same undesirable baggage that had supposedly been thrown out in 1927. Even Nikolai Klyshko, who had effectively been expelled during Curzon's time, managed to make four new visits to Britain during 1930 and 1931. And in the summer of 1934, a Soviet secret agent called Arnold Deutsch would take a walk in Regent's Park in London and recruit the Cambridge graduate Kim Philby, to start what became the most notorious spy scandal of the century.

And yet, from the end of the 1920s onwards – no matter how bad the crisis or how big the dispute – the United Kingdom never again tried to beat the Russians simply by ostracising them. Britain had discovered the futility of such gestures and the high risk of them backfiring. Like so many others throughout history, it had realised that Russia, which would not be tamed, could not be ignored either.

3561 De Kalb Ave.

September 25th, 1931.

Dear Charlie,

Your welcome letter received. Glad you are still in old haunts and keeping head above water.

There is little to write about myself. I am working on my pre-war job, now six days a week (used to be 7) and anyone here in steady job is pretty well off.

Boy already 8 years old. 3rd year in school. Life comfortabl enough and no worry about work.

First 2 years I almost got what one would call pettie bourgeoi stupor - did not interest about anything and could not really believe that no one intrigued me in work that free time was my own and no one was plotting intrigues on my account.

Then the last I heard of Carl and Peter Miller was in 1928 That was my last link which went with the past, but I have no regrets for I have always done the right thing.

This year in March I accidentally bought a white Russian paper published here and reading almost lost my senses. I did not know whether papers refers to times of Turkish atrocities or Spanish inquisition, but here it was - year 1928 in workers paradise - Russi Millers brother the cypher cler shot on arrival in Russia in 1927 for swallowing in the Arcos raid of old cypher instead of newest.

Peter Miller in the summer of 1928, while employed in Hamburg in soviet shipping office in charge of bunkering ships, forcefully taken from Hamburg and shot for being a British spy !
                          to Russia

Ye gods and little fishes ! That International Jewish criminal thresh has some sense of imagination ! But the real reason for shooting them both was that they knew too much of the dirty doings in upper sovietist circles in London. As far as I could check up through Latvia they both have been shot and wifes exterminated. One had a little girl the age of my boy and no one knows what became of her. The rest of acquaintance of that time in London are so terror- ised that they do not write, although some of them have parents living in neighbourhood of Millers parents in Latvia.

Jacob Kirchenstein nearly failed to make it back to the Bronx after leaving Britain in 1927. Standing in the Soviet diplomatic mission in Berlin, he suddenly realised that he would be killed if he returned to Russia. This letter, which he wrote in 1931, shows that he was almost certainly right.

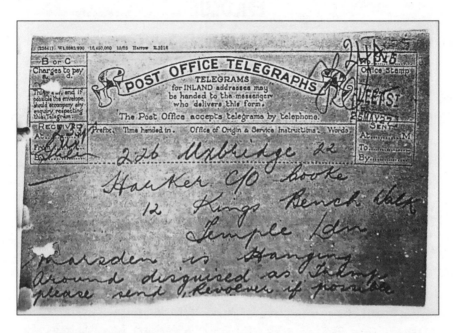

In case of emergency, Edward Langston had been told he could get a message
to his MI5 handler by wiring 'Harker c/o Cooke' at 12 King's Bench Walk.
This telegram was sent when the publican began fearing for his life in the
days after the ARCOS raid. The post office clerk in Uxbridge cannot have
been asked to send such requests — for a 'Revolver, if possible' — very often.

EPILOGUE

LIKE SHADOWS IN THE FAILING DUSK

By reputation, the 1920s buzzed and fizzed and roared right up until the moment when, falling victim to their love of speed, they crashed in Wall Street on 29 October 1929. But the decade was never so uniformly carefree as the stereotype suggests, and while there are many sources which demonstrate its true complexity, few are as persuasive or arresting as the declassified archives of MI5. The files tell a story of cultural transition, social upheaval and unprecedented political turbulence, but not from the perspective of those who were exhilarated by the changes, rather from the perspective of those who feared them.

From their uniquely privileged vantage point, right-wing intelligence officers catalogued the emergence of new threats and possibilities in interwar British society, and discharged the duty of determining on behalf of the rest of the population what was safe and what was not. Even after almost a century's self-censorship, pruning and weeding, the surviving MI5 paperwork reveals that the agency and its sister organisations in the 1920s were in the grip of paranoia, primed to see their own moral and social preferences as national security issues.

Writing of the later Cold War, the historian Corey Robin has described 'coalitions of fear' that elites manipulated in order to combat potential 'loss of privileges' or other threats to their 'power and standing'. The hallmark of such 'political fear', Robin writes, was 'a combination of rational concern and moral revulsion' – exactly what afflicted many parts of Britain's state and establishment in the 1920s.[1] Robin quotes Arthur Schlesinger, a Harvard academic writing in the 1940s, who said that at that time Western mankind was 'tense, uncertain [and] adrift'. Schlesinger's words might equally have been applied to the decade immediately after the Great War: 'We look upon our epoch as a time of troubles, an age of anxiety. The grounds of our civilization, of our certitude, are breaking up under our feet, and familiar ideas and institutions vanish as we reach for them, like shadows in the failing dusk'.[2]

It was certainly true that British Intelligence faced an almost impossible task after the Great War. Several of its agencies had to absorb swingeing financial cuts while also mastering a new, extensive and genuine threat from Russia. In many respects, they approached this unenviable endeavour with dedication and diligence. But from the start – and increasingly over time – they conceived of their work against the Soviets as being about far more than the dangers of Bolshevism. They saw alarming similarities between the Bolsheviks and the British Labour Party, as well as worrying links between Moscow and Britain's trade unions, the anger of the British unemployed, and even various aspects of modernist culture. While these conjectures had some roots in reality, they got woven into a hugely exaggerated, and often deliberately distorted, version of the truth. And this in turn warped the inquiries that British spies chose to focus on, the leads that they followed, and the cases they built up and passed on to Britain's elected politicians.

At times, British Intelligence and its political masters must have caught glimpses of the irrationality of their preferred interpretation of events. Without doubt, those involved in specific dirty-tricks campaigns must have known that they had created stories which had no basis in fact. The archives suggest that such individuals were partly motivated by the duplicitous and asymmetric nature of the Soviet threat itself. But partly their unreason stemmed from their own anxieties and general sense of dread.

The cat-and-mouse cruelty of the later Cold War has often been presented as a disaster that might have been averted. Yet the story of Britain's fight against the Russians in the 1920s strongly challenges that view. How difficult it was for people to know who and what to fear about the new enemy in the East. How inescapably prejudiced and personal were the choices that governments had to make about suspects and surveillance, and how hard it was to find a definitive response to a threat that was at once so sinister, so nebulous, and so resilient.

As we are now only too aware, the Soviet Union's principal successor state poses new quandaries and threats for world leaders of the twenty-first century. Today, Anglo-Russian relations continue to be far from smooth, and they are now only one element in a much broader nexus of possible threats, all of which British Intelligence must deal with. Britain's spooks are less monocultural than they once were, we are assured. They are also better resourced. And in some cases they have even been subjected to meaningful independent scrutiny.

Yet many of the dangers of the 1920s remain. The technical sophistication and sheer scale of today's data-collection capabilities mean that, to an even greater extent than a century ago, British Intelligence runs the risk of grabbing more data than it can ever meaningfully analyse. Meanwhile, the intelligence agencies continue to be, in essence, collections of individuals, each with his or her own beliefs and fears, and each still capable of being captured by groupthink or wider political and social agendas. The present-day need for democracies to practise espionage and counter-espionage is clear. That such work must take place in secret is axiomatic. But the lack of perspective that this inevitably brings will always be the system's greatest weakness, creating as it does the conditions for Wizard-of-Oz-style myths of omniscience and infallibility. And wherever such myths exist, it is we, the public, as much as any enemy secret agent, who should be wary.

NOTES

Throughout these notes the National Archives is abbreviated to TNA.

Prologue: Miss Lunn's misfortune
1. TNA, KV 2/2317, Lansbury to Klishko, 25 November 1920.
2. Ibid., Zika to Andriousha (British Intelligence translation), 17 August 1925.
3. Ibid., Mother to Edith, 13 November 1925.
4. Ibid., Andryusha to Edith, 8 December 1925. Author's translation from Russian.
5. Ibid., Index to file, note 32.
6. Ibid., Unknown to Phillips, 6 August 1925.

Introduction: Someone to watch over me
1. See in particular: David Burke, *The Spy Who Came in from the Co-op: Melita Norwood and the Ending of Cold War Espionage*, 2008; Christopher Andrew, *The Defence of the Realm: The Authorized History of MI5*, 2009; Keith Jeffery, *MI6: The History of the Secret Intelligence Service, 1909–1949*, 2010; Victor Madeira, *Britannia and the Bear: The Anglo-Russian Intelligence Wars, 1917–1929*, 2014; and Kevin Quinlan, *The Secret War between the Wars: MI5 in the 1920s and 1930s*, 2014.
2. There are many excellent histories that explore aspects of the United Kingdom in the 1920s. The works I have found especially useful are: Peter Clarke, *Hope and Glory: Britain 1900–2000*, 2004; Maurice Cowling, *The Impact of Labour, 1920–1924*, 1971; Ross McKibbin, *Classes and Cultures: England, 1918–1951*, 1998; and Martin Pugh, *Hurrah for the Blackshirts! Fascists and Fascism in Britain between the Wars*, 2005. There are also many fictional

works by people who lived through the 1920s and attempted to capture the essence of the decade. My favourites include: Aldous Huxley, *Antic Hay*, 1923; Evelyn Waugh, *Brideshead Revisited*, 1945; Angus Wilson, *No Laughing Matter*, 1967; and Virginia Woolf, *Mrs Dalloway*, 1925.

Part 1: A need for intelligence
1. Herodotus, *The Histories*, trans. Robert Waterfield, 1998, pp. 45–6.
2. Ibid., p. 47.
3. There have been very few survey histories of espionage through time. For an entertaining introduction, see Ernest Volkman, *The History of Espionage*, 2007. More detail on the period before 1500 can be found through R. M. Sheldon, *Espionage in the Ancient World: An Annotated Bibliography of Books and Articles in Western Languages*, 2003. For the nineteenth and twentieth centuries a similar guide is provided by James D. Calder, *Intelligence, Espionage and Related Topics: An Annotated Bibliography of Serial Journal and Magazine Scholarship, 1944–1998*, 1999.
4. Nigel West, *Historical Dictionary of British Intelligence*, 2014, p. 530.
5. For more information see Ray Wilson and Ian Adams, *Special Branch: A History: 1883–2006*, 2015.
6. Richard James Popplewell, *Intelligence and Imperial Defence: British Intelligence and the Defence of the Indian Empire, 1904–1924*, 1985.
7. Rather remarkably, fiction played an important role in making the case for a Secret Service Bureau. Among others, the novelist William le Queux published imaginary tales of what would happen if Britain were attacked by Germany. His 1906 work, *The Invasion of 1910*, was the most famous in the genre. It was commissioned by and serialised in the *Daily Mail*. See *The Great War with Germany, 1890–1914: Fictions and Fantasies of the War-to-come*, ed. Ignatius Frederick Clarke, 1997, p. 139.

1 For the good of the nation
1. *The Times*, 14 January 1919, p. 11.
2. TNA, CAB 24/76/67, para. 7.
3. Ibid., para. 4.
4. For a thorough account of this fascinating year, see Anthony Read, *The World on Fire: 1919 and the Battle with Bolshevism*, 2008.
5. There are many accounts of the Russian Revolution, its causes and consequences. To my mind, the best succinct account is still found in Robert Service, *A History of Modern Russia: From Nicholas II to Putin*, 2003.

6. Joseph Lee, *Ireland 1912–1985: Politics and Society*, 1989, pp. 40–1.
7. The additional repression only served to exacerbate matters. The Rowlatt Act, passed on 18 March 1919, led directly to yet more Indian unrest. Just weeks after its introduction, the Jallianwala Bagh, or Amritsar, massacre happened, a notorious clash in which British troops killed at least 379 civilians.
8. Cited in Jacqueline Jenkinson, *Black 1919: Riots, Racism and Resistance in Imperial Britain*, 2009, p. 42.
9. TNA, CAB 24/76/67, para. 5.
10. Ibid.
11. Ibid., para. 7.
12. Ibid., para. 5.
13. Ibid., para. 8.
14. Ibid., para. 10.
15. Ibid.
16. Ibid.

2 We need timber, fur and pig bristles

1. L. Muravyova, I. Sivolap-Kaftanova, *Lenin in London: Memorial Places*, trans. Jane Sayer, 1983.
2. Hugh D. Phillips, *Between the Revolution and the West: A Political Biography of Maxim M. Litvinov*, 1992, pp. 27–8.
3. *The Times*, 22 February 1919, p. 10.
4. *Hansard*, 5 November 1919, vol. 120, cc. 1473–4.
5. *The Times*, 3 June 1920, p. 7.
6. TNA, KV 2/500, Oldfield to Mugliston, 16 May 1920.
7. See Kevin Morgan, *Labour Legends and Russian Gold*, 2006. Also, for the personal recollection of one British socialist who was asked by Klyshko to store a suitcase full of platinum bars, Francis Meynell, *My Lives*, 1971, p. 125.
8. *Hansard*, 10 February 1920, vol. 125, cc. 9–64.
9. Richard H. Ullman, *Anglo-Soviet Relations, 1917–1921*, 3 volumes, vol. 3, *The Anglo-Soviet Accord*, 1972, p. 474.
10. Ullman, *The Anglo-Soviet Accord*, pp. 475–6.

3 The biggest jewel thieves in history

1. Anita Loos, *Gentlemen Prefer Blondes: The Illuminating Diary of a Professional Lady*, 1925, p. 207.
2. Andrew Campbell, 'Moscow's Gold: Soviet Financing of Global Subversion', *National Observer*, Autumn 1999.
3. Cited in Manuel Caballero, *Latin America and the Comintern, 1919–1943*, 2002, p. 14.

4. Meynell, *My Lives*, p. 122.
5. This fascinating event is described in detail in G. A. Solomon, *Among the Red Autocrats: My Experience in the Service of the Soviets*, 1935.
6. Klyshko's contact with H. G. Wells was friendly and even extended to spending weekends with the great author at his country house in Dunmow, Essex. In July 1921, Klyshko and his wife stayed there at the same time as Harold Laski, then a young academic. Laski wrote amusingly of his experiences in the following letter: '[Wells] has a corking country place at Dunmow with a fine old English garden and a great barn of which the importance will emerge presently. We got there on the Saturday afternoon and the other guests were the Klishkos. He is the assistant chief of the Soviet Bureau in London and somewhat of a mystery. His wife, whom we all cordially and thoroughly disliked, an English snob of the first water. Wells is a perfect dear – quick, agile, irrepressible, quite reckless in personal judgement and as generous as you please. The first evening we talked and talked and talked – Russia, Lloyd-George, Galsworthy as sentimentalist, Conrad, Henry James, and H. G. Wells. […] On the Sunday morning we played [Wells's] personal ball-game in the barn. Imagine a huge room full of angles and jutting beams, divided into two by a net 5.5 feet high. You play 3–4–5 a side with a ball about twice as big as a tennis ball. You can't hit it twice yourself and it must never bounce twice on your own side – otherwise you can do anything with the ball. Wells in a vest and trousers, Klishko half-naked, I in pyjama trousers and a vest for two hours on this ball. You become a mass of perspiration, intellectual problems cease to count, and you hate your partner who misses the ball as only Archibald Stevenson hates the Reds. Then music, lunch, talk, tea, ball-game, talk, dinner, talk, then bed and back to London early on Monday. We enjoyed it hugely and the house is full of books that would tempt your soul.' (Kingsley Martin, *Harold Laski 1893–1950: A Biographical Memoir*, 1969, pp. 52–3.)
7. TNA, CAB 24/129/10, 'Foreign Support of Communist Agitators in the United Kingdom'. Throughout this book, current values of old money have been derived using the Retail Price Index (RPI) and predecessor indices. Calculations have been made on the Measuring Worth website, www.measuringworth.com.
8. Ibid.
9. Ibid.
10. TNA, KV 2/1414, 'Northern Summary: Possible Sale of

Valuables Abroad: Implication of Soviet Delegation in London', 9 November 1922.

11. The majority of the papers are found in TNA, KV 2/1414, which now contains what survives of Klyshko's personal file.

12. TNA, KV 2/1414, HM to XQ, 26 October 1922.

13. Ibid. It is hard to get an accurate idea of the quantity of jewels involved, but the total amount at the Bolsheviks' disposal was enormous. At the end of the Russian Civil War, according to a primary source quoted by historian Sean McMeekin, the Bolsheviks controlled royal gems comprising '25,300 carats of diamonds, 1,000 carats of emeralds, 1,700 carats of sapphires, 6,000 carats of pearls, and many rubies, topazes, tourmalines, alexandrites, chrysoprases, beryls, chrysolites, turquoises, amethysts, agates, labradores [and] almadines' – and that was without counting the gold, Fabergé eggs and innumerable other baubles that the Romanovs had amassed, plus the wealth of all the other great noble and merchant families. Local Bolshevik committees, even in the most far-flung places, had been issued with instructions to collect the jewellery and precious stones of provincial notables and the Church and send them through to Moscow. Consignments started arriving at the rate of 400 per week, and sometimes even more, so that by the end of 1920 the new central State Treasury had amassed 23,000 uncracked safes and had to establish a Safes Commission to blow them all open. Around the same time, another body came into being with the chillingly industrial name, the Commission for the Depersonalisation, Sorting and Appraisal of Valuables. (Sean McMeekin, *History's Greatest Heist: The Looting of Russia by the Bolsheviks*, 2008, p. xix.)

14. Ibid.

15. Ibid., 'Northern Summary: Possible Sale of Valuables Abroad: Implication of Soviet Delegation in London', 9 November 1922.

16. Ibid.

17. Ibid.

18. Ibid.

19. Ibid., Special Branch to XQ, 25 October 1922, p. 2.

20. Ibid., SIS Section 1b to Captain Liddell, 19 March 1923.

21. Ibid.

22. Morgan, *Labour Legends and Russian Gold*, pp. 36–56.

23. Ibid., p. 40.

24. TNA, KV 2/1414, 'Memorandum on Soviet Policy in Great Britain as Expressed in Trade (1920–30)', 3[?] July 1930.

25. After the Soviet Union's collapse, further evidence would emerge to link Klyshko with India. In a document held in the Russian archives, one Indian nationalist writes in 1921, 'I applied to Comrade Klishko of the Soviet Trade Delegation in London to furnish me with funds to come to Moscow with a view to exploring the possibilities of Indian work. I was strongly recommended to Comrade Klishko by Russian comrades who knew me personally and my record of work. Comrade Klishko [...] provided me in December last year with the necessary funds to proceed to Moscow'. (*Indo-Russian Relations, 1917–1947: Select Documents from the Archives of The Russian Federation, Part 1: 1917–1928*, 1999, p. 143.)

4 Dear Mama!
1. For a full account of the CPGB in the 1920s, see Matthew Worley, *Class Against Class: The Communist Party in Britain Between the Wars*, 2002.
2. TNA, KV 2/1576, 'Home Office Warrant', 5 October 1920.
3. Rothstein's copy of *Pravda* seems to have begun arriving at the War Office main building in early 1922, specifically addressed to MI1c (the other name for SIS) but also, confusingly, marked for the attention of Andrew Rothstein. The publication came regularly for over six months and SIS's officers were both perplexed and unsettled by it. Was it possible that someone working at SIS or the War Office was in cahoots with Rothstein? Did the parcels contain something besides newspapers? Was some text in each edition of *Pravda* secretly encoded? Tests for invisible ink came back blank and all other avenues of inquiry also proved to be dead ends. Eventually, in mid-November, some in the British spy community began to wonder if it was 'possible that the "Pravda" people are pulling MI1c's leg'. 'Leave this mosquito alone,' a senior officer eventually wrote in the file on 22 November 1922, 'and go after the Elephants'. (TNA, KV 2/1576, File index, note 284.)
4. TNA, KV 2/1576, Andryusha to Mama, 10 November 1920. Author's translation from Russian.
5. According to Graham Stevenson, Rothstein was excluded on the personal advice of Lord Curzon, who was also a Balliol alumnus (see http://www.grahamstevenson.me.uk/index. php?option=com_content&view=article&id=493:andrew-rothstein-and-theodore-rothstein-&catid=18:r&Itemid=104, last accessed 24 September 2016).

6. TNA, KV 2/1576, MI5/B to DMI, 23 November 1920. The young Rothstein's penchant for exaggeration was remarked on by others he encountered. The noted screen actor Raymond Massey, who starred in *Arsenic and Old Lace* and *East of Eden*, was an undergraduate at Balliol at the same time as Andrew. In his memoirs, he wrote 'my next-door neighbour was Andrew Rothstein [...] He informed me that in the coming revolution, I would be the first to be put up against the wall and shot. Rothstein was the first Communist I had ever met. He was indignant that I had visited Siberia with a military force intended to interfere with the revolution, and I lost no opportunity of goading him into a rage'. (Raymond Massey, *When I was Young*, 1977, p. 225.)

7. Ibid., Andryusha to Mama, 10 November 1920.

8. Ibid., Febur to Andryusha, 19 January 1921.

9. Ibid., Extract from Secret Source, 29 September 1921.

10. Ibid., Schedule A, List of permanent staff of the Russian Trade Delegation, 21 March 1922.

11. Ibid., MI5/B to DMI, 23 November 1920.

12. Ibid., Esmond Ovey to unknown, 9 October 1921.

13. Ibid., Summary information on Andrew F. Rothstein, item 298A.

14. TNA, CAB 24/117, 'Report on Revolutionary Organisations in the United Kingdom', 16 December 1920, pp. 6–7.

15. TNA, KV 2/1576, Summary information on Andrew F. Rothstein, item 298A.

16. TNA, KV 2/1391, Confession of Jacob Kirchenstein, 27 September 1951, pp. 26–7. The actual reason for Basil Thomson's resignation has never been confirmed. While some continue to connect it with perceived failings in the fight against Bolshevism, others posit a personality clash with Lloyd George, and others still point to failures in the fight against Irish republicanism (see, for instance, Andrew Lycett, 'The Irish Volunteer', *History Today*, April 2016).

17. TNA, CAB 24/138/56, 'Report on Revolutionary Organisations in the United Kingdom', 10 August 1922, pp. 3–4.

18. TNA, CAB 24/159/44, 'Report on Revolutionary Organisations in the United Kingdom', 8 March 1923, pp. 4–5.

19. *Hansard*, 23 November 1922, vol. 159, cc. 111, 118.

20. TNA, KV 2/611–615.

21. TNA, CAB 24/134/27, 'Report on Revolutionary Organisations in the United Kingdom', 9 March 1922, p. 1. TNA, CAB 24/126/55, 'Report on Revolutionary Organisations in the United Kingdom', 21 July 1921, p. 2.

22. TNA, CAB 24/126/55, 'Report on Revolutionary Organisations in the United Kingdom', 21 July 1921, p. 2.
23. TNA, CAB 24/122/91, 'Report on Revolutionary Organisations in the United Kingdom', 28 April 1921, p.7.

5 A tour of Red Britannia
1. TNA, CAB 24/134/27, 'Report on Revolutionary Organisations in the United Kingdom', 9 March 1922, p. 3.
2. Ibid.
3. James Denman and Paul McDonald, 'Unemployment Statistics from 1881 to the Present Day', *Labour Market Trends*, January 1996, pp. 5–18, p. 6.
4. In addition to archival material, I have benefited greatly from Dan Jacobs's research in writing this chapter. See Dan Jacobs, *Borodin: Stalin's Man in China*, 1981, in particular pp. 97–107. See also Peter Hopkirk, *Setting the East Ablaze: Lenin's Dream of an Empire in Asia*, 1984.
5. Clare Sheridan, *Mayfair to Moscow – Clare Sheridan's Diary*, 1921, p. 107–8.
6. M. M. Borodin, *Istoriya velikoi izmeny*, 1922.
7. TNA, CAB 24/138/56, 'Report on Revolutionary Organisations in the United Kingdom', 10 August 1922, pp. 3, 5–6.
8. Jacobs, *Borodin: Stalin's Man in China*, p. 103.
9. TNA, CAB 24/159/77, 'Report on Revolutionary Organisations in the United Kingdom', 28 March 1923, p. 3. See also, the Red Clydeside section of Glasgow Digital Library, http://sites.scran.ac.uk/redclyde/redclyde/rc036.htm, last accessed 21 October 2016.
10. TNA, KV 2/1391, Confession of Jacob Kirchenstein, 27 September 1951, pp. 32–3.

Part 2 The truth about 'intelligence'
1. James Rusbridger, *The Intelligence Game: The Illusions and Delusions of International Espionage*, 1991, p. 1.
2. Sir Paul Dukes, *Red Dusk and the Morrow: Adventures and Investigations in Red Russia*, 1922, p. vii.
3. *The Times*, 9 December 1921, p. 11.

6 Getting away with it
1. TNA, KV 2/1391, Confession of Jacob Kirchenstein, 27 September 1951, p. 3.
2. Ibid.

3. For a full account of the second Comintern congress's place in the early Communist movement, see Jon Jacobson, *When the Soviet Union Entered World Politics*, 1994.

4. TNA, KV 2/1391, Confession of Jacob Kirchenstein, 27 September 1951, p. 11.

5. Throughout the Soviet period, it was common for wives and children to remain in Russia whenever agents went abroad: a very acute kind of insurance against defection. That Vallie was permitted to accompany Jacob may signal many things. He may have convinced his Comintern bosses that Vallie was vital to his cover story; she may have been understood as integral to the operation itself; or her presence with him may simply be an anomaly.

6. TNA, KV 2/1391, Confession of Jacob Kirchenstein, 27 September 1951, p. 13.

7. Ibid., p. 14.

8. Ibid., p. 15.

9. Ibid., p. 24.

10. Ibid., p. 16.

11. *Manchester Guardian*, 24 December 1920, p. 11.

12. TNA, CAB 24/129/10, 'Foreign Support of Communist Agitators in the United Kingdom', 15 October 1921, p. 9.

13. Ibid., p. 10.

14. TNA, KV 2/1391, Confession of Jacob Kirchenstein, 27 September 1951, pp. 26–7.

15. TNA, CAB 24/134/54, 'Report on Revolutionary Organisations in the United Kingdom', 16 March 1922, p. 12.

16. TNA, KV 2/1391, Confession of Jacob Kirchenstein, 27 September 1951, p. 21.

17. Ibid.

18. In the 1950s, Jacob said that five years after leaving New York he was desperate to restart a normal life, but he feared 'being declared a traitor' by the Soviet secret police, which he felt would lead to his photograph being circulated 'to all underground channels' worldwide, and probably 'my eventual assassination' (TNA, KV 2/1391, Confession of Jacob Kirchenstein, 27 September 1951, p. 35).

19. Vallie had already left Britain a few months earlier. She was pregnant and had travelled to the United States ahead of Jacob so that the couple's child could be born there and have automatic American citizenship. She, too, took the Stormonth passport, posting it back to Jacob after she had arrived. Unfortunately,

the couple's first child lived for only three days. (TNA, KV 2/1391, Confession of Jacob Kirchenstein, 27 September 1951, p. 28–9.)

7 From Mayfair to Moscow

1. These and other biographical facts are, unless otherwise referenced, taken from Anita Leslie, 'Sheridan, Clare Consuelo (1885–1970)', rev. *Oxford Dictionary of National Biography*, 2004, http://www.oxforddnb.com.ezproxy2.londonlibrary.co.uk/view/article/36064, last accessed 26 August 2016. See also Anita Leslie, *The Tempestuous Career of Clare Sheridan*, 1976.
2. Leslie, 'Sheridan, Clare Consuelo', *Oxford Dictionary of National Biography*.
3. *Observer*, 17 October 1920, p. 10.
4. Sheridan, *Mayfair to Moscow*, p. 27.
5. Ibid., p. 24.
6. Ibid., p. 25.
7. Details of Harker's marriage to Margaret Russell Cooke, including Sidney Cooke's and Sir Vernon Kell's presence at the wedding, are given in *The Times*, 27 October 1920, p. 15.
8. Sheridan, *Mayfair to Moscow*, p. 33.
9. Ibid., p. 35–7.
10. Ibid., p. 38.
11. Ibid., p. 50.
12. Ibid., p. 51.
13. Ibid., p. 95.
14. Ibid., p. 80.
15. Ibid., p. 184.
16. Ibid., p. 180.
17. TNA, KV 2/1033, File index, note 2.
18. Ibid., 'Note', 28 September 1923.
19. Ibid., Unnamed to Harker, 26 November 1925.
20. Ibid., OAH to CSI, 16 December 1925; TNA, KV 2/1033, File index, note 27.
21. Ibid., OAH to CSI, 16 December 1925.
22. Ibid., 'Note', 14 November 1923.
23. Ibid., File index, note 38.
24. Ibid., File index, note 42.
25. Ibid., Clare to Norman [Ewer], 6 October 1926.
26. Ibid., 'Press Cutting: Evening Standard, "I Shadowed Kameneff"', 25 August 1936. In this article Clare implies that she knowingly accepted a commission to shadow the Bolshevik for British

Intelligence in 1920. All other evidence points in the opposite direction, however, with both Kamenev and Sheridan being treated as suspects.

27. Sheridan, *Mayfair to Moscow*, p. 159–60.
28. Ibid., p. 198.
29. Ibid., p. 109.

8 Frolics

1. House of Commons, *A Collection of Reports on Bolshevism in Russia*, 1919, p. 32. Certainly, the Soviet state played a much bigger role in children's lives than democratic states did. It also ended the role of Christian churches in education and, in its early years, presided over an (unintended) increase in the number of orphans. However, there was no systematic attempt to remove the country's children from their parents on a permanent, ongoing basis.
2. *The Times*, 4 January 1919, p. 5.
3. Ironically, in the 1920s, MI5 was probably one of the few intelligence organisations in the world that boasted a woman among its high-ranking officers – a woman, moreover, whose role was most decidedly not that of seductress. Kathleen Sissmore, who was known as Jane, ran the agency's registry, with responsibility for keeping files and card indices up to date and identifying connections between suspects and cases. Sissmore (whose initials, KMMS, appear in almost every file I looked at) was a thoroughly modern, deeply serious woman, who studied for a law degree in her spare time and graduated with first-class honours in 1922, picking up an MBE in 1923, and being called to the Bar in 1924.
4. For a full examination of the truth and lies surrounding Mata Hari's story, and of its impact on the idea of the female spy, see Julie Wheelwright, 'The Language of Espionage: Mata Hari and the Creation of the Spy-Courtesan' in *Languages and the First World War: Representation and Memory*, ed. Christophe Declerq and Julian Walker, 2016, pp. 164–77.
5. Thomson describes his encounter with Mata Hari in Basil Thomson, *Queer People*, 1922, pp. 181–4. 'I am sure that she thought she had had the best of it' was his conclusion (p. 183).
6. TNA, KV 2/818, E. Gambs to H. S. Jackson, 17 March 1921.
7. TNA, KV 2/574, Phillips to Home Office (Mr Stephens), 19 October 1921.
8. Ibid.

9. TNA, KV 2/818, Extract from Major Aubrey MORRIS, 9 October 1922.
10. Ibid.
11. Ibid.
12. *The Times*, 20 May 1922, p. 7; *The Times*, 24 January 1923, p. 7.
13. *The Times*, 24 January 1923, p. 7.
14. Ibid.
15. G. A. Solomon", *Sredi krasnykh" vozhdei*, Paris, 1930, 2 volumes, vol. 2, p. 573. Author's translation from Russian.
16. Ibid., p. 576.
17. Ibid., p. 574–5.
18. Ibid., p. 577.
19. TNA, KV 2/1033, 'Copy' [document begins 'Mrs Clare Sheridan arrived in Rome']. Sheridan was said by an intelligence officer to have 'not only openly aired her views in favour of Bolshevism but tried to convince some of the guests of its advantages, especially in connection with free love'.
20. Yu. Fel'shtinskii, *Vozhdi v zakone*, 2008, pp. 21–2.
21. TNA, KV 2/574, Unknown to Mr Shortt, 1 May 1922.
22. Timothy Edward O'Connor, *The Engineer of Revolution: L. B. Krasin and the Bolsheviks, 1870–1926*, 1992, p. 266.
23. TNA, KV 2/574, Unknown to Bland, 12 November 1923.
24. Ibid., Unknown to X.P., 6 November 1923. Almost certainly, at least one of the British Intelligence agencies would have quickly opened a file on Tamara herself. To date this file has not been released and it may well have been destroyed. We do not, therefore, know how long she and her daughter were kept under surveillance.
25. TNA, KV 2/778, Unknown to Captain Miller, 21 October 1925.
26. TNA, KV 2/591, 'Cryptic Messages from the Personal Columns of "The Times", "The Morning Post" and "The Daily Mail"', various dates.
27. Adam Hochschild, *To End All Wars: A Story of Loyalty and Rebellion, 1914–1918*, 2011, pp. 366–7.

Part 3 We cannot stand idly by

1. John le Carré, *The Russia House*, 1989, p. 185.

9 Bulletins on Bolshevism

1. Research on the *Who Was Who* website reveals that Vernon Kell belonged to the Naval and Military club, Hugh Sinclair to the Army and Navy, Wyndham Childs to the Marlborough,

and Desmond Morton to the United Service, Royal Aero and Challoner clubs.

2. Gill Bennett, *Churchill's Man of Mystery: Desmond Morton and the World of Intelligence*, 2007, pp. 62–3. Bennett writes, 'Morton's purchase of a house so close to Chartwell must be more than coincidence. [...] It does not seem presumptuous [...] to assume that their shared antipathy to Bolshevism would have provided absorbing subject matter for their walks on the Chartwell estate, and their after dinner conversations that went on long into the night.' See also David Stafford, *Churchill and Secret Service*, 1997.

3. TNA, CAB 24/134/54, 'Report on Revolutionary Organisations in the United Kingdom', 16 March 1922, front page.

4. *Documents on British Foreign Policy, 1919–1939*, series 1, vol. 20, ed. W. N. Medlicott, Douglas Dakin and M. E. Lambert, 1977, p. 687.

5. Ibid., p. 788.

6. Ibid., p. 812.

7. TNA, CAB 24/159/44, 'Report on Revolutionary Organisations in the United Kingdom', 8 March 1923.

8. Ibid., pp. 1–2.

9. Ibid., p. 7.

10. Ibid., p. 11.

11. *Documents on British Foreign Policy, 1919–1939*, series 1, vol. 20, p. 967.

12. Ibid.

10 The Marquess's ultimatum

1. TNA, CAB 24/45/21, 'Conclusions of a Meeting of the Cabinet', 25 April 1923, p. 2.

2. TNA, CAB 24/45/23, 'Conclusions of a Meeting of the Cabinet', 2 May 1923, Note to Appendix 1.

3. Ibid., p. 1.

4. Ibid., pp. 2–3.

5. Ibid., pp. 1–2.

6. Ibid., p. 3.

7. Davidson had been accused of running a fuel cartel during the civil war and using the proceeds to fund anti-revolutionary activity; he was shot after spending four months in prison, in full accordance, or so the Soviets claimed, with prevailing legislation at the time (see Stephen White, *Britain and the Bolshevik Revolution: A Study in the Politics of Diplomacy, 1920–1924*, 1979,

pp. 151–2). Mrs Stan Harding (born Sedine Milana) survived her ordeal and later published her own account: Stan Harding, *The Underworld of State*, 1925.

8. TNA, CAB 24/45/23, 'Conclusions of a Meeting of the Cabinet', 2 May 1923, Appendix 1, p. 3.

9. Ibid., p. 4.

10. Ibid., p. 5.

11. Ibid., p. 2. *The Times*, 9 May 1923, p. 11.

12. TNA, CAB 24/45/23, 'Conclusions of a Meeting of the Cabinet', 2 May 1923, p. 2.

13. *The Times*, 9 May 1923, p. 13.

14. *Sunday Times*, 13 May 1923, p. 12.

15. *The Times*, 10 May 1923, p. 16.

16. *Economist,* 12 May 1923, pp. 986–7.

17. *Manchester Guardian*, 10 May 1923, p. 8.

18. *New York Times*, 10 May 1923, p. 21.

19. *Time*, 19 May 1923, p. 9.

20. *Manchester Guardian*, 14 May 1923, p. 7. For a full account of Arthur Ransome's fascinating experiences in Russia, including his own run-ins with the secret services, see Roland Chambers, *The Last Englishman: The Double Life of Arthur Ransome*, 2010.

21. Ibid.

22. Mikhail Bulgakov, 'Benefis lorda Kerzona', *Nakanune*, 19 May 1923, reprinted in Mikhail Bulgakov, *Sobranie sochinenii v 5 tomax*, 5 volumes, vol. 2, 1992. Author's translation from Russian.

23. *The Times*, 12 May 1923, p. 12.

24. *Manchester Guardian*, 14 May 1923, p. 7.

25. Ibid.

26. *Documents on British Foreign Policy, 1919–1939*, series 1, vol. 25, ed. W. N. Medlicott, Douglas Dakin and Gillian Bennett, 1984, p. 105.

27. *Manchester Guardian*, 16 May 1923, p. 9.

28. Ibid. 'Members smiled on hearing from the Under Secretary that Mr Krassin was understood to be in London with the intention of seeking an interview with the Foreign Secretary. Nor was their amusement without justification, for at that moment Mr Krassin [...] happened to be seated in the Distinguished Strangers' Gallery, not far distant from another well-known figure of the shifting Russian drama in the person of Mrs Stan Harding.'

29. *Manchester Guardian*, 24 May 1923, p. 7.

30. Ibid.
31. *Documents on British Foreign Policy, 1919–1939*, series 1, vol. 25, p. 135.
32. *The Times*, 24 May 1923, p. 11.
33. G. H. Bennett and Marion Gibson, *The Later Life of Lord Curzon of Kedleston – Aristocrat, Writer, Politician, Statesman: An Experiment in Political Biography*, 2000, pp. 205–6.
34. At the time that the Queen invited him to form a government, in 1963, Sir Alec Douglas Home was the Earl of Home and sat in the House of Lords. However, he immediately disclaimed his peerage and stood in a by-election for a safe Conservative seat to enable him to enter the House of Commons.
35. Kenneth Rose, *Superior Person: A Portrait of Curzon and His Circle in Late Victorian England*, 1969, p. 384.
36. Malcolm Pearce and Geoffrey Stewart, *British Political History, 1867–2001: Democracy and Decline*, 2013, p. 392.
37. *Baldwin Papers: A Conservative Statesman, 1908–1947*, ed. Philip Williamson and Edward Baldwin, 2004, p. 93.
38. *Manchester Guardian*, 31 May 1923, p. 15.
39. *The Times*, 14 June 1923, p. 16.
40. G. H. Bennett, *British Foreign Policy during the Curzon Period, 1919–24*, 1995, pp. 73–4.

11 The apparition of a monstrosity

1. *Daily Mail*, 31 December 1923, p. 8.
2. *Daily Mail*, 7 January 1924, p. 8.
3. *The Private Diaries of Sir H. Rider Haggard*, ed. D. S. Higgins, 1980, p. 269.
4. *Champion Redoubtable: The Diaries and Letters of Violet Bonham Carter, 1914–1945*, ed. Mark Pottle, 1998, p. 159. Violet's response to Churchill, in a letter of 18 January 1924, was 'I think the Labour Govt. will suffer from the timidity & inefficiency of its members not from their violence.' (p. 160).
5. *The Times*, 1 January 1924, p. 9.
6. Maurice Cowling, *The Impact of Labour*, 1971, p. 365.
7. Ibid.
8. Labour Party, *Manifesto*, 1923, http://labourmanifesto.com/1923/, last accessed 2 September 2016.
9. Cited in Harvey Wish, 'Anglo-Soviet Relations during Labour's First Ministry (1924)', *Slavonic and East European Review*, 1939, vol. 17, no. 50, pp. 389–403, p. 391.
10. Wish, *Slavonic and East European Review*, 1939, vol. 17, no. 50, p. 391.

11. Keith Neilson and T. G. Otte, *The Permanent Under-Secretary for Foreign Affairs, 1854–1946*, 2009, p. 181.
12. Ibid.
13. See Trevor Barnes, 'Special Branch and the First Labour Government', *Historical Journal*, 1979, vol. 22, no. 4, pp. 941–51.
14. Barnes, *Historical Journal*, 1979, vol. 22, no. 4, p. 944.
15. Andrew, *The Defence of the Realm*, p. 146–7.
16. TNA, KV 2/1414, Unknown to X.P., 27 May 1924.
17. Morgan, *Labour Legends and Russian Gold*, p. 52.
18. The text of the general treaty can be read in *The Times*, 8 August 1924, p. 6. A summary of the contents of the two treaties is in *The Times*, 8 August 1924, p. 12.
19. Wish, *Slavonic and East European Review*, 1939, vol. 17, no. 50, p. 398.
20. *Hansard*, 7 August 1924, vol. 176, cc. 3131–65.
21. See, for instance, *The Times*, 7 August 1924, p. 12.
22. *The Times*, 20 August 1924, p. 6.
23. Ibid., 23 August 1924, p. 11.
24. See, for instance, N. D. Siederer, 'The Campbell Case', *Journal of Contemporary History*, 1974, vol. 9, no. 2, pp. 143–62.

12 The big lie

1. Laura Beers helps to situate this moment within the longer history of British media representations and misrepresentations of the Labour Party. See Laura Beers, *Your Britain: Media and the Making of the Labour Party*, 2010.
2. Wish, *Slavonic and East European Review*, 1939, vol. 17, no. 50, p. 392.
3. *Sunday Times*, 18 November 1923, p. 11.
4. *The Times*, 10 October 1924, p. 7.
5. Quoted in Paul Addison, 'Churchill's Three Careers' in *Winston Churchill in the Twenty-First Century*, ed. David Cannadine and Roland Quinault, 2004, pp. 9–25, p. 22.
6. *Sunday Times*, 5 October 1924, p. 17.
7. *Hansard*, 9 October 1924, vol. 177, cc. 728–30.
8. Many of the details in this account rely on the scholarship of Gill Bennett who, as the Foreign and Commonwealth Office's Chief Historian, published a definitive account of this episode in 1999: Gill Bennett, *'A Most Extraordinary and Mysterious Business': The Zinoviev Letter of 1924*, 1999.
9. Bennett, *'A Most Extraordinary and Mysterious Business'*, pp. 93–5.
10. Ibid., p. 36.

11. Ibid., p. 39.
12. Ibid., p. 35.
13. Ibid., p. 39.
14. Ibid., p. 31.
15. Ibid., p. 82.
16. *Daily Mail*, 25 October 1924, p. 9.
17. *The Times*, 27 October 1924, p. 8.
18. *The Times*, 25 October 1924, p. 13.
19. *The Private Diaries of Sir H. Rider Haggard*, ed. Higgins, p. 277.

Part 4 Dragnet
1. *Documents on British Foreign Policy, 1919–1939*, series 1, vol. 25, p. 655. The government and Conservatives more generally would continue to insist that the Zinoviev Letter was genuine for the remainder of the interwar period.
2. *Baldwin Papers*, ed. Williamson and Baldwin, p. 163.
3. Ibid., p. 166.
4. *Sunday Times*, 5 October 1924, p. 17.
5. *Baldwin Papers*, ed. Williamson and Baldwin, p. 168.

13 The old business goes on
1. On Jacob's earlier period in London, see Chapter 6.
2. TNA, KV 2/1392, 'The Russian Trade Delegation and Revolutionary Organizations in the United Kingdom', 7 December 1925, Appendix A, Letter 20.
3. Ibid., Letter 40.
4. TNA, KV 2/1391, 'Jacob Kirchenstein', H.O. File Misc. 2750, 21 September 1925.
5. Ibid., 'Extracts from a Report on the Russian Trade Delegation and Revolutionary Organizations in the United Kingdom dated 7th December, 1925', pp. 2–3.
6. TNA, KV 2/643, 'Cross-Reference. Subject: VLADIMIROF', 6 December 1923.
7. TNA, KV 2/1391, 'Notes on information contained in S.F. 450/U.K. Serial 3 (11b)', [circa 16 May 1927].
8. Ibid.
9. Ibid., File index, note 90.
10. Another agent, Klaus Fuchs, had been convicted in March 1950, after confessing to giving nuclear secrets to the Soviets. He was sent to prison for more than a decade and stripped of his British citizenship. Kirchenstein may well have feared incarceration or deportation if he owned up to similar activities, albeit decades earlier.

11. TNA, KV 2/1391, Confession of Jacob Kirchenstein, 27 September 1951, p. 46.

12. Ibid., 'Comments on Kirchenstein's Interrogation', 26 November 1951.

13. TNA, KV 2/1101, 'The Daily Herald, 21.11.24', 21 November 1924.

14. Ibid., Item 18A, 29 November 1924.

15. Ibid., Item 18A, 20 December 1924.

16. Ibid., 'Q.X. to D. A. Reinmann Esq.', 9 January 1925.

17. Ibid., 'Federated Press of America', 24 April 1950.

18. Ibid., 'Reinmann ('D') Report', 3 February 1925, p. 1.

19. Ibid., 'Reinmann ('D') Report', 3 February 1925, p. 2.

20. Ibid., 'Federated Press of America', 30 January 1950, p. 1.

21. TNA, KV 2/1016, 'Clandestine Activities of William Norman Ewer 1919–1929, Part I. Narrative', September 1949, p. 2.

22. Ibid., Part III. The "Kenneth Milton" Correspondence', September 1949, p. 1.

23. Ibid., H. Miller to Harker, 7 May 1925.

24. Ibid., 'Clandestine Activities of William Norman Ewer 1919–1929, Part I. Narrative', September 1949, p. 4.

25. For more information about the police strikes of the late 1910s and the connection to Ewer and the FPA, see Madeira, *Britannia and the Bear*, pp. 29–60.

26. TNA, KV 2/989, Item 66a, 1 August 1928, p. 4.

27. TNA, KV 2/1395, Rosa to [Ewer], 28 March 1926.

28. The identities of most of these people or organisations remain a mystery. Careful reading of the files reveals, however, that the Bink, so far from being a dangerous Russian spy, was actually Trilby's first son, whom he had with his wife, the successful novelist Monica Ewer.

29. *Documents on British Foreign Policy, 1919–1939*, series 1, vol. 25, p. 664.

30. *The Times*, 29 October 1925, p. 8.

31. TNA, KV 2/1101, 'Federated Press of America', 30 January 1950, p. 3.

14 Bolshevism is catching

1. For an excellent analysis of the SCR's first two decades, see Emily Lygo, 'Promoting Soviet Culture in Britain: The History of the Society for Cultural Relations between the Peoples of the British Commonwealth and the USSR, 1924–45', *Modern Language Review*, 2013, vol. 108, no. 2, pp. 571–96. See also,

Ludmila Stern, *Western Intellectuals and the Soviet Union, 1920–1940*, 2007.

2. *Manchester Guardian*, 11 July 1924, p. 10.

3. Ibid., p. 16.

4. See, for instance, *Russia in Britain, 1880–1940: From Melodrama to Modernism*, ed. Rebecca Beasley and Philip Ross Bullock, 2013.

5. TNA, KV 2/1109, C. B. Hutchinson to Rothstein, 15 July 1925.

6. Worley, *Class Against Class*, p. 5.

7. TNA, KV 2/1109, Rev. Wm. Dick to Andrew Rothstein, 13 June 1925.

8. TNA, KV 2/1111, 'Extract [from] PFR 3911 SOC. for the PROMOTION of CULTURAL RELATIONS WITH RUSSIA', 27 January 1926.

9. Cited in Giles Dostaler, *Keynes and his Battles*, 2007, p. 93.

10. The most important examples to come to light *after the fact* include the RAF serviceman Anthony Wraight, who defected to Russia in the 1950s after spending years spying on his employers, and Wilfred Burchett, a *Daily Express* journalist, who allegedly moonlighted for the Soviets in Cold War hotspots such as China and Vietnam. In a similar vein, we now know that Anthony Blunt began his espionage career after taking an organised trip to Russia in 1935, the trip having been arranged through Inturist, a body that was run by the same department of the Soviet state as the SCR. Blunt went in search of pictures and architecture, he told his brother, but the KGB scouts spotted him and reeled him in all the same.

11. Files in the KV series on all these individuals have been declassified in recent years and can be viewed at the National Archives. Some have also been digitised and can be downloaded online.

12. For a detailed history of the development of British film censorship, see James C. Robertson, *The Hidden Cinema: British Film Censorship in Action, 1913–1972*, 1989.

13. TNA, HO 45/24871, Note by S.W.H., 24 June 1926.

14. Ibid., O. A. R. Murray to Anderson, 21 June 1926.

15. Ibid., Sir William Bridgeman to Sir William Joynson-Hicks, 1 July 1926.

16. Ibid., Brooke Wilkinson to S. W. Harris, 30 June 1926.

17. *Observer*, 11 July 1926, p. 10.

18. TNA, HO 45/24871, Clipping from the *Workers' Weekly*, 16 July 1926.

19. Ibid., 'Memorandum', 9 September 1926, p. 1.

20. Ibid., pp. 1–2.

21. Ibid., p. 3.
22. Ibid., p. 4.
23. Ibid.
24. Ibid., Exterior file cover, 'Armoured Cruiser Potemkin Film', 9 September 1926.
25. Ibid., Interior file cover, 'Armoured Cruiser Potemkin Film', 9 September 1926.
26. Ibid., H. Miller to Scott, 30 December 1926.
27. Ibid., H. Miller to Newsam, 13 October 1927.
28. Ibid., Untitled memorandum, 14 September 1928, p. 5.
29. Ibid., H. Miller to Scott, 13 October 1927.
30. Ibid., Ivor Montagu to Union der Socialistischen Sowjet Republiken, 2 September 1927.
31. Leon Trotsky, 'Problems of the British Revolution', www. marxists.org, last accessed 10 September 2016.
32. Cited in Sarah Smith, *Children, Cinema and Censorship: From Dracula to the Dead End Kids*, 2005, pp. 181–3.
33. TNA, HO 45/24871, Interior of file cover, no. 495038, 16 July 1926.
34. Denise J. Youngblood, *Soviet Cinema in the Silent Era, 1918–1935*, 2014.
35. I learned about Eisenstein's presence at the screening through the fascinating exhibition on the director at London's GRAD gallery in the spring of 2016.
36. Cited in Lawrence Napper, *British Cinema and Middlebrow Culture in the Interwar Years*, 2009, pp. 69–70.

15 Spies, Fascists and the General Strike

1. See, for instance, Read, *The World on Fire*.
2. Cited in Peter M. Slowe, *Manny Shinwell: An Authorised Biography*, 1993, p. 88.
3. The most famous critical analysis of the Chancellor of the Exchequer's policy is John Maynard Keynes's *The Economic Consequences of Mr Churchill*, which was published in 1925 by Leonard and Virginia Woolf and contains a chapter on the coal industry.
4. *Manchester Guardian*, 1 August 1925, p. 10.
5. Ibid.
6. Ibid.
7. TNA, CAB 23/50/22, 'Conclusions of a Meeting of the Cabinet', 30 July 1925, p. 3.
8. *Manchester Guardian*, 13 October 1925, p. 6.

9. We have already seen that Oswald Harker and Sidney Russell Cooke remained in touch after the latter left MI5, though this was due to a direct family connection. More generally, old spies were positively encouraged to stay in contact with former colleagues. Sir Vernon Kell created one means for doing so in the aftermath of post-war budget cuts, the IP Dining Club (IP stood for Intelligence and Police). See Andrew Staniforth, *Routledge Companion to UK Counter Terrorism*, 2012, pp. 30–1, and also, for what is surely a fictionalised account of this same institution, the descriptions of the 'Thursday Club' in John Buchan's novel *The Three Hostages* (1924).

10. *The Times*, 29 July 1924, p. xxix.

11. Bennett, *Churchill's Man of Mystery*, pp. 71–2.

12. Ibid., pp. 72, 128. See also John Hope, 'Surveillance or Collusion? Maxwell Knight, MI5 and the British Fascisti', *Intelligence and National Security*, vol. 9, no. 4, 1994, pp. 651–75, and Henry Hemming, *M: Maxwell Knight, MI5's Greatest Spymaster*, 2017.

13. Stephen Dorril, *Blackshirt: Sir Oswald Mosley and British Fascism*, 2007, pp. 196–8.

14. Colin Holmes, *Searching for Lord Haw-Haw: The Political Lives of William Joyce*, 2016, p. 297. See also J. Hope, 'Fascism, the Security Service and the Curious Careers of Maxwell Knight and James McGuirk Hughes', *Lobster*, November 1991, no. 22, pp. 1–5.

15. John G. Hope, 'Surveillance or Collusion? Maxwell Knight, MI5 and the British Fascisti', pp. 651–75.

16. Bennett, *Churchill's Man of Mystery*, p. 81.

17. Cited in R. C. Maguire, '"The Fascists … are … to be Depended Upon": The British Government, Fascists and Strike-breaking during 1925 and 1926' in *British Fascism, the Labour Movement and the State*, ed. N. Copsey and D. Renton, 2005, pp. 6–26, p. 8.

18. *The Times*, 1 October 1925, p. 11.

19. Charles Ferrall and Douglas McNeill, *Writing the 1926 General Strike*, 2015, p. 36.

20. Ibid., p. 37.

21. Ibid., p. 36.

22. For more on the *Morning Post*'s important role in interwar anti-socialism, see Keith M. Wilson, *A Study in the History and Politics of* The Morning Post, *1905–1926*, 1990.

23. Andrew, *The Defence of the Realm*, pp. 125–6.

24. Cited in John Campbell, *F. E. Smith: First Earl of Birkenhead*, 1983, p. 785.
25. Cited in Stephen Lee, *Aspects of British Political History, 1914–1995*, 1996, p. 88.
26. TNA, KV 2/2317, H. R. Vyvyan to Col. Sir V. G. W. Kell, 31 August 1925.
27. Daniel F. Calhoun, *The United Front: The TUC and the Russians, 1923–1928*, 2008, p. 237.
28. TNA, KV 2/1111, Excerpt from A. Rosengolz to A. Rothstein, 9 June 1925.
29. James Hinton, *Labour and Socialism: A History of the British Labour Movement, 1867–1974*, 1983, p. 138.
30. *The Times*, 29 June 1926, p. 18.
31. Cited in Jeffery, *MI6*, p. 227.
32. Ibid.
33. *The Times*, 21 June 1926, p. 8.
34. Ibid.

Part 5 The ARCOS raid
1. *The Times*, 9 October 1926, p. 7.
2. The Rasputin allegation is found in Richard Rhodes, *The Making of the Atomic Bomb*, 2012, p. 195.
3. Ian Thomas, 'Confronting the Challenge of Socialism: The British Empire Union and the National Citizens' Union, 1917–1927', unpublished M.Phil. thesis, University of Wolverhampton, 2010, p. 157.
4. *The Times*, 17 September 1926, p. 14.
5. Austen Chamberlain, *The Austen Chamberlain Diary Letters: The Correspondence of Sir Austen Chamberlain with his Sisters Hilda and Ida, 1916–1937*, ed. Robert C. Self, 1995, p. 310.

16 The landlord of The Dolphin
1. Advertising pamphlet for the *Morning Post* newspaper, mid-1920s, John Johnson Collection, Bodleian Library, University of Oxford.
2. TNA, FO 371/12586, J. P. Leigh to Captain Liddell, 6 April 1927.
3. I identified Edward Langston by making a systematic comparison of names in ARCOS staff lists, which are contained in TNA file HO 144/8403, with the names of pub landlords in contemporary west London business directories. (It is clear from elsewhere in the MI5 files that the unnamed 'Y' took over a pub in Uxbridge.)

4. TNA, KV 3/15, 'Arcos Ltd.: A Chronological Note of Events', 14 May 1927, p. 2.
5. *The Times*, 8 March 1927, p. 18.
6. TNA, KV 3/15, 'Signal Training, Volume 3, Pamphlet no. 11', 1926.

17 One in the eye for Lenin
1. TNA, KV 3/15, 'Raid on 49 Moorgate on 12th May, 1927: Report on Documents Obtained by the Police', undated, p. 3.
2. TNA, HO 144/8403, 'A Short Statement by Insp. Clancy', 16 May 1927.
3. Ibid., 'Note by Sir Wyndham Childs', undated, p. 1.
4. TNA, KV 3/15, 'Raid on 49 Moorgate on 12th May, 1927: Report on Documents Obtained by the Police', undated, p. 4.
5. TNA, HO 144/8403, Clippings from the *Daily Mail*, 13 May 1927.
6. *Daily Mail*, 14 May 1927, p. 11. The Black Museum, now called the Crime Museum, is a department of the Metropolitan Police that collects and curates important artefacts from the force's cases.
7. TNA, HO 144/8403, Clippings from *The Times*, 14 May 1927.
8. *The Times*, 26 May 1926, p. 17.
9. TNA, HO 144/8403, Clippings from the *Daily Mail*, 17 May 1927.
10. *Hansard*, 24 May 1927, vol. 206, cc. 1842–54.
11. *Hansard*, 26 May 1927, vol. 206, cc. 2195–326.
12. Ibid.
13. Ibid.
14. Ibid.
15. Ibid.
16. Frederick Winston Furneaux Smith Birkenhead, *F.E.: The Life of F. E. Smith, First Earl of Birkenhead*, 1960, p. 539.
17. *Morning Post*, 25 May 1927, p. 14.
18. TNA, KV 2/2379, 'H.O. File 510225/70 (Formerly B.2614)', 22 July 1927.
19. *The Times*, 16 July 1927, p. 7.

18 One in the foot for Britain?
1. *Manchester Guardian*, 13 May 1927, p. 10.
2. *The Times*, 18 May 1927, p. 18.
3. The Commissioner of the Metropolitan Police, Sir William Horwood, wrote to Jix on 14 May 1927 exposing his poor

grasp of the finer points of international diplomacy. He said that 'I do not think that [...] the question of diplomatic status and immunity of the Soviet Trading Delegation [*sic*] matters at all, but, as a matter of fact, we discovered last night a graph which shows that the head of the Trading Delegation is in direct control of ARCOS. This in itself would have justified anything we have done. It exposes the farce of the separate organisation.' (TNA, HO 144/8403, Horwood to the Home Secretary, 14 May 1927, p. 2.)

4. TNA, HO 144/8403, Draft search warrant, 12 May 1927.
5. Ibid., 'The Raid on the Buildings of ARCOS', undated, p. 1.
6. Ibid., pp. 1–2.
7. *The Times*, 14 May 1927, p. 12.
8. TNA, HO 144/8403, Copy of 'The Raid on ARCOS Ltd. and the Trade Delegation of the USSR: Facts and Documents'.
9. Leo Stennett Amery, *The Leo Amery Diaries: Volume 1: 1896–1929*, ed. John Barnes and David Nicholson, 1980, p. 506.
10. TNA, FO 1093/73, Untitled Memorandum on the Recent Arcos Case, 28 June 1927, p. 6.
11. TNA, KV 3/15, Copy of 'Russia No. 2 (1927). Documents Illustrating the Hostile Activities of the Soviet Government and Third International against Great Britain', pp. 1–31, p. 29.
12. Ibid., p. 31.
13. *Hansard*, 24 May 1927, vol. 206, cc. 1842–54.
14. TNA, FO 1093/73, Untitled Memorandum on the Recent Arcos Case, 28 June 1927, p. 1.
15. *Saturday Review*, 21 May 1927, p. 769–70, 773.
16. Ibid., 28 May 1927, p. 813.
17. *Spectator*, 28 May 1927, pp. 929–30.
18. Ibid., p. 932.
19. Ibid., p. 935.
20. TNA, FO 1093/71, Minutes of the Meeting Held on Friday, June 24th, p. 5.
21. Ibid., Minutes of the Meeting Held on Thursday, June 30th, p. 4.
22. TNA, KV 3/17, Liddell to Kell, 22 December 1926, pp. 1–3.
23. TNA, FO 1093/73, Untitled Memorandum on the Recent Arcos Case, 28 June 1927, pp. 4–5.
24. Ibid., p. 7.
25. Andrew, *The Defence of the Realm*, p. 156.

19 Escapes, lucky and unlucky

1. *New Statesman*, 21 May 1927, p. 169.

2. *Documents on British Foreign Policy, 1919–1939*, series 1A, vol. 3, ed. W. N. Medlicott, Douglas Dakin and M. E. Lambert, 1970, p. 318.
3. Ibid., p. 356.
4. *The Times*, 11 June 1927, p. 12.
5. *Documents on British Foreign Policy, 1919–1939*, series 1A, vol. 3, pp. 354–5.
6. Michael Hughes, *Inside the Enigma: British Officials in Russia, 1900–1939*, 1997, p. 219.
7. *The Times*, 13 June 1927, p. 13.
8. TNA, KV 2/1391, Confession of Jacob Kirchenstein, 27 September 1951, p. 69.
9. TNA, KV 2/1391, Confession of Jacob Kirchenstein, 27 September 1951, p. 70.
10. TNA, KV 2/1391, Confession of Jacob Kirchenstein, 27 September 1951, p. 70.
11. Ibid., p. 71.
12. Ibid., p. 72.
13. Ibid., p. 73.
14. Ibid.
15. Ibid., Jacob Kirchenstein to Charles Douglas, 25 September 1931.
16. Ibid., Minute no. 90, 10 October 1950.
17. TNA, KV 3/15, Untitled document, no. 17A, 13 May 1927, p. 1.
18. Ibid., 're "Y"', 26 May 1927, p. 1.
19. We do not know how many more times MI5 used Sidney Russell Cooke's flat as a safe house. But the possibility of doing so abruptly ended in 1930, when Cooke himself was found shot dead there, with a double-barrelled gun at his side. Most agreed that this was suicide, though the coroner's official verdict was that it had been an accident. Some saw a connection to Cooke's life as a spy and wondered if he had been murdered. As Andrew Lycett wrote in a history of the City firm where Cooke worked, 'an inquest recorded that Cooke had shot himself accidentally while cleaning his gun, but rumours of Soviet involvement persisted. Hugo Pitman, who was not a great fabricator of tales, told a young colleague specifically that Cooke had been shot by the Russians'. (Andrew Lycett, *From Diamond Sculls to Golden Handcuffs: A History of Rowe and Pitman*, 1998, p. 46.)
20. TNA, KV 3/15, Copy of telegram, 25 May 1927.
21. Ibid., 're "Y"', 26 May 1927, p. 1.
22. Ibid., p. 2.

23. Ibid., Clipping from the *New Leader*, 3 June 1927.
24. Ibid., Minute sheet, item 15A, 10 May 1927.
25. TNA, KV 2/999, 'Copies of Entries in the Diary of W. E. Dale', p. 26.
26. Wilfred Macartney, *Zigzag: Autobiographical Reminiscences*, 1937.
27. TNA, KV 2/647, 'Wilfrid Francis Macartney' character description, undated.
28. Sir Compton Mackenzie, 'Prologue' in Wilfred Macartney, *Walls Have Mouths: A Record of Ten Years' Penal Servitude*, 1936, pp. 21–2.
29. *The Times*, 13 February 1929, p. 16.
30. Labour Party, *Manifesto*, 1929, http://labourmanifesto.com/1929/, last accessed 24 September 2016.

Epilogue Like shadows in the failing dusk

1. Corey Robin, *Fear: The History of a Political Idea*, 2004, p. 182.
2. Ibid., p. 13.

FURTHER READING

Readers who would like to understand more about some or all of the subjects in this book will find many other sources of information, both primary and secondary. Below, I have collected details of the archives and texts I have found most useful.

Archives

The core of this book is the contents of the 1920s files of MI5. These are held at the United Kingdom's National Archives and, due to subsequent consolidations and organisational changes, contain, in addition to the surviving MI5 papers, a great deal of material from Special Branch. Each file begins with the reference letters KV. A small but increasing number of files have been digitised and may be viewed online, sometimes for a small fee. Otherwise, the records may be consulted in person by anyone who visits the National Archives.

The records of 1920s cabinet discussions and the papers that informed these discussions, both of which I have found invaluable, are also held at the National Archives, under references CAB 23 and CAB 24 respectively. All can be viewed and searched online for free at the dedicated 'Cabinet Papers 1915-1988' website: www.nationalarchives.gov.uk/cabinetpapers/default.htm.

The official report of debates in parliament, *Hansard*, has largely been digitised and can be viewed and searched online for free too: hansard.millbanksystems.com.

The archives of *The Times*, the *Sunday Times*, the *Manchester Guardian* and the *Observer* are also available online, for a fee.

General histories of espionage

Calder, James D., *Intelligence, Espionage and Related Topics: An Annotated Bibliography of Serial Journal and Magazine Scholarship, 1944–1998*, 1999.

Rusbridger, James, *The Intelligence Game: The Illusions and Delusions of International Espionage*, 1991.

Sheldon, R. M., *Espionage in the Ancient World: An Annotated Bibliography of Books and Articles in Western Languages*, 2003.

Volkman, Ernest, *The History of Espionage*, 2007.

General histories of British Intelligence

Andrew, Christopher, *The Defence of the Realm: The Authorized History of MI5*, 2009.

Jeffery, Keith, *MI6: The History of the Secret Intelligence Service, 1909–1949*, 2010.

Staniforth, Andrew, *Routledge Companion to UK Counter Terrorism*, 2012.

West, Nigel, *Historical Dictionary of British Intelligence*, 2014.

Wilson, Ray and Ian Adams, *Special Branch: A History: 1883–2006*, 2015.

British Intelligence and the Bolsheviks in the 1920s

Barnes, Trevor, 'Special Branch and the First Labour Government', *Historical Journal*, 1979, vol. 22, no. 4.

Bennett, Gill, '*A Most Extraordinary and Mysterious Business': The Zinoviev Letter of 1924*, 1999.

Burke, David, *The Spy Who Came in from the Co-op: Melita Norwood and the Ending of Cold War Espionage*, 2008.

Copsey, N. and D. Renton (eds.), *British Fascism, the Labour Movement and the State*, 2005.

Hemming, Henry, *M: Maxwell Knight, MI5's Greatest Spymaster*, 2017.

Hope, J., 'Fascism, the Security Service and the Curious Careers of Maxwell Knight and James McGuirk Hughes', *Lobster*, 1991, no. 22.

Hope, John, 'Surveillance or Collusion? Maxwell Knight, MI5 and the British Fascisti', *Intelligence and National Security*, 1994, vol. 9, no. 4.

Mackenzie, Sir Compton, 'Prologue' in Macartney, Wilfred, *Walls Have Mouths: A Record of Ten Years' Penal Servitude*, 1936.

Madeira, Victor, *Britannia and the Bear: The Anglo-Russian Intelligence Wars, 1917–1929*, 2014.

Maguire, R. C., '"The Fascists . . . are . . . to be Depended Upon": The British Government, Fascists and Strike-breaking during 1925 and 1926' in N. Copsey and D. Renton (eds.), *British Fascism, the Labour Movement and the State*, 2005.

Popplewell, Richard James, *Intelligence and Imperial Defence: British Intelligence and the Defence of the Indian Empire, 1904–1924*, 1985.

Quinlan, Kevin, *The Secret War between the Wars: MI5 in the 1920s and 1930s*, 2014.

Wish, Harvey, 'Anglo-Soviet Relations during Labour's First Ministry (1924)', *Slavonic and East European Review*, 1939, vol. 17, no. 50.

General Anglo-Soviet contacts in the 1920s
Beasley, Rebecca and Philip Ross Bullock (eds.), *Russia in Britain, 1880–1940: From Melodrama to Modernism*, 2013.

Bennett, G. H., *British Foreign Policy during the Curzon Period, 1919–24*, 1995.

Borodin, M. M., *Istoriya velikoi izmeny*, 1922.

Calhoun, Daniel F., *The United Front: The TUC and the Russians, 1923–1928*, 2008.

Hughes, Michael, *Inside the Enigma: British Officials in Russia, 1900–1939*, 1997.

Indo-Russian Relations, 1917–1947: Select Documents from the Archives of The Russian Federation, Part 1: 1917–1928, 1999.

Lygo, Emily, 'Promoting Soviet Culture in Britain: The History of the Society for Cultural Relations between the Peoples of the British Commonwealth and the USSR, 1924–45', *Modern Language Review*, 2013, vol. 108, no. 2.

Medlicott, W. N., Douglas Dakin and M. E. Lambert (eds.), *Documents on British Foreign Policy, 1919–1939*, series 1A, vol. 3, 1970.

Medlicott, W. N., Douglas Dakin and M. E. Lambert (eds.), *Documents on British Foreign Policy, 1919–1939*, series 1, vol. 20, 1977.

Medlicott, W. N., Douglas Dakin and Gillian Bennett (eds.), *Documents on British Foreign Policy, 1919–1939*, series 1, vol. 25, 1984.

Morgan, Kevin, *Labour Legends and Russian Gold*, 2006.

Neilson, Keith and T. G. Otte, *The Permanent Under-Secretary for Foreign Affairs, 1854–1946*, 2009.

Solomon, G. A., *Among the Red Autocrats: My Experience in the Service of the Soviets*, 1935. Originally published as G. A. Solomon", *Sredi krasnykh" vozhdei*, 2 volumes, 1930.

Stern, Ludmila, *Western Intellectuals and the Soviet Union, 1920–1940*, 2007.

Ullman, Richard H., *Anglo-Soviet Relations, 1917–1921*, 3 volumes, 1961–72.

White, Stephen, *Britain and the Bolshevik Revolution: A Study in the Politics of Diplomacy, 1920–1924*, 1979.

The United Kingdom in the 1920s

Beers, Laura, *Your Britain: Media and the Making of the Labour Party*, 2010.

Clarke, Peter, *Hope and Glory: Britain 1900–2000*, 2004.

Cowling, Maurice, *The Impact of Labour, 1920–1924*, 1971.

Denman, James and Paul McDonald, 'Unemployment Statistics from 1881 to the Present Day', *Labour Market Trends*, January 1996.

Dorril, Stephen, *Blackshirt: Sir Oswald Mosley and British Fascism*, 2007.

Dostaler, Giles, *Keynes and his Battles*, 2007.

Ferrall, Charles and Douglas McNeill, *Writing the 1926 General Strike*, 2015.

Hinton, James, *Labour and Socialism: A History of the British Labour Movement, 1867–1974*, 1983.

Holmes, Colin, *Searching for Lord Haw-Haw: The Political Lives of William Joyce*, 2016.

Jenkinson, Jacqueline, *Black 1919: Riots, Racism and Resistance in Imperial Britain*, 2009.

Keynes, John Maynard, *The Economic Consequences of Mr Churchill*, 1925.

Lee, Joseph, *Ireland 1912–1985: Politics and Society*, 1989.

Lee, Stephen, *Aspects of British Political History, 1914–1995*, 1996.

McKibbin, Ross, *Classes and Cultures: England, 1918–1951*, 1998.

Pearce, Malcolm and Geoffrey Stewart, *British Political History, 1867–2001: Democracy and Decline*, 2013.

Pugh, Martin, *Hurrah for the Blackshirts! Fascists and Fascism in Britain between the Wars*, 2005.

Robertson, James C., *The Hidden Cinema: British Film Censorship in Action, 1913–1972*, 1989.

Siederer, N. D., 'The Campbell Case', *Journal of Contemporary History*, 1974, vol. 9, no. 2.

Thomas, Ian, 'Confronting the Challenge of Socialism: The British Empire Union and the National Citizens' Union, 1917–1927', unpublished M.Phil. thesis, University of Wolverhampton, 2010.

Wilson, Keith M., *A Study in the History and Politics of* The Morning Post, *1905–1926*, 1990.

Worley, Matthew, *Class Against Class: The Communist Party in Britain Between the Wars*, 2002.

The rise of the Bolsheviks and the new Soviet state

Bulgakov, Mikhail, 'Benefis lorda Kerzona', *Nakanune*, 19 May 1923, reprinted in Mikhail Bulgakov, *Sobranie sochinenii v 5 tomax*, vol. 2, 1992.

Caballero, Manuel, *Latin America and the Comintern, 1919–1943*, 2002.

Fel'shtinskii, Yu., *Vozhdi v zakone*, 2008.

Hopkirk, Peter, *Setting the East Ablaze: Lenin's Dream of an Empire in Asia*, 1984.

House of Commons, *A Collection of Reports on Bolshevism in Russia*, 1919.

Jacobson, Jon, *When the Soviet Union Entered World Politics*, 1994.

McMeekin, Sean, *History's Greatest Heist: The Looting of Russia by the Bolsheviks*, 2008.

Muravyova, L. and I. Sivolap-Kaftanova (trans. Jane Sayer), *Lenin in London: Memorial Places*, 1983.

Read, Anthony, *The World on Fire: 1919 and the Battle with Bolshevism*, 2008.

Service, Robert, *A History of Modern Russia: From Nicholas II to Putin*, 2003.

Youngblood, Denise J., *Soviet Cinema in the Silent Era, 1918–1935*, 2014.

Biography and memoir

Addison, Paul, 'Churchill's Three Careers' in David Cannadine and Roland Quinault (eds.), *Winston Churchill in the Twenty-First Century*, 2004.

Amery, Leo Stennett, *The Leo Amery Diaries: Volume 1: 1896–1929*, ed. John Barnes and David Nicholson, 1980.

Bennett, G. H. and Marion Gibson, *The Later Life of Lord Curzon of Kedleston – Aristocrat, Writer, Politician, Statesman: An Experiment in Political Biography*, 2000.

Bennett, Gill, *Churchill's Man of Mystery: Desmond Morton and the World of Intelligence*, 2007.

Birkenhead, Frederick Winston Furneaux Smith, *F.E.: The Life of F. E. Smith, First Earl of Birkenhead*, 1960.

Campbell, John, *F. E. Smith: First Earl of Birkenhead*, 1983.

Cannadine, David and Roland Quinault (eds.), *Winston Churchill in the Twenty-First Century*, 2004.

Chamberlain, Austen, *The Austen Chamberlain Diary Letters: The Correspondence of Sir Austen Chamberlain with his Sisters Hilda and Ida, 1916–1937*, ed. Robert C. Self, 1995.

Chambers, Roland, *The Last Englishman: The Double Life of Arthur Ransome*, 2010.

Dukes, Sir Paul, *Red Dusk and the Morrow: Adventures and Investigations in Red Russia*, 1922.

Harding, Stan, *The Underworld of State*, 1925.

Higgins, D. S. (ed.), *The Private Diaries of Sir H. Rider Haggard*, 1980.

Jacobs, Dan, *Borodin: Stalin's Man in China*, 1981.

Leslie, Anita, *The Tempestuous Career of Clare Sheridan*, 1976.

Macartney, Wilfred, *Walls Have Mouths: A Record of Ten Years' Penal Servitude*, 1936.

Macartney, Wilfred, *Zigzag: Autobiographical Reminiscences*, 1937.

Meynell, Francis, *My Lives*, 1971.

O'Connor, Timothy Edward, *The Engineer of Revolution: L. B. Krasin and the Bolsheviks, 1870–1926*, 1992.

Phillips, Hugh D., *Between the Revolution and the West: A Political Biography of Maxim M. Litvinov*, 1992.

Pottle, Mark (ed.), *Champion Redoubtable: The Diaries and Letters of Violet Bonham Carter, 1914–1945*, 1998.

Rose, Kenneth, *Superior Person: A Portrait of Curzon and His Circle in Late Victorian England*, 1969.

Sheridan, Clare, *Mayfair to Moscow – Clare Sheridan's Diary*, 1921.

Slowe, Peter M., *Manny Shinwell: An Authorised Biography*, 1993.

Stafford, David, *Churchill and Secret Service*, 1997.

Thomson, Basil, *Queer People*, 1922.

Williamson, Philip and Edward Baldwin (eds.), *Baldwin Papers: A Conservative Statesman, 1908–1947*, 2004.

Fiction from and about the 1920s
Buchan, John, *The Three Hostages*, 1924.

Huxley, Aldous, *Antic Hay*, 1923.

Waugh, Evelyn, *Brideshead Revisited*, 1945.

Wilson, Angus, *No Laughing Matter*, 1967.

Woolf, Virginia, *Mrs Dalloway*, 1925.

Other sources

Campbell, Andrew, 'Moscow's Gold: Soviet Financing of Global Subversion', *National Observer*, Autumn 1999.

Clarke, Ignatius Frederick (ed.), *The Great War with Germany, 1890–1914: Fictions and Fantasies of the War-to-come*, 1997.

Declerq, Christophe and Julian Walker (eds.), *Languages and the First World War: Representation and Memory*, 2016.

Hochschild, Adam, *To End All Wars: A Story of Loyalty and Rebellion, 1914–1918*, 2011.

Robin, Corey, *Fear: The History of a Political Idea*, 2004.

Smith, Sarah, *Children, Cinema and Censorship: From Dracula to the Dead End Kids*, 2005.

Wheelwright, Julie, 'The Language of Espionage: Mata Hari and the Creation of the Spy-Courtesan' in Christophe Declerq and Julian Walker (eds.), *Languages and the First World War: Representation and Memory*, 2016.

ACKNOWLEDGEMENTS

The principal events described in this book took place over the course of seven years, which is also approximately how long the book took to write. While archives are marvellous things – the truest record of our past beyond the span of living memory – they are also unwieldy and resistant to taming. As I fell in love with and then sometimes fell out with my remarkable primary sources, I required the assistance, kindness and support of many individuals and institutions, and there is no doubt that, without them, I would never have made it to the end of this endeavour.

My first and greatest thanks are to the editors and others at Granta who have believed in this project and nurtured it from the start. I am particularly grateful to Laura Barber, who has been an inspirational and energising editor over the past four years; to Sara Holloway, who commissioned the book; and to Pru Rowlandson and Lamorna Elmer, whose publicity efforts are so intelligent and the first thing that really allows an author to believe that the finishing line has been crossed. Veronique Baxter of David Higham Associates has also been a source of calm belief from beginning to end.

I researched and wrote the book in many places. I acknowledge the help of staff in the National Archives in Kew and the National Archives in Washington DC, and in the British Library, the Bodleian Library, and the libraries of the University of Michigan and the University of North Carolina. With regard to the latter two, I want to commend the enlightened policy of allowing anyone to use the collections and work in the reading rooms without applying for membership. A stay at the Landmark Trust's Lynch Lodge provided a vital leap forward during the spring of 2016. But if the book has a true home, it is undoubtedly the basement and back stacks of the London Library, which has been my haven on Fridays and Saturdays for many years. My friends Simon Dunton and Yasmin Khan offered invaluable comments on early drafts. Bill Nesbitt first introduced me to the culture and language of Russia. Catriona Kelly helped me to start my career as a writer, and she and Polly Jones provided helpful advice on a Russian dimension of this story. Ben Wright has taught me so much about how British politics work, past, present and future. And I am also grateful for opportunities to reflect on the subject matter of the book at conferences organised by Rebecca Beasley, Philip Bullock, and Emily Lygo.

The book is dedicated to Nini Rodgers, who has been my friend for almost thirty years. Nini was the first person to show me that history did not need to be oversimplified to be interesting. I know no one who can tell a story better. I also want to thank the many other friends, colleagues and family members who have sustained me and helped to develop the ideas in this book: John and Wendy Phillips; Ruth and John Bale; Annie Auerbach; Mel Bach; Mark Blacklock; Stefan Collini; Annie Crombie; Barbara Davidson; Candy Davies; Michael Fealy; Naomi Foxwood; Mark Flugge; Jane Garnett; Eliane Glaser; Caroline Goodson; Keren Gorodeisky; Nat Hansen; Claire Hardy; Helen and Robert Irwin; Bridget Jackson; Karen Jackson; James Kidd; Ceri Lawrence; Lord Lexden; Rebecca Loncraine (much missed); Steve Luxford; Ben Lyttleton; Megan McNamee; Susie Mesure; George Miller; Paul Mills; Poppy Mitchell-Rose; James Morgan; Ruth Morse; Aileen Murphie;

Carla Nappi; Mark Parrett; Richard Phillips; Lydia Prior; Mernie Reisner; Gervase Rosser; Bruce Rusk; Jessica Shattuck Flugge; John Shields; Victoria Sowerby; Paul Strohm; Piers Torday; Will Tosh; Alex von Tunzelmann; Harry Wallop; and Matthew Wilkins.

Two individuals, above all others, walked with me each step of the way while the book took shape: Percy, my beloved cat, who moved silently through the house and seldom let me out of his sight as I typed, a top-class spy who is greatly missed; and Anthony Bale, who has never stopped backing me, even when I lacked faith in myself. He is, quite simply, brilliant.

ILLUSTRATION CREDITS

In the following credits the National Archives is abbreviated to TNA. The author has made every effort to trace the copyright holders of the images. Please contact the publisher if you are aware of any omissions.

1. TNA, KV 2/2317
2. TNA, CAB 24/76/67
3. TNA, KV 2/500
4. Oh So Romanov website, ohsoromanov.tumblr.com
5. TNA, KV 2/1111
6. *Ogonek* website, www.kommersant.ru/ogoniok
7. TNA, KV 2/1391
8. TNA, Series BT26
9. *Mayfair to Moscow: Clare Sheridan's Diary*, 1921
10. Art of the Russias blog, artoftherussias.wordpress.com
11. TNA, CAB 24/159/44
12. Indian History Pinterest board, uk.pinterest.com/raghubalan/indian-history/
13. Mary Evans Picture Library
14. *Punch*, 29 October 1924
15. TNA, KV 3/17
16. TNA, KV 2/1101
17. TNA, KV 2/1109
18. TNA, HO 45/24871
19. Private source
20. TNA, KV 3/15
21. TNA, KV 3/15

INDEX